Approaches to Teaching the Works of John Dryden

Approaches to Teaching World Literature

For a complete listing of titles, see the last pages of this book.

Approaches to Teaching the Works of John Dryden

Edited by

Jayne Lewis

and

Lisa Zunshine

The Modern Language Association of America
New York 2013

Library of Congress Cataloging-in-Publication Data

Approaches to teaching the works of John Dryden / edited by Jayne Lewis and Lisa Zunshine.
pages cm.—(Approaches to teaching world literature, ISSN 1059-1133; 126)
Includes bibliographical references and index.
Summary: "Offers pedagogical techniques . . . including bringing issues of translation, adaptation, religion, literary rivalry, criticism, and occasional poetry. . . . Genres covered include satire, elegy, heroic tragedy, and comedy. Includes information on editions, translations, reference works, biographies, and online resources" — Provided by publisher.
ISBN 978-1-60329-125-5 (cloth : alk. paper)
ISBN 978-1-60329-126-2 (pbk : alk. paper)
1. Dryden, John, 1631–1700—Study and teaching. 2. Dryden, John, 1631–1700—Criticism and interpretation. I. Lewis, Jayne Elizabeth, editor of compilation. II. Zunshine, Lisa, editor of compilation.
PR3427.S78A67 2013
821′.4—dc23 2013011835

Approaches to Teaching World Literature 126
ISSN 1059-1133

ISBN 978-1-60329-167-5 (EPUB)
ISBN 978-1-60329-168-2 (Kindle)

Cover illustration of the paperback and electronic editions: *Aeneas at the Court of Latinus*.
By Ferdinand Bol, c. 1661–63. Oil on canvas, 218 × 232 cm.
Courtesy of the Rijksmuseum (object SK-A-614)

Published by The Modern Language Association of America
26 Broadway, New York, NY 10004-1789
www.mla.org

CONTENTS

PREFACE

The prospect of bringing John Dryden (1631–1700) into the twenty-first-century college classroom begs one question right away: Which Dryden? The rehabilitator of the ancients? The first of the moderns? The ambivalent laureate? The sidelined convert to Rome? The literary theorist? The translator? The playwright? The poet? And if the poet, the elegist? the satirist? the panegyrist? Or if the playwright, Shakespeare's renovator? Purcell's collaborator? the tragedian? the trenchant critic of modern manners? One moral of the remarkable versatility of Dryden is that he is almost inevitably approached through his modes and the conflicts that he staged among them, often in a single work.

The present volume aims to highlight these intermodal conflicts and their pedagogical value while working in the time-tried parameters established by the MLA series Approaches to Teaching World Literature. The first part of the volume, "Materials," offers a guide to teaching editions of Dryden's work and a discussion of the background resources, from biographies and literary criticism to social, cultural, political, and art histories, that will enhance his classroom presence. It is based on a survey completed by habitual and committed teachers of Dryden's work. The second part, "Approaches," is divided into three sections: "Poetry," "Drama," and "Prose and Translation." This division both reflects Dryden's facility in most of the literary genres known to him and foregrounds his experiments with literary forms in and across genres.

The editors are grateful to the survey participants, who obligingly wended their way through a long questionnaire designed to ascertain not just which Drydens are taught today but also why and how; to Sonia Kane, who served as assistant director of Book Publications at MLA; her successor, James Hatch; the anonymous MLA readers whose insightful suggestions shaped the project at every stage; our long-suffering copyeditor, Michael Kandel; and to the volume's contributors, whose dedication to Dryden made this project possible in the first place. Dryden's epigraph to *Absalom and Achitophel* borrows from Horace to warn his reader that "the closer you stand, the more captivated you will be." Thanks to so many helping hands, we are able to offer twenty-one examples of how to bring twenty-first-century students closer to Dryden's poetry, drama, and prose—and thereby captivate them.

JL and LZ

Part One

MATERIALS

Primary Works

The editions that bring Dryden into any given classroom depend on the kind of study under way there. As one might expect, the more advanced the class, the more the depth and quality of the editing matter. Those who teach Dryden in advanced and specialized classes are hampered by a scarcity of affordable and fully representative editions of his poetry; those who rely on the three standard anthologies of British literature—the Longman (Damrosch et al.), the Blackwell (DeMaria), and the Norton (Greenblatt et al.)—often bemoan their limited offerings. For example, the most recent (ninth) edition of the *Norton Anthology of English Literature* eliminates Dryden's "To the Pious Memory of . . . Mrs. Anne Killigrew," even though, outside of *Absalom and Achitophel* and "Mac Flecknoe," it may be the most frequently taught of all his poems. Thus those who teach Dryden in survey courses frequently prefer the Longman.

In the available editions of Dryden's work, one difficulty is the editorial idiosyncrasy that inevitably decides the principle of selection. Although no one could level the charge of idiosyncrasy against the venerable and now complete California Dryden (*Works of John Dryden* [ed. Hooker and Swedenberg])—still so indispensable to Dryden scholarship—this edition seldom finds its way into the undergraduate classroom, either in PDF or photocopy form, though it is occasionally made available as a background resource through library reserves. The other two scholarly editions of Dryden's work—the five-volume Longman collection of his poetry, edited by Paul Hammond (*Poems of John Dryden*), and the James Kinsley edition (*Poems and Fables*)—are less likely to be afforded this honor, partly because each spotlights only one genre.

Lower-division surveys of the history of English poetry tend to draw on the pleasingly healthy sample of Dryden's work that appears in the *Norton Anthology of Poetry* (Ferguson, Salter, and Stallworthy). The Norton includes much of *Absalom and Achitophel* (omitting lines 569–932 and thus most of Dryden's ad hominem satire, which can fell even the most advanced graduate students), "Mac Flecknoe," "A Song for Saint Cecilia's Day," and "To the Memory of Mr. Oldham." *Mac Flecknoe* and "To Oldham" are by far the most frequently assigned texts in introductory poetry courses.

Both lower- and upper-division surveys of Restoration and eighteenth-century English literature in which Dryden is taught rely on one of four anthologies of British (sometimes "English") literature: the Norton, the Longman, the Blackwell, and occasionally the Broadview (Black et al.). All include *Absalom and Achitophel* and "To Oldham," but thereafter selections vary. The Longman, Blackwell, and Norton all feature "Mac Flecknoe," a staple on syllabi in survey courses, while the Broadview inexplicably omits it; the Blackwell alone offers the epistle to Charleton; only the Broadview bothers with an excerpt from *Dramatick Poesie*, and only the Longman with "A Secular Masque," though both the Longman and the Norton offer the preface to *Fables, Ancient and Modern*. From *Fables* the Broadview selects "Cymon and Iphigenia," the Blackwell "Pygmalion and the Statue." None of the standard anthologies includes *Astraea Redux*, though that work yields a vivid sense of Charles II's Restoration and of the ways its legitimacy could be manipulated poetically. Nonetheless, since these anthologies typically support far-reaching sophomore-level survey courses that can begin in the Anglo-Saxon period and end as late as 1800, this omission is unlikely to derail most syllabi.

The absence of poems such as *Astraea Redux* is more likely to pose a problem for upper-division literature surveys that focus on the Restoration and eighteenth century, though here the standard anthologies (often in breakaway volumes, if these exist) still often suffice. Otherwise, the once-standard Geoffrey Tillotson, Paul Fussell, and Marshall Waingrow anthology, *Eighteenth-Century English Literature*, has gone the way of all print, supplanted by Martin Price's *Restoration and Eighteenth Century* volume of the *Oxford Anthology of English Literature*. A number of our respondents use Price's edition in upper-division surveys that focus on the long eighteenth century, especially if they engage Dryden as a critic. Price's volume boasts a broad selection of Dryden's commentary on figures as diverse as Shakespeare, Chaucer, Jonson, and Juvenal. Price also includes Dryden's translations of Lucretius and Juvenal's sixth satire, as well as the Killigrew ode and lines on Milton, and of course *Absalom and Achitophel* and "Mac Flecknoe." Restoration and eighteenth-century survey courses that foreground satire are also well served by Price's anthology.

Depending on how colleges and universities divide them, Dryden can either begin or end the historical survey courses that remain the backbone of many an undergraduate curriculum. In some cases, he sees an old age out; in others, he launches a new one. A different kind of historical flexibility underwrites the preference expressed by several of our respondents for teaching his translations, which can provide lively illustrations both of cultural conservation and of cultural creation. In the same vein, some use *The State of Innocence* (photocopied from the California Dryden) to teach Milton's *Paradise Lost*. Admittedly, no one seems inclined to turn *Paradise Lost* into a gloss on *The State of Innocence*, but nor does it seem that Dryden would have resented this interpretation. *All for Love* remains the most frequently taught of Dryden's plays, often turning up in Shakespeare classes. Many of our respondents found Dryden most teachable as a dramatic writer regardless of the genre at hand, so it's a special pity that all the standard literature anthologies should neglect the drama in favor of the poetry and criticism.

In the thematic rubrics of survey courses that focus on the Restoration and eighteenth century and in terms of the special topics that often organize upper-division literature courses, Dryden is sometimes understood as a transitional, indeed transformational, figure. This is particularly true from the perspective of genre. The generic hybridity of individual works goes hand in hand with the debates they stage, and in Dryden's satires, odes, and translations many respondents find an opportunity to examine how generic forms respond to historical contingency. Those who regularly teach Dryden's drama or poems like "Alexander's Feast," "A Song for Saint Cecilia's Day," or the odes to William Congreve and Godfrey Kneller foreground his collaborations and rivalries with other artists, including Henry Purcell. Such pairings can dramatize the process of pollination across the arts, so lively in the period. The Killigrew ode may realize the contemporary conceit of the sister arts (and illuminate the sexual politics buried therein) even as the same poem might, like the one to Oldham, map the fault lines of elegy under pressure or test the limits of poetic reference.

Many historically or thematically based upper-division courses not necessarily aiming for coverage make extensive use of Dryden's poetry. Such courses are typically served by the three editions of Dryden's work that are presently available: the one-volume Longman edited by Hammond and Hopkins (*Selected Poems*); the Oxford World's Classics *The Major Works*, edited by Keith Walker; and the Penguin *Selected Poems*, edited by Steven N. Zwicker and David Bywaters. Several respondents regretted the disappearance of Earl Miner's once standard *Select Poetry and Prose of John Dryden* (Modern Library). Of the editions we do have, Walker's has been the most often used, though in the view of some its wide margins and abundant text are offset by its relative lack of textual apparatus and sometimes overly terse notes. Walker is unique in his attention to numerous prologues from the plays, in the range of odes and songs that he offers, and in his generous incorporation of Dryden's translations of Lucretius, Ovid, Juvenal, Vergil, and Horace. The translations make Walker's edition indispensable in upper-division courses that focus on Dryden's classicism. Both Dryden's translations and criticism serve classes that emphasize his place in reception. (Penguin's full edition of the *Aeneid*, edited by Frederick Keener [*Virgil's* Aeneid], is portable, not terribly expensive, and a useful supplement in such a course.) The disadvantage of Walker's affordable edition, noted by several frustrated respondents, is that it goes in and out of print.

Not so the Penguin *Selected Poems*, almost as generous as the Oxford in its inclusion of Dryden's translations of the Latin poets and covering more of Dryden's early polemical poetry. Thus courses that stress the historical and political contexts of the Restoration may be better served by the Penguin. Finally, several respondents reported using the Longman, edited by Hammond and Hopkins. Drawn from the complete five-volume edition of Dryden's work, also edited by Hammond, the Longman uniquely includes, along with the standards, *The Hind and the Panther*. Because *Religio Laici* also appears in it, it is especially attractive to those who fix Dryden in the lens of contemporary religious conflict. It also includes part of Dryden's *Iliad* and an unusually healthy sampling from *Fables, Ancient and Modern*, so that it might rival Walker's Oxford edition as a source for a classically oriented course. Its notes are unparalleled in scope and substance. The Longman is, however, considerably more expensive than either the Penguin or the Oxford. A persistent complaint is that none of the Dryden anthologies includes any of Dryden's plays or critical prose.

The plays, of course, are staples in many a Restoration drama course, where the clientele is often upper-division English and drama majors. The plays can also anchor courses on neoclassical or baroque tragedy in a more broadly European context and courses designed to trace Shakespeare's legacy alongside his plays. Respondents who teach Dryden in connection with Shakespeare often regret the absence of a teachable edition of *The Tempest* and perforce rely on *All for Love* (available in many forms) as a rejoinder to *Antony and Cleopatra*. Dryden often measures up to Shakespeare: left to their own devices, students won't necessarily realize that *All for Love* is "supposed to be bad" and may well prefer it to its Shakespearean template. Of course, the question of whether the play is indeed "bad" is arguable. One respondent's students, priding themselves on their sophistication, as manifest in their attraction to unorthodox reading lists, usually conclude that the play is good. If they haven't been assigned the Penguin edition of *Shakespeare Made Fit*, edited by Sandra Clark, students will almost certainly encounter *All for Love* in the well-edited and affordable Norton New Mermaids edition; the New Mermaids *Marriage à-la-Mode* prevails for the same reasons in drama classes where only one Dryden play is taught.

Restoration drama courses that feature Dryden are also likely to draw on these two plays, which may be found in J. Douglas Canfield and Maja-Lisa von Sneidern's widely adopted *Broadview Anthology of Restoration and Eighteenth-Century Drama*. This volume includes a range of more and less canonical plays of the period and is edited by some of the liveliest scholarly minds in the field. Dryden is, for example, treated by Tanya Caldwell (*All for Love*), Brian Corman (*Marriage à-la-Mode*), and Robert Markley and Jeannie Dalporto (*Amphitryon*). *Amphitryon* appears to be taught much less often than the other works but can be contextualized in versions of the Amphitryon legend by Molière, Kleist, and Plautus. Here, as elsewhere, Dryden plays well in version-centered courses that foreground his role as a modernizer and mediator. Teachers of *Amphitryon* can also profit from Judith Milhous and Robert Hume's rich discussion of its staging in their *Producible Interpretation: Eight English Plays, 1675–1707*.

Anthologies that include at least one play by Dryden are sometimes assigned in Restoration drama courses. David Womersley's *Restoration Drama: An Anthology*, for example, contains *The Conquest of Granada (Part One)* and *All for Love*. The same plays are represented in Arthur Ellicott Case and George Henry Nettleton's more venerable *British Dramatists from Dryden to Sheridan* (see Nettleton, Case, and Stone). Of the tragedies not adapted from other sources, *Aureng-Zebe* figures most prominently both in classes on specific themes in Restoration literature (e.g., baroque tragedy) and in those that spotlight tragedy and its variants in the period. The play is available in two affordable freestanding editions, one drawn from the digital archives of the Cornell University Library and printed with part of William Somervile's *The Chace*, with notes and a biography by Kenneth Deighton. Far more popular, however, is the Bison Regents Restoration Drama edition, conscientiously curated by Frederick Link. Many of our respondents lamented the decline of the University of Nebraska's once stellar series of individual titles and the absence of editions of *The Tempest* and *Troilus and Cressida*.

This feast-or-famine dynamic—multiple versions of two plays to choose from, moderate representation of two more, and a dearth of all the rest—no doubt affects which plays turn up in the classroom, though by this argument *The Conquest of Granada* would be taught more often than it is, especially at the undergraduate level. It is more likely to be offered at the graduate level, in seminars on Restoration drama, cross-cultural encounter in the period, or the poetics of sovereignty, and it is occasionally excerpted so as to credit Dryden with the coinage of the term "noble savage." Upper-division courses that examine the politics of empire could draw profitably on *The Indian Emperour* or *The Indian Queen*, if affordable print versions of these plays were readily available. More's the pity that they are not, since performances of these plays, which still take place, can be woven into students' experience of Dryden's work. In 1998, for example, the Long Beach Opera created a golden pedagogical opportunity when it transposed *The Indian Queen* into a range of Southern California dialects (from Spanglish to surfer drawl), thereby mining the play's deep potential as a medium for multicultural encounter.

For purists, Purcell's music for the play makes it a strong candidate for teaching in courses that explore links between music and drama. Dryden and Purcell's *King Arthur* holds sway in a number of upper- and lower-division music courses on various topics—for example, opera and society or the history of European music. *Secret Love* turns out to be a dark-horse favorite in interdisciplinary courses taught between drama and literature departments. Both plays may be assigned from photocopies made from the California Dryden or the database *Early English Books Online*. *King Arthur* is conveniently reprinted in Michael Burden's *Henry Purcell's Operas*, a standard teaching text for this play in courses that seek to reconstruct the musical culture of the period. Drama classes occasionally use Dryden's *Essay of Dramatick Poesie* (usually excerpted, either by the editor of the course text or by the instructor) to frame contemporary generic debate but mainly incorporate selections in photocopy or PDF.

Online Resources, Recordings, and Artwork

Dryden found all his literary voices in the cacophony of vigorous media competition and change; we can help students hear those voices thanks to the very similar conditions that prevail today. There is first the possibility of reading Dryden's work online: several of our respondents allow their students to download poems from *Literature Online* (*LION*) and *Google Books*. The database *Early English Books Online* (*EEBO*) can give students a sense of the ways Dryden's work would have looked to his readers. *EEBO*'s fraternal twin, *Eighteenth-Century Collections Online* (*ECCO*) reproduces a number of eighteenth-century editions and makes many texts available that are out of print. Those with access to both databases, however, find these resources a bit too decontextualized for undergraduates to navigate with ease.

More enthusiasm was expressed for the possibility of drawing on other media resources: for example, portraits of Charles II's mistresses are often commissioned for filling in the opening lines of *Absalom and Achitophel*. The course that emphasizes neoclassical contexts of Dryden's thought can draw sustenance from Philip J. Ayres's magnificently illustrated *Classical Culture and the Idea of Rome in Eighteenth-Century England* (1997). Ayres presents many fine specimens of neo-Palladian architecture, innumerable echoes of the Pantheon and the Maison Carré, and a veritable gallery of poets and statesmen posing in Roman garb or immortalized as Roman busts.

Classes with a performance emphasis sometimes use videos that demonstrate eighteenth-century physical movement (postures, fan handling). Indeed, Dryden's avid participation in the musical culture of his day yields a recipe for incorporating some of that music in the classroom. Those who teach *King Arthur* can draw on the recordings of three historically informed performances: one directed by William Christie, which John Eliot Gardiner and Trevor Pinnock recorded during the Purcell tercentenary in 1995; a 2000 recording by Alfred Deller; and Nikolaus Harnoncourt's 2004 production by the Salzburg Opera (unfortunately for English speakers, in German). Video clips from these productions may be available on *YouTube*—clearly a popular destination among our survey respondents.

Those who underscore Dryden's intimacy with the music of his day do so primarily through "A Song for Saint Cecilia's Day" and "Alexander's Feast" and occasionally with reference to some of the songs from his plays that appear in many of the anthologies. Here it's practically essential to draw not just on James Winn's splendid essay "Dryden's Songs" but also on the CD provided with *Enchanted Ground*, the tercentenary volume in which Winn's essay appears (Lewis and Novak). The CD includes "Why Should a Foolish Marriage Vow," from *Marriage à-la-Mode*; "Ah, Fading Joy," from *The Indian Emperour*; "Two Daughters of This Aged Stream," from *King Arthur*; and "The Soft Complaining Flute," from "A Song for Saint Cecilia's Day." The recordings are an invaluable supplement to each of these works, whether Dryden is a passing feature in a survey course or the star of a more conceptually focused one. Purcell's and Handel's settings of "A Song for Saint Cecilia's Day" are widely available on CD and on *YouTube*.

Students themselves may track down other *YouTube* resources, such as the full recording of Purcell and Tate's *Dido and Aeneas*, which one respondent uses to bring Dryden's classicism to life and specifically to enhance the poet's neo-Ovidian "Dido to Aeneas." Others have treated Purcell's works, especially his adaptation of the *Aeneid*, as an occasion to discuss some of the aesthetic and gender relations as Dryden represents them. One respondent has incorporated excerpts from the Opus Arts production on DVD of Rameau's *Indes Gallant* to explore how the Restoration period uses artificiality and spectacle to address key aesthetic and moral issues, from decorum to colonialism.

Other auditory connections can be made through the many available recordings of Purcell's setting of "Alexander's Feast." But for the sound of Dryden's own poetry, several respondents recommend the recording of John Richetti mellifluously reading several of Dryden's poems; it is available on the University of Pennsylvania's *PennSound* Web site. Richetti delivers the poems to Charleton, Oldham, Killigrew, and Congreve as well as "Mac Flecknoe," "Alexander's Feast," and "A Song for Saint Cecilia's Day." LibriVox offers sound recordings of three of Dryden's songs and of the *Aeneis*. The Poetry Foundation Web site includes numerous poems, from the major pieces like "Mac Flecknoe," "To the Memory of Mr. Oldham," and "The Secular Masque" to songs from the plays, though none has as yet been recorded. *YouTube* supplies video recordings of several works: "To the Memory of Mr. Oldham," "Mac Flecknoe," and "A Song for Saint Cecilia's Day."

One advantage of *YouTube* is that students may be encouraged to keep up with its mutable and capacious archive on their own. They have been known to direct their instructors to postings like "Dr. Hal Recites *Paradise Lost*," a seven-minute animated dramatization of the poem that bears ironic comparison with *The State of Innocence* and helps foreground questions of adaptation. Also recommended is the Yale professor John Rogers's lecture on book 1 of *Paradise Lost*; ninth in the Academic Earth lecture series, it references *The State of Innocence*.

Several of our respondents recommend the online anthology *Luminarium*, though most often as a link to course Web sites. *Luminarium* provides not only a rich cultural and visual guide to Dryden's life and selected works but also notes on *Annus Mirabilis*, "Mac Flecknoe," "A Song for Saint Cecilia's Day," and *An Essay of Dramatick Poesie*. None of our respondents assigned work from the *Luminarium* anthology (which draws its texts from sources as far-flung as *Google Books* and the *Perseus Project*), but several have directed their students to it for background material. *Luminarium* produces the title page of *Sylvae*, a photograph of Dryden's grave, and several contemporary portraits. While its appearance is at present at once sumptuous and haphazard, *Luminarium* may someday become a primary pedagogical resource. Certainly it sidesteps some of the difficulties posed by print anthologies, which tend not to include the plays (*Luminarium* itself is still rather light on them) or much critical material.

Google Books and *Project Gutenberg* are also potential teaching resources. *Project Gutenberg* contains all of Scott's edition of Dryden, though its relevance is limited to more advanced and specialized readers. Nonetheless, these resources raise the question of how Dryden might fare in the medium of electronic publishing. At least one of our respondents is convinced that it is only a matter of time before instructors begin publishing their own selections of copyright-free texts on electronic readers like Kindle for free. Since Kindle and other electronic files can be downloaded from the Internet onto personal devices, there seem to be relatively few technological obstacles to this approach—one that would certainly create the possibility of individualized editions of Dryden's work. Such versions of Dryden can only be objects of speculation here, but one loss would surely be the collective sense of the writer and his work that a liberal arts education was once obliged to create. But then again the elusive, multifarious Dryden himself might well have warmed to his own Kindling.

Background Materials and Criticism

Print still remains a far more reliable source of background material than the Internet. Print resources fall into two broad categories: works that provide a strong sense of political and social history and works that offer a specific cultural context for Dryden's writing and thus illustrate the musical, aesthetic, theatrical, and literary institutions and practices with which Dryden was actively involved. The notes and introductions to individual works in the California Dryden harbor vast troves of information of both kinds but will be of more use to the instructor than to the student. Two often recommended student-friendly titles that double as pedagogical aids for the instructor are Tim Harris's *London Crowds in the Reign of Charles II* (1987) and, unrivaled in liveliness and readability, Liza Picard's *Restoration London* (1997).

Our respondents turned more often to Winn's *John Dryden and His World* than to any other work of reference, uniformly praising its depth, specificity, and powerful evocation of the contemporary cultures that forged Dryden even as he helped forge them. It may be supplemented with Winn's *"When Beauty Fires the Blood": Love and the Arts in the Age of Dryden*. Hopkins's searching study *John Dryden* attends specifically to the commercial, literary, and political pressures on Dryden's work.

When our respondents wish to illuminate the special circumstances of the Restoration theater, they single out Curtis Price's *Henry Purcell and the London Stage*. Cedric Reverand II's erudite yet approachable "Dryden's *Essay of Dramatick Poesie*: The Poet and the World of Affairs" sets both the *Essay* and Dryden's drama in the light of their times. Though it does not address the traditions of seventeenth- and eighteenth-century European neoclassical drama that often frame Dryden's plays, *The Cambridge Companion to English Restoration Theatre* (Fisk) is a treasure box well stocked with essays on various aspects of theater in the late Stuart period. The volume's overarching emphasis is on generic modes; less attention is given to such shaping forces as architecture, economics, science, and certain technical aspects of stagecraft. Richard Kroll's *Restoration Drama and the "Circle of Commerce"* offers a tendentious but deeply informed reading of some of these forces. Milhous and Hume's *Producible Interpretation* brings to life both the technical intricacies of contemporary staging and the interpretive issues that they raise.

Some monographs devoted exclusively to Dryden can clarify the debates, both internal and external, that typify his writing across genres. Three perennially useful monographs are Phillip Harth's *Contexts of Dryden's Thought*, Alan Roper's *Dryden's Poetic Kingdoms*, and Zwicker's *Politics and Language in Dryden's Poetry*. Though it heavily emphasizes *Annus Mirabilis*, Michael McKeon's *Politics and Poetry in Restoration England* has been found to place Dryden usefully in the overlapping realms of literary practice and political dilemma. H. F. Mason's essay "Dryden's Dream of Happiness" familiarizes a writer whom students can find it difficult to grasp as a personality, and always fresh, relevant, and accessible are Samuel Johnson's "Dryden" and T. S. Eliot's "John Dryden." Several of our respondents teach Dryden in history of literary criticism courses along with Eliot and Johnson, who can also be used to foreground some of the more pressing and permanent concerns in Dryden's work. Dryden's own literary criticism is helpfully framed in two works our respondents often cited: H. James Jensen's *Glossary of John Dryden's Critical Terms* and John M. Aden's *Critical Opinions of John Dryden*.

The many who foreground Dryden's classicism will be grateful for Hammond's *Dryden and the Traces of Classical Rome* as well as for two books by Tanya Caldwell, *Time to Begin Anew: Dryden's* Georgics *and* Aeneis and *Virgil Made English: The Decline of Classical Authority*. Reverand's *Dryden's Final Poetic Mode: The Fables* is an especially elastic and viable resource for those who teach the late poems. Paul Davis's chapter on Dryden in his book *Translation and the Poet's Life* can animate not just Dryden's classicism but also the writing and interpretive practices through which it was mounted.

While our respondents found its essays to vary in pedagogical usefulness, Zwicker's *Cambridge Companion to John Dryden* touches on several vital contexts of Dryden's work: art, politics, religion, social life (especially Will's Coffee House culture). Likewise, four tercentenary volumes provide valuable essays for teachers of Dryden even as they model current analytic approaches to individual works: *John Dryden: A Tercentenary Miscellany* (Green and Zwicker); *John Dryden: Tercentary Essays* (Hammond and Hopkins); *John Dryden, 1631–1700: His Politics, His Plays, and His Poets* (Rawson and Santesso); and *Enchanted Ground: Reimagining John Dryden* (Lewis and Novak).

For assistance with Dryden's poetics, we recommend two essays in the *Cambridge Companion*: Christopher Ricks's "Dryden's Triplets" and Anne Cotterill's "Dryden's Fables and the Judgment of Art." Frederick Keener's discussion of Dryden's couplet art in his Penguin edition of the *Aeneis* also provides an unusually luminous guide to the nuts and bolts of Dryden's verse. With respect to the Killigrew ode, an essay that also gives unusually teachable insight into

Dryden's gender politics is Carol Virginia Pohli's "Formal and Informal Space in Dryden's Ode."

Further Reading Recommendations

Those teaching Dryden in specialized upper-division or graduate courses may wish to develop the historical background, and especially the political context, of Dryden's work. Especially helpful studies of the period are Ronald Hutton's *The Restoration: A Political and Religious History of England and Wales, 1658–1667*, Mark Kishlansky's *A Monarchy Transformed: Britain, 1603–1714* (1996), N. H. Keeble's *The Restoration*, John Miller's *The Restoration and the England of Charles II*, Craig Rose's *England in the 1690s*, and John Spurr's *England in the 1670s*.

Instructors wishing to stress cultural life in Dryden's era are encouraged to turn to John Brewer's *The Pleasures of the Imagination: English Culture in the Eighteenth Century*. As enlivening as they are enlightening are John Butt's *The Augustan Age*, Donald Greene's *The Age of Exuberance: Backgrounds to Eighteenth-Century English Literature*, A. R. Humphreys's *The Augustan World: Life and Letters in Eighteenth-Century England*, and Jean Hagstrum's *Sex and Sensibility: Ideal and Erotic Love from Milton to Mozart*. Also useful are Harold Love's "Dryden's London," Gerald MacLean's *Culture and Society in the Stuart Restoration: Literature, Drama, History*, and Graham Parry's *The Seventeenth Century: The Intellectual and Cultural Context*.

Dryden's plays can be understood—hence taught—more completely in the context of contemporary theater. Relevant drama studies are Richard W. Bevis's *English Drama: Restoration and Eighteenth Century, 1660–1789*, Edward Burns's *Restoration Comedy: Crises of Desire and Identity*, J. Douglas Canfield and Deborah C. Payne's *Cultural Readings of Restoration and Eighteenth-Century Theater*, Brian Corman's *Genre and Generic Change in English Comedy, 1660–1710*, Baxter Hathaway's "John Dryden and the Function of Tragedy," Peter Holland's *The Ornament of Action: Text and Performance in Restoration Comedy*, Blair Hoxby's "Dryden's Baroque Dramaturgy: The Case of *Aureng-Zebe*," Elizabeth Howe's *The First English Actresses: Women and Drama, 1660–1700*, Derek Hughes's *English Drama, 1660–1700*, Robert D. Hume's *The Rakish Stage: Studies in English Drama, 1660–1800*, R. J. Kaufman's "On the Poetics of Terminal Tragedy," Frances M. Kavenik's *British Drama, 1660–1779: A Critical History*, Richard Leacroft's *The Development of the English Playhouse: An Illustrated Survey of Theatre Building in England from Medieval to Modern Times*, Nancy Maguire's *Regicide and Restoration: English Tragicomedy, 1660–1671*, David Roberts's *The Ladies: Female Patronage of Restoration Drama, 1660–1700*, Laura J. Rosenthal's *Playwrights and*

Plagiarists in Early Modern England: Gender, Authorship, Literary Property, Hanna Scolnicov and Peter Holland's *Reading Plays: Interpretation and Reception*, Susan Staves's *Players' Scepters: Fictions of Authority in the Restoration*, Earl R. Wasserman's "The Pleasures of Tragedy," and Harold Weber's *The Restoration Rake-Hero: Transformations in Sexual Understanding in Seventeenth-Century England*.

Among earlier book-length studies of Dryden that have weathered particularly well are Earl Miner's *Dryden's Poetry*, George Wasserman's *John Dryden*, David Wykes's *A Preface to Dryden*, and Zwicker's *Dryden's Political Poetry*.

Finally, many of these essays will be useful for illuminating individual works: Laura Brown's "Dryden and the Imperial Imagination," Paul Davis's "Dryden and the Invention of Augustan Culture," Jerome Donnelly's "John Dryden and the Failure of Political Categories," Jack D. Durant's "*Religio Laici*: The Poem as Product," Katsuhior Engetsu's "Dryden and Modes of Restoration Sensibility," David Hopkins's "Dryden and His Contemporaries," Anne K. Krook's "Satire and the Constitution of Theocracy in *Absalom and Achitophel*," Harold Love's "Dryden's London," Michael McKeon's "Historicizing *Absalom and Achitophel*," James Ogden's "Dryden's Satirical Tendency," Ronald Paulson's "Dryden and the Energies of Satire," Thomas Reinert's "Theater and Civility in Dryden's Essay," Randy Robertson's "The Delicate Art of Anonymity: The Case of *Absalom and Achitophel*," Roper's "Who's Who in *Absalom and Achitophel*?," R. J. Stove's "Dryden in His Time and Ours," A. E. Wallace Maurer's "The Form of Dryden's *Absalom and Achitophel*, Once More," and Zwicker's "Dryden and the Poetic Career" and "Composing a Literary Life."

Survey Issues

College-level instructors from across Britain, Canada, and the United States report that the exhilaration, challenge, convenience—and ultimately the relevance—of Dryden's work are all born of the multiplicity of voices that argue in and through it, a multiplicity to which our respondents' own diversity bears witness. Their syllabi at once echo the plaintive question posed in *Religio Laici*—"[M]ust all tradition then be set aside?"—and mobilize a common commitment to pedagogical adventure. Above all, the results of our survey affirm Dryden's fitness for an age skeptical of disciplinary boundaries, one surely as transitional as his own.

Our respondents teach at four-year liberal arts colleges and professionally oriented institutions with large working student bodies, at private research universities and large public ones, some with open admissions policies. They are affiliated with music, literature, and drama departments, and they regularly introduce Dryden into a wide array of pedagogical settings, from surveys of English literature to cross-listed seminars on baroque dramaturgy. Dryden often plays a pivotal role in freshman-level introductions to poetry that fulfill general education requirements. But he also ties surveys of literary criticism together and features in special author courses on Shakespeare or Milton. Our respondents have teamed him with Purcell and Kneller, Jonson and Hobbes, Racine and Corneille, Behn and Rochester, Johnson and Pope. They put Scott's "glorious John" in conversation with the libertine coteries of the Restoration but also with religious controversialists, musicians, and actors.

Every kind of class summons—to some extent creates—its own Dryden. In historical surveys of anglophone literature, Dryden the poet is definitely taught more often than Dryden the dramatist, and the poet of "Mac Flecknoe," *Absalom and Achitophel*, and the Killigrew and Oldham odes more than the one of *Astraea Redux*, *Religio Laici*, or *The Hind and the Panther*. This preference holds whether or not a survey is limited to the Restoration and eighteenth century. In more advanced special-topics classes (often also historically delimited), Dryden the translator makes a surprisingly strong showing, primarily through the *Aeneis* and *Fables, Ancient and Modern* but also through his translations of other poems by Vergil and poems by Juvenal. Bucking the stubborn cult of romantic personality in almost every particular, Dryden cuts a significant figure in four kinds of classes: lower-division introductions to English poetry, whose clientele often includes non–English majors; lower-division surveys of British literature designed for English majors and typically beginning in the medieval period and ending in 1800; upper-division surveys of Restoration and eighteenth-century literature, often riveted on specific themes or problems (neoclassicism, genres in transition); and upper-division seventeenth- and eighteenth-century drama courses.

In this general distribution, two trends emerge. It perhaps reflects our profession's descent into melancholy that Dryden's odes and elegies, particularly those to Anne Killigrew and John Oldham, are now taught at least as often as the standard satires, *Absalom and Achiotophel* and "Mac Flecknoe." The Killigrew ode often does double duty as a way of foregrounding late-seventeenth-century sexual politics. Its inconsistencies of tone and motive also allow some to smuggle satire in the back door, "Mac Flecknoe" sometimes bringing up the rear. The second trend is that although several respondents focused (usually upper-division literature) courses on the still viable triumvirate of Dryden, Pope, and Johnson or tied Dryden to Jonson or Shakespeare in seventeenth-century drama courses that breach the Interregnum, Behn has become his favored partner. Indeed, what once was called the Age of Dryden is now more likely to be understood as the Age of Behn, and it would be hard to find two writers whose stock has risen or fallen so dramatically or in such a perfectly inverse proportion. Yet for the teaching of Dryden, the gains from the rise of Behn are real: Dryden proves to be as deeply, resonantly, and ambivalently engaged with sexual politics and the poetics of empire as the Behn of *Oroonoko*, and association with that work, as with plays like *The Widow Ranter* or *The Rover*, can amplify this significant strain in Dryden's work. For some respondents, the two writers' common move toward the Roman Catholic faith provides a vital frame for the other political and religious questions raised in their writing. One respondent teaches *The Rover* alongside *Amphitryon* on the grounds of their shared fascination with masked or assumed identities, a pairing that highlights the manipulative mystique of the concept of personal essence for the Restoration stage.

We wanted to know which aspects of Dryden carry best into the classroom. One aspect turns out simply to be his capacity to give imaginative, human, and narrative pleasure. Several respondents cited the confidence of his voice and tone, his control of genre and manipulation of the tensions between genres. Still others appreciate his creative engagements with the past and the startling modernity of his English. Perhaps most resonant, though, is simply the grandeur and urgency of his themes. These were justly summarized by one of our respondents as "adventure, peril, the fall of great cities, the allure and terrible cost of empire, the allure and threat of ambition or exorbitant wishes; sex and passionate obsession, getting philosophical about sex and passionate obsession, erotic betrayal and regret; recollections of the dead, the meaning of life, atoms and the void. How could a twenty-year-old not be interested?"

How indeed? Dryden's work throws down three significant gauntlets. First, as Crites admits in *An Essay of Dramatik Poesie*, "many things appear flat to us, the wit of which depended on some custom or story which never came to our knowledge" (17: 20–21). Largely lost on many of our students are the customs and stories that motivate and deepen so much of Dryden's work, especially its historical and political contexts. Dryden's topical and densely allusive public voice easily frustrates novice readers remote from the particularities of Restoration culture and politics. Although many of the controversies and conflicts that shaped that culture harmonize uncannily with our own unstable times, the hapless instructor must still depend on background materials and historical resources not simply to enhance the poetry and drama but also to explain it in the first place.

Some instructors refer their students to such background material, while others simply build it into their presentation of Dryden's work. One respondent, who regularly centers a semester-long upper-division course on Dryden and Behn, sends her students to the *Dictionary of Literary Biography*, where (for credit) they can uncover for themselves the historical actors of the period. Others rely on who's who handouts and attempt to involve students in the decoding. It's also possible to develop illustrated lectures on the history of the period or simply to concentrate on close reading, filling in historical reference as one goes and foregrounding the difference made when literary language must respond to its immediate environment or the politics of representation.

A related concern is our students' innocence of Dryden's classical antecedents and so of the source of so many of his allusions and templates. Without such references at the undergraduate fingertip, much of Dryden's achievement, and especially his humor, can be lost. The same is also true of the biblical customs and stories that confront novice readers of the often taught *Absalom and Achitophel* and the sometimes taught *Religio Laici*. Finally, students can fault Dryden for lacking the values of lyric intensity and privacy of mind so easily caught from the Romantics; they may find his formality off-putting, his vigor somehow misdirected. His English sometimes needs heavy paraphrasing, though several respondents noted not just its striking modernity alongside, say, Shakespeare's but also the ways in which it can be used to model the stabilizing power of modern print culture. From here, class discussion might turn to print's significance, if not its tyranny, as a medium for the modern writers of whom Dryden would be counted the first.

Barriers breached, one way or another, students laugh with Dryden, and they come to appreciate the qualities that our respondents want them to. In our survey, the most mentioned of these is his complex relation to genre. Dryden very often serves to introduce the rules of literary modes, from satire to pastoral. For instance, the Killigrew and Oldham poems may be taught alongside elegies by Vergil, Milton, Shelley, Tennyson, Arnold, Plath, and even Phillis Wheatley. In this context, Dryden can serve as a connecting link between inherited elegiac traditions and emergent variations on them, and the internal conflicts that characterize his work—involving Christian consolation, for example—can be more teachable than, say, the intractable disruptions of Milton's "Lycidas."

Self-reflexive critical awareness of particular genres makes Dryden a genial conduit for the rules of panegyric, mock epic, and neoclassical tragedy. Our respondents offer upper-division courses that team *All for Love* not just with the inevitable Shakespeare but also with Milton's *Samson Agonistes*, Racine's *Berenice*, and Addison's *Cato*. Others offer upper-division period courses that focus on double-plot tragicomedy, ranging from *The Rover* and *The Man of Mode* to the nondramatic *Oroonoko*—works that both *Amphitryon* and *All for Love* can elucidate. Shift the scene, and Dryden's *Iliad* (bk. 1) or his *Aeneis* (bks. 1, 2, 4, and 6) can launch course-long investigations of epic and mock epic, even as his translations of Vergil introduce pastoral and georgic and dramatize these forms' capacity to respond to historical pressure. Dryden's translations of Lucretius make lucid and compelling introductions to the didactic poem and philosophical verse, while his translations of Juvenal set the stage for the study of satire, including his own. Neo-Ovidian poems like "Dido to Aeneas" put the intimate verse epistle on a trajectory that can be traced through Rochester to Behn and Pope's "Eloisa to Abelard."

Perhaps as notable as Dryden's often exploited versatility across a range of genre-based teaching modules is the currency of those modules. Queried as to their general methodological approach to teaching Dryden, our respondents laid claim primarily to historically informed formalism, preferring genre approaches, reading-based interpretive models, and, in the case of the plays, performance history over critical theory. Some approached the plays (and occasionally their music), along with such works as the Killigrew ode, through gender studies, and many brought reception history to bear, noting, moreover, that a reader-response approach is appropriate for an author who continually responded to the expectations and values of his readers. Better yet, such an approach can reveal Dryden's poems as dynamic works of art and rhetoric.

No matter which Dryden comes to light on today's college campuses—the elegist, the satirist, the translator—virtually all our respondents stress the internal tensions that govern his work. These tensions elucidate what one respondent termed the "competitive and vituperative modes of Restoration literary culture." Some treat Dryden as a window onto his time; others use him to open the multiple potentials of literary expression. Both Dryden's investment in public discourse and his willingness to bring multiple generic perspectives to bear on a single work inevitably remind his students—those behind the podium and those behind the desk—that there is more than one viable literary mode and that modality itself is an ironic constant through the vagaries of literary history.

Unless otherwise indicated, the edition of Dryden used by the contributors to this volume is the twenty-volume *Works of John Dryden* (ed. Hooker and Swedenberg).

Part Two

APPROACHES

Introduction

Jayne Lewis

Dryden: The Poetics and Politics of Transition

When Walter Scott set about editing his magisterial 1808 *Works of John Dryden*, he did so with an eye to "the thousands of young persons who seem[ed] to be growing up in contented ignorance of one of the greatest of our masters" (*Life* 156). One might expect that what was true a century after Dryden's death would be all the more so another two centuries on. Today, after all, mastery is held in high suspicion, and "contented ignorance" has given way to the endless distraction faced by "young persons" living through dramatic social, cultural, political, and ecological change. But in fact no literature speaks more directly or fluently to our own moment of historical transition than that of the English Restoration. And if one seeks a representative text of this turbulent period, it is likely to have been written by Dryden. Dryden was poet laureate through much of the reign of Charles II, falling from that position only with the Revolution of 1688 and the official arrival of aesthetic and sociopolitical modernity—a modernity that his own work at once resisted and helped bring into being. He was his conflicted age's wittiest and most influential satirist and the author of some of its most compelling and self-reflexive drama. Dryden composed several of the seventeenth century's preeminent odes and panegyrics, and he was the chief architect of its most innovative (and synthetic) literary theory. Samuel Johnson famously praised him for having "found [English poetry] brick, and left it marble" ("Dryden" 155)—a feat Dryden achieved partly as the translator of authors from Vergil, Horace, and Juvenal to Lucretius and Boccaccio. Two of his longer poems, *Religio Laici* (1682) and *The Hind and the Panther* (1687), give shape and voice to the urgent religious problems of the later seventeenth century.

Dryden's creative life spanned four decades and encompassed every major genre outside prose fiction. His poetic career was launched in 1659 with his *Heroic Stanzas* in praise of Oliver Cromwell, an incongruous prelude to a literary life spent otherwise celebrating the restored Stuart dynasty through such major poems as *Astraea Redux* (1660), *Annus Mirabilis* (1666), and *Absalom and Achitophel* (1681). Portions of *Absalom*—along with "Mac Flecknoe," his 1678 skewering of the poetaster Thomas Shadwell, and the more generalized invective of *The Medall* (1681–82)—still stand among the most brilliant (and most often anthologized) satires of the period. But Dryden also wrote unforgettable odes celebrating the poets John Oldham and Anne Killigrew and two major poems on the power of music, "Song for Saint Cecilia's Day" (1687) and "Alexander's Feast" (1697). These last four works all double as skeptical meditations on the nature and power of art, while Dryden's Anglican poem *Religio*

Laici and his Roman Catholic *The Hind and the Panther* raise questions about religious authority from radically different credal positions.

As a dramatist, Dryden wrote several of the most successful plays to appear on the Restoration stage. They range from political tragedies like *Don Sebastian* (1690), *Aureng-Zebe* (1675), and his strikingly postcolonial drama about the defeat of Montezuma at the hands of Spain, *The Indian Emperour* (1665), to the witty comedy of manners *Marriage à-la-Mode* (1673) and definitive updatings of Shakespeare. Dryden's *All for Love* (1677) rivals its Shakespearean template, *Antony and Cleopatra*, while his partnership with William Davenant in their 1667 adaptation of *The Tempest* remains an exemplary guide to the sometimes baffling tastes of late-seventeenth-century audiences. As a translator, Dryden Englished all Vergil's major poetry, including the *Aeneid*, and in the eighteenth century he was best known, especially among women readers, for his modernizations of Ovid and Boccaccio in *Fables, Ancient and Modern* (1700). Finally, out of Dryden's copious body of literary criticism, his *Essay of Dramatick Poesie* (1668) and "Discourse concerning . . . Satire" (1693) remain staples in courses on the history of literary theory and genre, not least because they so brilliantly arbitrate between competing views—ancient and modern, English and Continental—of their topics.

The splendor and scope of Dryden's oeuvre could hardly be more obvious; as James Russell Lowell remarked in 1868, Dryden was "the earliest complete type of a literary man" (220). The legendary vigor of his engagement with literary history has often cast him as one of our most virile writers. Editing Dryden for early-nineteenth-century readers, Scott vowed never to "castrate" work that seemed to him "marked strongly by a masculine character" (*Life* xxxii). The Victorian critic George Saintsbury likewise admired Dryden's "masculine strength and originality" (81), as did Saintsbury's contemporaries Gerard Manley Hopkins, who hailed Dryden as the "most masculine of our poets" (268), and Leslie Stephen, who noted his "masculine sense of power" (205). But if nineteenth-century writers like Hopkins found Dryden to "lay the strongest stress of all our literature on the naked thew and sinew of the English language" (268), today it is his work's inherent contradictions, its perennial difference from itself, that we notice, value, and urge our students to appreciate. A writer closer to Dryden's day, Johnson, found him "always *another and the same*" ("Dryden" 123), and it is Dryden's differences with himself that speak most directly to our world. His world, like ours, was aggressively politicized, drenched in new media, and suspended among seemingly irreconcilable visions of past, present, and future. As Scott maintained in the wake of the French Revolution, another notably unstable moment in political, social, and literary history, the time for bringing up Dryden is now.

The contradictions that make Dryden relevant to us arise from the uniqueness of his time. The second half of the seventeenth century saw a collective transition into print culture, constitutional monarchy, commodity capitalism, and globalization. Dryden's work is profoundly responsive to a world that could not know where it was headed—a world with many worries and obsessions and populated by an idiosyncratic cast of characters: Thomas Shadwell, Shaftesbury, even Charles II. Yet the personalities and problems that shaped Dryden's writing are seldom remembered today. As Scott put it, Dryden "had to write for those around him, rather than for posterity" (*Life* 144). J. G. Lockhart, a biographer of Scott, supposed that "the obsoleteness of [late-seventeenth-century] party politics" alone was likely to make Dryden himself obsolete (2: 69). Topicality distinguishes Dryden from his contemporary John Milton, whose charm for readers has waxed and waned much less dramatically over time. Intimacy with the likes of Oliver Cromwell, Henry Vane, and the house of Stuart is not a prerequisite for grasping *Paradise Lost*.

An open, vigorous, and buoyantly public style also distinguishes Dryden from Milton. As Johnson's tribute to English's marble maker recognizes, it is this style that did more than that of any other writer to modernize English literary language. But because Dryden's style was put out to so many different kinds of service, it is easy for today's students to accuse it of hypocrisy or simple indecision. The tragicomedy of Dryden's sexual politics, his splicing of originality and imitation, and the backward glances that his modernism casts are as contradictory and baffling as they are fascinating. Then too there is the mystery of the person behind the page, for Dryden will never address us as directly as a Milton, a Johnson, or a Keats. Dryden's Bloomsbury biographer, Allan Lubbock, remarked that, reading Dryden, "one is aware of the presence of a character as solid as Dr. Johnson, but look for him, and he is not there: the lines of the human figure dissolve, as you turn, into those of the literature of his age" (5).

This dissolution is in itself a reason to make certain that Dryden's writing, if not Scott's "glorious John" himself (Scott, *Pirate* 2: 9), stays in the foreground of the English literature we want our students to read and understand. Dryden's dissolving figure opens the way for that literature's formative conflicts to be experienced directly, even as it allows us to glimpse all the things that English literature, in the wake of the Romantic revolution, has not been in some time. As T. S. Eliot appreciated in his famous homage to Dryden, "to those whose taste in poetry is formed entirely upon the English poetry of the nineteenth century . . . it is difficult to explain or excuse Dryden" (264). At the bottom of the matter we find William Wordsworth's complaint that Dryden's "language . . . is not in the highest sense of the word poetical, being neither of the imagination or the passions" (641). The Romantic poet's statement now sounds rather narrow and tendentious, but we can recover a sympathetic understanding of Dryden's "imagination" and "passions" by realizing how deeply they were structured by his contemporary politics and poetics of transition.

Many of the contributors to this volume emphasize that Dryden's poetry, drama, and criticism were all products of contingency and circumstance. They foreground his involvement with a social, political, and cultural environment whose essence was the struggle for power. This is a struggle that today's students grasp intuitively—and for that very reason they need to examine it at a distance. As Margaret Anne Doody points out in her essay, Dryden "understands that power is made. It is there, up for grabs as we say—but it is to be made or transformed rather than merely grabbed." The Restoration struggle for power played in the houses of Parliament, at court, and on the stage of nascent empire. But sexual, political, and cultural battles were also waged in the new media environments of the late seventeenth century. Today's Facebooking, YouTubing, Twittering students will immediately understand the newness of these environments and find in Dryden a model for negotiating them.

Dryden's Reception

Although conceived as a practical guide for use in the classroom, this collection of essays also participates in the history of Dryden's critical reception. As we find in Scott's view of Dryden, and in the California edition of Dryden's work, history has often coincided with the project of making Dryden available to a new generation. In that history, attitudes toward history—especially political history as it relates to literary practice—has fluctuated wildly, and evaluations of Dryden have tended to match this fluctuation.[1] In his own day, he earned the praise even of prickly contemporaries like John Dennis, for having "refin'd the Language of our Rhyming Poetry, and improv'd its Harmony" ("Reflections" 259). But along with his conversion to Roman Catholicism, his fall from political grace with the revolution of 1688 also meant that one strand of his memory was kept alive by cultural subalterns like the women who contributed appreciations to one of the most famous volumes of elegiac poetry published after his death, *The Nine Muses* (1700). Samuel Garth's 1717 "Memorial" registered the persistence of a fundamentally political—thus local and historical—understanding of Dryden, whose grave had been denied a proper headstone because of the Jacobite bent of his late politics: he was, for Garth, "the sad and shameful instance of [the] truth" that politics can deform cultural memory (xx). It was Johnson, of course, whose biography of the poet turned him into a hero of the English language, though Johnson may have done so partly to avoid addressing "the curiosity which his reputation must excite" ("Dryden" 79). Johnson's account of Dryden is strangely evasive, even uneasy. This evasion eventually justified the Irish lawyer Edmond Malone's late-eighteenth-century edition of Dryden's prose works, an edition distinguished by a biography based on thousands of pages of authentic documents that Johnson had not consulted.

Scott was Dryden's major early-nineteenth-century editor. Unlike Malone, he interpreted his task liberally, famously—or, rather, infamously—"correcting" many of Dryden's lines. Saintsbury defended the liberty that Scott took by insisting that Scott had merely reedited Dryden as "[Dryden] might have re-edited it himself had he been alive today" (81). In any case, the emergent historical novelist saw something of himself in the seventeenth-century writer. He was not alone. In 1868, Lowell, an American, found Dryden "a type of the kind of poet America would have produced by the biggest-river-and-tallest-mountain recipe" (220). But in Britain, Dryden's perceived range and masculine vigor could alienate decorous Victorian readers who cultivated both a Romantic taste for lyric interiority and the Whig interpretation of history. As T. B. Macaulay put it, almost dismissively, Dryden proved that "'tis the age that forms the man, not the man that forms the age." Come to think of it, "on no man did the age exercise so much influence" (31). Politics and religion—both topics that made many Victorians queasy—affected so many of Dryden's poems that Matthew Arnold's highest praise of them was also a dismissal. "Dryden and Pope are not classics of our poetry," he decided in 1880, "they are classics of our prose" (31).

After World War I, Eliot saw in Dryden a kindred dissident from Victorian literary sensibilities, one for whom nineteenth-century "tastes and fashions had no place." The modern poet, playwright, and critic saw his own tripartite mission modeled in Dryden, a "defender of sanity" for whom "the larger forms of poetry should have a moral influence" and to whom "it would not have occurred . . . that there was or should be anything irrational in poetic imagination" (308). For Eliot, Dryden's rationality was expressed in his sense of form, itself a response to the extraliterary questioning of political, social, and religious forms in his time.

The New Critical movement, which in Eliot's own lifetime became one of high modernism's signature expressions, is famous for its insistence on the isolated and autonomous properties of literary art. But the movement still found time for Dryden. The New Critic Mark Van Doren produced one of the most important studies of the author to be published in the twentieth century. To read Van Doren's *John Dryden* is to realize that the New Criticism's obsessive attention to form is precisely what gave its practitioners insight into Dryden's rhetorical method and historical milieu. At the height of the movement, Louis Bredvold's *The Intellectual Milieu of John Dryden* stimulated a genuinely new phase of appreciation for the ways in which historical environments condition verbal art, often dividing it against itself. During this time too, the mid-1950s, the first volumes of the California Dryden made their debut, gracefully integrating practical criticism with a rich and layered attention to historical detail.

Against this background, the proliferation of critical studies and biographies of Dryden that accompanied the repoliticization of literature and the rise of the new historicism in the 1980s seems more like the continuation of an ironically consistent strain in literary history. Sometimes dissident, sometimes dominant, this strain stretches all the way back to Dryden's own reflections, in *An Essay of Dramatick Poesie* on art's complicity with a history that is always about "disputed . . . command" (*Works* 17: 8). In any event, if Dryden's stock took a dip with the opening of the literary canon in the 1980s, today he is back in a new guise, one that blends attention to his poetics (especially their classical genealogy) with increasingly complex understandings of the vulnerability and contradiction that attend art's explicit admission of political and social change.

None of the essays in this volume sees formal and contextual approaches to Dryden as mutually exclusive. On the contrary, many blend formal critical scrutiny with a lively appreciation of context and collaboration, and many embrace conflict and uncertainty as sources of both historical and aesthetic interest. The essays themselves are organized generically, but virtually all their authors acknowledge that Dryden tests generic boundary. He does so in his criticism, in dramatic works that blend comedy and tragedy, and in poetry that oscillates between heroic and satiric modes.

Our contributors all embrace the debates and dilemmas that structure Dryden's work as rich teaching opportunities. The extent to which that work is unresolved is, for many, the extent to which it is modern and the extent to which it reveals that we have never been modern. Adam Potkay's buoyant guide to teaching Dryden's "pollinating art of translation" strikes deftly at the heart of this matter. "[T]o what degree is Orpheus's task the same as Vergil's, and Vergil's the same as Dryden's?" Potkay wonders. His larger point is that this task is also ours, and like other contributors he shows how it can be turned into our students' task as well.

Teaching within and across Genres and Media

While the essays in this volume fall into broad and basic categories—namely, poetry, drama, and prose and translation—these categories say little about how we presently organize our thinking about Dryden. The reader of this volume may prefer to track the essays through the conversations they conduct across section boundaries, conversations that are ongoing in contemporary Dryden scholarship. Overlap is inevitable, since often our contributors have published influential critical work on Dryden in recent years.

For example, as they and others do on the page, in the classroom many of our contributors organize a historical approach to Dryden through a particular controversy. For Anna Battigelli, that controversy is primarily religious; her essay shows how *Religio Laici* can draw students into then (and in fact still) lively clashes over the status of scriptural authority and how religious polemic of Dryden's day can be used to animate *Religio Laici*. In Jennifer Brady's hands, *Marriage à-la-Mode* and *Aureng-Zebe* come to life amid the partisan literary rivalries of the Restoration, most particularly Dryden's with Rochester. If Brady shows how students can be taught to cringe at Dryden's lack of shame in his competitive quest for aristocratic patronage, Will Pritchard sets *Marriage à-la-Mode* in a very different scene: that of contestation over the meaning of marriage in the 1670s. Ann Huse teaches Dryden at New York's John Jay College of Criminal Justice. She accordingly uses "To His Sacred Majesty" and "The Secular Masque" to illuminate problems of Restoration crowd control. Consideration of these problems can open up issues of sovereign authority and social stratification even as they speak to the challenges of mob management in present-day Manhattan. Elizabeth Bobo cross-references Dryden's *The State of Innocence* and Milton's *Paradise Lost* in the lively setting of late-seventeenth-century print culture. As students learn how publication practice reflected the political and theological spectrum of the day, Bobo shows, they develop a more nuanced understanding of two writers who occupied opposite ends of that spectrum.

They may also gain a more sophisticated sense of genre, since Bobo's pairing of Milton and Dryden necessarily spotlights the differing projects of epic and drama. Indeed, a number of essays foreground Dryden's experiments with literary forms from elegy and georgic to the heroic play and the critical essay. Such experiments proceed now by mobilizing the dynamics of conflict, now by tapping the energy released by genres in transition. For John Richetti, emphasizing the conversational, dramatic, and dialogic elements of Dryden's odes can lead to "a lesson in genre criticism." Cedric Reverand approaches the elegies to Oldham and Killigrew quite differently, sorting through Dryden's affronts to the elegiac tradition so that students can see how Dryden exposes that tradition to the slings and arrows of outrageous satire. After noting the synchrony of *All for Love* with Restoration libertine poetry, Blair Hoxby wrests the play out of the conventions of Shakespearean tragedy (and adaptation) to emphasize its engagement with the principles of Continental neoclassical tragedy. Potkay sets Dryden's translations of Lucretius and especially Vergil in the light of ongoing ecological crisis. His ingenious linking of this content to the mysterious and possibly tragic fate of honeybees allows new insight into the power and potential reflexivity of the generic forms—the didactic poem and the eclogue—that convey them.

Recent criticism tends to stress that Dryden wrote at the crossroads of diverse media as well as multiple literary genres. What Dianne Dugaw calls the inherently multimedia orientation of his writing carries especially well to the ears and eyes of students accustomed to mixing and matching various media forms. The essays in our second section, "Drama," draw on Dryden's intimacy with the nonliterary arts, from music and performance to painting. In their playful essay, Thomas F. Bonnell, a literature professor, and Katie Sullivan, a professor of drama, show how mounting a performance of *Secret Love* transports upper-division students into Dryden's work. Dance and voice supply vital threads through the labyrinth of the play. In a different but still cross-disciplinary vein, Amanda Eubanks Winkler and Kathryn Lowerre show how Dryden's fascination with music can seduce even nonmusical students. The juxtapositions of music and spoken word that Winkler and Lowerre foreground through Dryden's collaboration with Henry Purcell in *King Arthur* animate other tensions—between the court and popular culture, between high and low styles, between mythic and patriotic versions of English identity, even between competing constructions of gender.

Similarly contrapuntal arrangements structure Dugaw's account of how to make use of Dryden's strong ties to both music and the visual arts, ties that reveal a Dryden deeply invested in the baroque aesthetic of Catholic Europe. Dugaw forges a path into *All for Love* by way of both baroque instrumental music and the art of Artemisia Gentileschi. Dryden's engagements with both media forms demonstrate an entrancing "interplay of earthly and mythic, individual and collective, interpersonal and imperial"—an interplay deeply influenced by Gentileschi's staging of the same play. Dugaw also suggests ways today's students can exploit today's favorite media form, the *YouTube* video, to gain access to Dryden's drama.

Margaret Anne Doody's meditation on "Dryden the dramatic" wittily marries the Dryden of the poems with the Dryden of the stage, mixing pagecraft with stagecraft to uncover the depth of his engagement with contemporary forms of power. J. Caitlin Finlayson shows how Dryden's Shakespearean adaptations, *The Tempest* and *All for Love*, can double as lively media for teaching performance theory and theater history. As she works with some of the practical issues of transferring Shakespeare from the Elizabethan stage to that of the Restoration, Finlayson also shows how Dryden addresses one of power's favorite media, the law.

Teachers in search of an approach to Dryden will still need, no matter what the approach, to take their students through the lines that Dryden wrote. Our collection therefore consistently attends to individual works and the question of how students can be taught simply to read them. The reader will find contrasting approaches to the two poems that are taught especially often, *Absalom and Achitophel* and the Killigrew ode. As Christopher Dyer Johnson's lively discussion of how Dryden engages the reader of *Absalom and Achitophel* suggests, even the most resistant student may be taken outside the poem by moving deeper into it. Johnson sets this polyphonic work in the context of a culture "saturated with misleading information from media that were both partisan and ruthless." He promises that as students learn how and why so many of Dryden's ideas were reduced to rhetorical ploys, they develop new and more sophisticated ways of reading. But Kirstin Wilcox, teaching, boldly throws out the paratexts and footnotes that seem essential to the poem. Her students read their way through *Absalom and Achitophel* on their own, then build specific biblical and contemporary resonances back in for themselves. Drawing on Johnson's verdict that the Killigrew ode is "undoubtedly the noblest ode that our language ever has produced" ("Dryden" 137–38), Deborah Kennedy uses the metrical and melodic dimensions of the work to open up the music of Dryden's verse. In her hands, the ode's discrete stanzaic form also encourages students to unpack self-contained points of reference.

Scott MacKenzie treats "Mac Flecknoe" as a model for practical criticism. He accesses everything from Dryden's fury to his anagrams and acrostics, converting each property of the poem into both an exercise in close reading and a guide to the contemporary contexts and long literary traditions in which

Dryden's most famous satire participates. Aaron Santesso shows how Dryden's "Discourse concerning . . . Satire" can let students witness the birth of both the unreliable narrator and the modern author; how to make the discourse personal, lively for students; and even how to seduce them from the Romantic cult of authorial personality. Differently but just as admirably devious is Philip Smallwood's lyrical account of teaching *Fables, Ancient and Modern*, which smuggles aesthetic appreciation and close reading under cover of the sexual and identity politics that the *Fables* overtly engage and that are the default for many university students today.

Our contributors, then, approach Dryden's work from many different directions. Some of these directions are institutionally motivated, since today Dryden is taught both in classes that meet general education requirements and in classes that operate at the most esoteric levels of an English or drama major. Our contributors, working in institutions of higher learning in Britain, Canada, and the United States, represent small and medium-sized liberal arts colleges, large public and private research universities, and professionally oriented schools where most of the teaching happens under cover of darkness. Dryden carries across all these settings, just as he has carried across three centuries.

NOTE

[1] On Dryden's reception, see Amarisinghe; Miner, "On Reading Dryden"; and Lewis.

POETRY

John Dryden's Trojan Horse: *Religio Laici*

Anna Battigelli

Writing about John Dryden, Harold Love rightly noted that "it is easy for us to overlook that the eighteenth century could see him as an alien, even a dangerous spirit" ("Dryden's Unideal Vacancy" 74). Dryden's willingness to question cultural pieties, his habitual irony, his tendency to evoke multiple and even competing points of view at once, and his persistence in asking readers to weigh these oppositions carefully in order to understand more fully the complexity of an issue—each of these qualities ran counter to the polarized polemical energies of the public sphere. Dryden was always a poet first, a polemicist second. We might say that he devised an experiential poetics that forced readers to sense, review, and reflect on the full force of ideas at play in Restoration London. Reading Dryden, "one breathes in the atmosphere of political conflict and senses the pervasive presence of alternative opinions" (Piper 21). Paradox and contradiction, not consistency, confessional alignment, or orthodoxy, are the hallmarks of his style.

These same characteristics complicate the task of teaching Dryden's religious poems. Yet both *Religio Laici* (*Poems of John Dryden* 2: 85–134) and *The Hind and the Panther* (3: 39–180) offer rich opportunities to expose students to Dryden's interest in combating the polarized polemical combat of the public sphere. *Religio Laici*, although a more practical choice for both undergraduate survey courses and upper-level eighteenth-century courses than the longer *The Hind and the Panther*, is a difficult poem, not least because it will not yield a single, fixed reading. Teaching *Religio Laici* requires familiarizing students with a series of contexts: they must understand the differences among Anglican, Catholic, and deist approaches to the rule of faith; the gist of Richard Simon's argument in his *Critical History of the Old Testament*; the anti-Catholic response to James Stuart's public profession of Catholicism; and Catholic book history. Some lecturing can make these contexts intelligible to students, but students must also evaluate the poem's arguments for themselves. Once they are familiar with the contexts, they can try to identify whether the poem presents one rule of faith as preferable to others. Ideally, they will examine both Dryden's careful presentation of arguments and his prosody. Disagreement about which rule of faith the poem advances may be a sign of successful teaching, indicating that the poem has retained its stubbornly and, for its time, shockingly open-ended character.

Though it might at first appear to be so, *Religio Laici* is not Dryden's personal confession of faith. Samuel Johnson famously labeled the poem a "voluntary effusion" ("Dryden" 139), and readers since have consistently scoured it for clues to Dryden's confessional allegiance in 1682.[1] Such readings are abetted by Dryden himself, who took the unusual step of attaching his name to the poem, thereby giving it "a special voltage" by presenting it in the guise of a confession of faith (Mullan 178). He presents his arguments as those of an orthodox Anglican, claiming in his preface to have taken many of his arguments from "our reverend divines of the Church of England" (86). He adds that he has received approval for most of his arguments from "a judicious and learned friend, a man indefatigably zealous in the service of the church and state" (87). This friend is often identified as John Tillotson, an Anglican divine. Additionally, the poem's three-part structure seems to posit two alternatives to the Church of England, deism and Catholicism, as extremes to be avoided. *Religio Laici* takes as its subject the problem of identifying the source of religious authority, which Anglicans resolved through the doctrine of *scriptura sola*, the notion that scripture is clear on all matters necessary for salvation. A deist interlocutor counters that reason alone, not scripture, provides a sufficient rule of faith. A Catholic interlocutor insists on the need for church tradition as a guide to scripture. Wedged between these two extremes, the *via media* of Anglicanism appears to be advanced as preferable to either. Dryden concedes elements of each argument but concludes with the need for "waiving each extreme" (line 427). If we stop with this conclusion, we join many distinguished scholars in reading the poem as an orthodox Anglican confession of faith.

Yet the poem's forceful dialogic presentation of competing arguments works against such a fixed interpretation. In particular, its attention to outlawed Catholic arguments functions as a kind of Trojan horse, injecting forbidden arguments into the public sphere, thereby allowing a fuller consideration of the problem of determining the rule of faith. Dryden's seeming orthodoxy is inconsistent, for example, with his claim that the poem was inspired by the publication of Henry Dickinson's translation of the *Critical History*, by Richard Simon, a French Oratorian priest whose pioneering biblical criticism included blistering attacks on the Protestant doctrine of *scriptura sola*. Simon demonstrated that all extant scriptural texts were copies of lost originals and therefore vulnerable to errors transmitted by scribes over time. For Simon, Church tradition was necessary in order to help the layman with the textual difficulties of scripture. "*[I]f*," he insisted, "*the truth of Religion remain'd not in the Church; it would be unsafe to search for it at present in Books which have been subject to so many alterations, and have in many things depended upon the pleasure of Transcribers*" (sig. [a4]v). Only those who were "either ignorant or prejudic'd" could possibly affirm that the "Scripture is plain of it self" (sig. b1r). Stalwart Anglicans were horrified by Simon's work; John Evelyn wrote immediately to John Fell, bishop of Oxford, that Simon "exposes not only the Protestant and the whole Reformed Churches abroad, but (what ought to be dearer to us) the Church of England at home, which with them acknowledges the Holy Scriptures alone to be the canon and rule of faith." Noting that the *Critical History* "hugely prevails," he hoped that the "pens and chairs" of Oxford might respond to it (663). No such volume was produced, and Dickinson's English translation of Simon's work might have remained forbidden reading, because of its exposition of Catholic arguments.[2] Yet Dryden did not just popularize Simon's arguments by discussing them in his poem; according to Phillip Harth, when Dickinson's translation encountered difficulties getting printed in England, Dryden helped his publisher, Jacob Tonson, package the volume by securing commendatory poems (188–90). Why, students might be asked, was an allegedly orthodox Anglican both writing about a Catholic priest's biblical criticism and actively involved in seeing an English translation of his controversial work through the English press?

Dryden's determination to allow Simon's arguments to be heard was particularly defiant, given the intensity of the debate between Restoration Anglicans and English Catholics over the self-sufficiency of scripture. During the 1670s, anti-Catholic agitation escalated and was even promoted by the Anglican hierarchy, which was unsettled by the Duke of York's public profession of Catholicism in 1673. When York subsequently married a young Italian princess, the Anglican hierarchy was forced to confront the possibility that he might beget Catholic heirs. As John Spurr notes, "Popery became the dominant issue of English politics" (*Restoration Church* 66). Eager to protect its monopoly over religious doctrine and its establishment as the nation's sole religious authority, the Anglican hierarchy became more intransigent and more anti-Catholic, enforcing the Test Acts of 1673 and 1678 and launching a propaganda campaign depicting Catholics as credulous, idolatrous, superstitious, and servilely subservient to authority. Edward Stillingfleet, an Anglican divine, had long established himself as the leader of this anti-Catholic campaign. He presented the doctrine of *scriptura sola* as a counterauthority to papal authority. For Stillingfleet, the act of reading scripture conveyed reliably the scriptural teachings essential to salvation.

English Catholics, however, viewed the Church not solely as a community believing in the moral tenets of scripture but also as a community enacting scripture's teachings through the sacraments; for them, Stillingfleet's confidence in the layman's ability to read scripture alone was unfounded. Vincent Canes, a Franciscan, summarized the argument by insisting on the need for Church authority to serve as a living judge, capable of resolving interpretive disputes over scripture: "Experience hath now taught us clear enough, that the scriptur [sic] is a dangerous edged tool to put into the hands of the rude and boisterous vulgar" (*Fiat Lux* 56). Repeatedly, Catholics pointed to the example of the Socinians, who derived their heretical beliefs from scripture. No clear agreement regarding religious issues could be possible, they argued, without an authoritative guide to the controversies.

Stillingfleet and his fellow Anglicans had a distinct advantage over Catholics in this religiopolitical paper war, in that they could publish their arguments legally. The Licensing Act of 1662 forbade anything to be printed contrary to the doctrines of the national Church. Somewhat disingenuously, Stillingfleet invited Catholics in 1671 with anything to say "either against our Church or in Defence of their own, [to] . . . come into the open Field, from which they have of late so wisely withdrawn themselves, finding so little success in it" (sig. a2r). Fully aware that the conditions of minority printing precluded an "open field" of printed debate, he nevertheless had a copy of his attack on Catholicism, *Discourse concerning the Idolatry* (1671), delivered personally to the Catholic controversialist Thomas Godden, whose argument it partly addressed.[3] Godden viewed the delivery as a challenge, claiming to receive Stillingfleet's text "*with the same regard, that Men look upon a* Glove, *when sent by a Person, with whom they have happened formerly to have some* difference" (sig. [a1]r). Canes ventured that Catholics were perfectly willing to "fit their Slings into their Arms, and meet [Stillingfleet]" but that they were obstructed by the legal restrictions of Catholic printing. He noted in particular one inquisitor's entering printing houses, crying "*[H]ave ye here any thing against the Doctour Stillingfleet*?" (*Account* 3). Serenus Cressy, a Benedictine, corroborated Canes's complaint, noting that since Stillingfleet's challenge

> *searches* into *Presses* have been more solicitously exact, and more frequent dayly and hourly, then they have been all the years taken together since his *Majesties Restauration*, *Inquisitors* searching into every hole, turning over every small paper, and rigorously examining both Maisters and Servants whether any thing has been written against *Doctour Stillingfleet*. (sig. a3r–a3v)

When Catholics did respond to Stillingfleet's challenge, they were doomed to publish their work in formats announcing the work's unlicensed and thus extralegal status, which delegitimized their arguments. Canes summarized his frustration by lamenting that fencers

> meet in Bear-garden[s] without any controul, there to baste one another lustily for the peoples pleasure. And it would be a pastime I think equally delightful, not less profitable, and somewhat more civil, to see two men

> reason down one another. We poor men should esteem it a great favour to us, if our adversary might read his charge and we our defence, even in [a] Bear-garden. Since neither in churches, Halls, Universities, or Schools are we permitted to speak; or print any thing to speak for us.
>
> (*Account* 73–74)

Religio Laici might thus be read as a response to the need for a more "open field" of debate than the public sphere permitted in the early 1680s. Students can be asked to consider the effect of Dryden's decision to sign his name to the poem. How does the poem's ascription to Dryden, who was the nation's poet laureate, package and even legitimize the poem's blend of orthodox and unorthodox arguments? His decision to popularize Simon's work, with its explicit censuring of *scriptura sola*, suggests his interest in hearing the play of competing arguments regarding the rule of faith. Note that when Narcissus Luttrell, an anti-Catholic diarist and book collector ever vigilant in ferreting out papist material, read Dryden's poem, he inscribed his copy with the warning "Atheisticall."[4] An ecumenical spirit was largely alien to Restoration thinkers. The very openness of Dryden's poem was clearly disturbing to readers like Luttrell and Evelyn, who were eager to link Englishness with Protestantism.

Once students understand these contexts, they will want to look at the way the poem maps out competing arguments for the rule of faith. They should familiarize themselves with the deist's arguments (lines 42–61, 168–83), the answers to them (62–167, 184–223), the review of Simon's work (224–75), the Catholic's arguments (276–81, 305–15), and the interlaced responses to those arguments. A preliminary discussion should consider whether Dryden's reviews of deist and Catholic arguments are balanced.

Students might then be asked to respond to the following set of questions:

1. In the preface, Dryden claims that "a poem designed purely for instruction ought to be plain and natural, yet majestic" (105–06). Similarly, his epigraph insists, "The subject itself refuses to be ornamented; it is content to be explained." Consider the poem's range of styles, from its majestic eleven-line exordium to its deflated concluding couplet. Is Dryden's style "plain and natural"?
2. Why are the deist's couplets (lines 42–61, 168–83) end-stopped? Why are the Catholic interlocutor's couplets (276–81, 305–15) enjambed? What effect do end-stopping and enjambment have on the credibility of their arguments? How might we link Dryden's attention to style in these passages with his dismissal of style in the poem's concluding lines?
3. Dryden twice raises the problem posed by the Socinians, who contested the divinity of Christ, first in the preface (93) and again in the poem (line 312). In his *Critical History*, Simon thought that the example of the Socinians revealed the need to appeal to Church authority:

> There have . . . been very few Protestant Divines who have sufficiently answer'd the *Socinians*, who affirm that there can be no medium held betwixt their Religion, and the *Roman Catholic*: for if we take the Scripture, Reason, and Experience for our Rule, we must, say they, be of their Opinion, whereas if we follow the prejudices of Tradition, we must of necessity joyn with the *Roman Catholicks*, in a word the Protestants in their Disputes against *Socinians*, have much ado to [forbear] the making use of the Authority of the Ancient Fathers of the Church; wherefore the *Socinians* have reason to blame them for not standing to their Principle. (118 [bk. 3])

To what purpose does Dryden mention the Socinians in the preface? in the poem? Does the poem refute or emphasize Simon's concern?

4. Dryden's angry comments on William Tyndale's translation of the Bible (99 [preface]) and on the Reformation's placing the Bible into the hands of the illiterate (lines 400–26) echo Catholic concerns. Yet Protestants, like Dryden's irenic and pious tutor at Trinity, John Templer, also worried about this problem, noting that those whose "understandings being coloured with a false light, . . . look through it upon the Scripture, and so make the Scripture appear to them of the same colour; just as men, that put green or blew glass before their eyes, all the objects round about will appear blew or green" (Templer 15). How are we to understand Dryden's outbursts regarding the Reformation and reading? Might these outbursts be considered unresolved concerns pertaining to Reformed thought? Are the attacks on biblicists balanced by criticisms of Catholic tradition (lines 370–97)?
5. Is the poem a Trojan horse or an expression of orthodox Anglican faith?
6. What does Dryden's poem suggest about the nature of Restoration religious experience? Was it confident and self-assured? self-questioning? informed? Compare and contrast it with modern religious experience.

Students are no more apt than scholars to agree on answers to these questions. But they will acquire an appreciation for Dryden's interest in using poetry to awaken readers to complexities, contradictions, and paradoxes that the polarized polemic of the public sphere too often either ignored or disallowed. It was likely the probing intellectual curiosity evident in this poem that led contemporaries to consider Dryden "an alien, even a dangerous spirit."

NOTES

[1] Louis Bredvold viewed the poem's philosophical skepticism as an indication of Dryden's receptivity to Catholicism. Phillip Harth countered that such skepticism as Dryden possessed was strictly methodological, not philosophical. For Harth, *Religio Laici* was an

expression of Anglican orthodoxy. Steven Zwicker departed from such readings to argue that Dryden lacked an interest in religion ("Dryden and the Poetic Career").

[2] Edward Stillingfleet characteristically dismissed Simon's work in a sermon at Whitehall in early 1683 by describing Simon as "a late Writer in great vogue among those who are glad to find any thing that seems to reflect on the Authority of the Scriptures" (qtd. in Reedy 147).

[3] Thomas Godden was a pseudonym for Thomas Tilden or Tylden.

[4] Luttrell's copy of *Religio Laici* is part of the Percy J. Dobell collection at the Folger Shakespeare Library. Some have attributed Luttrell's dismay to the poem's deistic arguments. Such dismay is unlikely, given the affinities between radical Protestant defenses of reason and Anglican anti-Catholic polemic, which defended reason on similar grounds. But see Mullan 173.

Dryden the Elegist: "To the Memory of Mr. Oldham" and "To the Pious Memory of . . . Anne Killigrew"

Cedric D. Reverand II

In both upper-division 1660–1750 British literature classes and graduate classes, I teach "To the Memory of Mr. Oldham" (*Works* 2: 175) together with the ode to Anne Killigrew (3: 109–15), but I begin with Milton's "Lycidas." This strategy introduces students to the elegy, a rather important literary genre and one that they will encounter again; it also has the advantage of introducing them to "Lycidas," which they are unlikely to have read in preliminary survey courses, largely because my colleagues seldom teach it, thinking the density of references makes it too difficult.

Students generally regard the Oldham poem as a simple, straightforward tribute. It is short, a mere twenty-five lines, not terribly difficult syntactically. Their first response tends to be, "So what?" They do not know the complicated publication history of Dryden's and Oldham's satires, which means they cannot quite make sense out of "The last set out the soonest did arrive" (line 8), unless they read the line as "The guy who was born last died first," which is true enough. Nor do they know the complexities entailed in the classical allusions, particularly the allusion to Nisus and Euryalus, and student editions typically say only that in book 6 of the *Aeneid* Euryalis beats Nisus in a footrace. So what?

"To the Pious Memory of . . . Anne Killigrew" presents a different problem. It is so extravagant that students simply do not know what to make of it. Then there are those wild images. She's treading with the seraphims and adopted to a star? The planets shined on her horoscope? She conquered the realm of painture? Realm? Painture? How can he be serious?

What do "Lycidas," "To Oldham," and the Killigrew ode have in common, aside from being elegies? Well, they are all written by a poet about dead poets. Then, with "Lycidas" in hand, we look for the basic parts of the elegy. First, the narrator establishes the occasion: "For *Lycidas* is dead, dead ere his prime" (line 8). Then, somewhere along the way, the narrator identifies with the dead Lycidas:

> Together both, ere the high Lawns appear'd
> Under the opening eyelids of the morn,
> We drove afield, and both together heard
> What time the Gray-fly winds her sultry horn,
> Batt'ning our flocks. . . . (25–29)

At this point, I have to explain that this is a pastoral elegy, that Lycidas is the classical name for Edward King, that the two of them battened their flocks, as it were, on that "self-same hill" (23)—that is, Cambridge. For the moment, we skip the central issues and look for the resolution: "Weep no more, woeful Shepherds, weep no more, / For *Lycidas* your sorrow is not dead" (165–66). Though he is drowned, "Sunk . . . beneath the wat'ry floor," like the "day-star," he will rise again "Through the dear might of him that walk'd the waves" (173). Big change: we have gone from "*Lycidas* is dead" to "*Lycidas* . . . is not dead."

Now, we look for the same elements in Dryden, starting with the Oldham poem. The occasion? Students are likely to think you have just asked them a ridiculously simple question, and they quickly quote the title, "To the Memory of Mr. Oldham," and point both to the word *memory* and to the first word of the poem, "Farewel." Dryden wastes no time getting to the identification either, beginning in lines 3–4: "For sure our Souls were near ally'd; and thine / Cast in the same Poetick mould with mine." Now, we look for the resolution:

> Once more, hail and farewel; farewel thou young,
> But ah too short, *Marcellus* of our Tongue;
> Thy Brows with Ivy, and with Laurels bound;
> But Fate and gloomy Night encompass thee around.
> (22–25)

Whoops. Something is wrong: no heaven, no afterlife, no daystar rising. Dryden is supposed to say, "You died, but your fame will live on"; instead, he says, "You won some fame, but you're dead."[1] But students can recognize that the ending is unusual only when they learn how an elegy is supposed to end: when you expect "For Oldham, your sorrow, is not dead," and instead get Oldham not just dead but encompassed by fate and the gloomy night, it is a stunning reversal.

Now, we look for these elements in the Killigrew ode. The occasion gives no problem: "Memory" in the title usually provides a sufficient clue, and the poem opens with "Thou Youngest Virgin-Daughter of the Skies" (line 1), with the poet-painter rolling above us, "call'd to more Superiour Bliss" (10), singing a celestial song, and the students can figure out that the reason Killigrew is up there and not down here is that she is dead. When I ask them to find the moment of identification, however, their usual reaction is to bury their heads in their books in hopes of becoming invisible.

All right, then we look for the resolution, which is found easily enough. It is the entire final stanza, where Dryden depicts "the last Assizes," with the "Judging God" closing the book of fate and the dead being noisily resurrected (181–82). When the "Golden Trump" signals the event,

> The Sacred Poets first shall hear the Sound,
>   And formost from the Tomb shall bound:
> For they are cover'd with the lightest Ground,
> And streight, with in-born Vigour, on the Wing,
> Like mounting Larkes, to the New Morning sing.

> There Thou, Sweet Saint, before the Quire shalt go,
> As Harbinger of Heav'n, the Way to show,
> The Way which thou so well hast learn'd below.
> (188–95)

The question this passage immediately raises is, Why, in the Oldham poem (1684), does Dryden end with his poet encompassed by fate and the gloomy night, while just two years later (1686), his young poetess is not only resurrected but grandly resurrected, leading all mankind to heaven at the Last Judgment? Why does Oldham end up "bound" in the sense of being restricted and tied down, while Killigrew will "bound" in the sense of leaping upward?

If the students have read "Mac Flecknoe" by this point (*Works* 2: 54–60; first circulated in manuscript in 1676, it precedes both elegies), they may well ask another question: How could Dryden be so savage to Thomas Shadwell, an undistinguished poet, and yet praise Anne Killigrew, who was no better? This difference troubled David Vieth, who years ago argued that Dryden must have been satirizing Killigrew, which, as Howard Weinbrot has pointed out, is almost certainly wrong (359–72). Why do students have difficulty finding the moment of identification? It is there, in stanza 4, but they miss it. For now, we simply leave the question hanging in the air.

Back to Milton. Here, I give a little background, explaining that Milton was reading day and night so that he could one day write a sacred epic that would encompass large areas of human knowledge. Then, he learned that King, a fellow poet whom he knew at Cambridge, a man who had intended to take sacred orders, had drowned. I ask them how *they* would feel if they discovered that somebody roughly their age, somebody like them, had suddenly died (this is not an uncommon experience: in a class of twenty-five students, there will be at least one who knows somebody who was killed in a car accident or struck down by a devastating disease). How would Milton respond? He would wonder why he was studying so hard—this is something students understand pretty well—when death, "the blind *Fury* with th'abhorred shears" (line 75), could cut everything away in an instant. Instead of working hard and sacrificing, so that he could one day write his great epic, perhaps he should "sport with *Amaryllis* in the shade" (68), at which point we all try extremely hard to imagine Puritan Milton sporting with somebody named Amaryllis (this bit, I think, is one of the funniest in all of Milton). Such a death leads us to ask why. "What hard mishap hath doom'd this gentle swain?" (92). Then, Could the death have been prevented? "Where were ye Nymphs when the remorseless deep / Clos'd o'er the head of your lov'd *Lycidas*?" (50–51). But no, "Ay me! I fondly dream! / Had ye been there—for what could that have done?" (55–56). We also wonder why death should take him and not somebody less valuable: Camus reflects, "How well could I have spar'd for thee, young swain, / Enough of such as for their bellies' sake / Creep and intrude and climb into the fold?" (113–15). There are memories of happy times together, now forever lost: "But O the heavy change, now thou art gone" (38). Sometimes, during extreme stress, the mind focuses on simple, minor details as a way of distracting itself from overwhelming emotion. Milton accordingly tries to "interpose a little ease" (152) and imagines flowers being piled on the tomb (since King was lost at sea, this image is pure fancy).

What are the issues in "Lycidas"? I spend less time on the poem's issues than on its formal properties, but I do point out that the two main topics—Why should I continue studying in hopes of one day writing a Christian epic? Why should I believe in God?—are connected. If Milton plans to write *Paradise Lost* (the first issue), he must sustain his belief in a loving God (the second issue). That King was both a poet and intended to be a minister conveniently combines the two. In short, I push students toward discovering that this extremely formal poem actually traces the psychological steps a person goes through when grieving, from shock and disbelief, to questions about justice and fate, through memories and distractions, and finally, to recovery. Along the way, the students may come to realize that this occasional poem is not about the occasion itself, but launches from the occasion to matters troubling Milton. As one of my students once observed at this point, "When you grieve for the dead person, you're really grieving for yourself."

Now we can return to Dryden, and I begin by fleshing out the biographical background. First of all, Dryden was fifty-three at the time of the Oldham poem, whereas Oldham died at the age of thirty. Clearly, they were not nursed on the selfsame hill. They were separated by age, by achievement, Dryden, the prolific, established poet laureate, Oldham, the author of a handful of poems and one book. Where Milton thought he might have been an Edward King and died unfulfilled, Dryden, by contrast, thinks Oldham, had he lived, could have become another Dryden.

Like Milton's occasional poem, Dryden's also is about the author: the central issue is Dryden versus Oldham, the fruitful poet laureate versus the poet whose "generous fruits" were "gather'd ere their prime" (line 19), which brings us to the Nisus-Euryalis allusion.

> To the same Goal did both our Studies drive.
> The last set out the soonest did arrive.
> Thus *Nisus* fell upon the slippery place,
> While his young Friend perform'd and won the Race.
> (7–10)

I put a list of titles and publication dates on the board to demonstrate that Dryden was the first verse satirist, having written "Mac Flecknoe" around 1676 and having started *Absalom and Achitophel* probably before 1678, but Oldham was the first published verse satirist, since *Satires upon the Jesuits* appeared in 1681, ten months before *Absalom and Achitophel* ("Mac Flecknoe" was first published, spuriously, in 1682). We also know that Dryden influenced Oldham, because there exists in the Bodleian Library a long extract of "Mac Flecknoe" written in Oldham's hand, dated 1678, before Oldham wrote *Satires upon the Jesuits*. Now we can understand the relevance of the Nisus-Euryalis story. Nisus (Dryden) is the faster runner (he was winning the race before he slipped in a pool of blood)—that is, he is the more accomplished poet. And he helps "his young Friend" Euryalis win by tripping the lead runner intentionally, just as Dryden, by his example of "Mac Flecknoe," helped Oldham learn how to write verse satire.

I review the give-and-take in the poem, where every time Dryden says something critical of Oldham, he then undercuts it, criticizing him for not having smooth "numbers," but saying "Satyr needs not those" (14–15), pointing out the "harsh cadence of a rugged line," but calling this fault a "noble Error" (16–17), with the criticism implicit in "Error" more or less canceled out if the error is "noble."

I turn again to the ending, the nonresolution, and students can see that although Oldham was a Dryden in training, Dryden, too, has to look forward to fate and gloomy night. I explain that Nisus and Euryalis appear later in the *Aeneid*, when they go on a plundering expedition to the enemy camp and die together in a pool of blood (an echo of the pool in which Nisus slipped during the race). Students can figure out the implications: it does not matter, ultimately, that Nisus is the faster runner or Dryden the better poet. After Nisus loses the footrace, Salius, the runner he tripped, complains that he was fouled, and Aeneas gives him a prize. Nisus remarks that as long as prizes are being given for falling down, he too fell down, and indeed he too gets rewarded. That is, winning does not matter, since everybody wins the race, . . . and in the end everybody loses the race, because everybody dies. While it is clear throughout the poem that Dryden appreciates his own superior skill, it is also clear that he realizes this skill affords him no advantage against fate and gloomy night. The poem ends with a grimly realistic, classical, unredemptive vision of darkness burying all.

Yet the Killigrew poem ends with Anne triumphantly leading all mankind at the Last Judgment. What happened? I explain that somewhere around 1685, between the two poems, Dryden converted to Catholicism. Students know enough about religious conversions (primarily from the media in the context of politics) that they can grasp the possibility of sudden religious enthusiasm. They can also understand sudden guilt for the sins of the past, accompanied by the fervent desire to start anew. The key now comes in the moment of identification, which they had missed:

> O Gracious God! How far have we
> Prophaned thy Heav'nly Gift of Poesy?
> Made prostitute and profligate the Muse,

Debas'd to each obscene and impious use,
Whose Harmony was first ordain'd Above
For Tongues of Angels, and for Hymns of Love?
O wretched We! why were we hurry'd down
 This lubrique and adult'rate age,
 (Nay added fat Pollutions of our own)
 T' increase the steaming Ordures of the Stage?
What can we say t' excuse our Second Fall?
Let this thy *Vestal*, Heav'n, attone for all! (56–67)

In part, they missed the identification because Dryden uses "we" instead of "I." But also, even if they read the introduction, they did not reflect upon, or notice, Dryden's conversion, and they know nothing about Dryden the playwright or about the racy plays of the Restoration stage. This is a reverse identification: Oldham and Dryden are alike, in that each is a potential version of the other, but Killigrew is conspicuously unlike Dryden. "Her *Arethusian* Stream remans unsoil'd, / Unmixt with Forreign Filth, and undefil'd" (68–69). She did not allow herself to be "hurry'd down / This lubrique and adult'rate age," and I take some time telling students about the obscene plays of the period, which has the auxiliary advantage of getting students to look forward to future reading assignments.

We can now address the question of why Dryden would pillory Shadwell and exalt Anne Killigrew. Shadwell was a competitor when Dryden was writing his supposedly polluted plays, which Dryden charmingly refers to as "steaming ordures of the stage" (unlike students from an urban environment, those at a rural university like mine have an earthy awareness of ordure, and they know that it steams). Killigrew, by contrast, is what a poet should be, the pure Arethusan stream rather than the lubric and adulterate river that Dryden had been hurrying down. Turning to stanza 2, we discover that Killigrew was a "Præexisting Soul" that "did through all the Mighty Poets roul / Who *Greek* or *Latine* Laurels wore" (29, 31–32), which metamorphically, or by metempsychosis, makes her all great classical poets rolled into one. Whether she was a good poet or a minor talent does not matter if she represents all poets. What matters is that her heart was in the right place, her soul was pure. What might a poet as accomplished as Dryden have done, what might he yet do, if his motivation were similarly elevated?

This exercise accomplishes a number of things. We end up reading two contrasting poems in the context of Dryden's biography, but also in the context of a genre, and I explain that one of the things that makes the Killigrew ode transcendent is Dryden's choice of writing a Pindaric ode, which makes grandiose claims (if I am teaching a graduate class, I will most likely assign odes by Cowley to give students a taste of the genre). With any luck, students learn something not only about elegies but also about the range of an elegy's possibilities, from pastoral to restrained and classical to Pindaric. And they will perhaps see that formal, initially distant poems can deal with human experiences and feelings they understand, with such things as ambition, pride, self-doubt, guilt. They even may learn about Dryden's restless mind, always turning issues inside out, in this case writing a poem that expresses supreme confidence in his powers, then a poem that confesses his failure to live up to the requirements of his genius.

NOTE

[1] I borrow the sharp remark from Dustin Griffin's fine article on the poem.

Reading Dryden's Verse: Generic Control in the Killigrew Ode and Oldham Elegy

John Richetti

I have taught Dryden's verse in undergraduate poetry surveys for English majors and a specialized graduate seminar on poetic genres in the English Restoration and eighteenth-century. In both settings, I always begin by discussing the crucial differences between cultural attitudes to poetry at the end of the seventeenth and the beginning of the eighteenth century and those that have prevailed, more or less, since the early nineteenth century. For exploring those differences, I can think of no better guide than J. Paul Hunter's "Couplets and Conversation." As this essay title indicates, one difference that is immediately apparent in many poems from the period is their affinity for "conversation," hence my preference for the word *verse* over *poetry*, since *verse* is a fairly neutral marker of an organizing form of language, whereas *poetry* has since the Romantics acquired an aura of special insight or vision or even prophetic intensity. As Hunter puts it, couplet poems are artful precisely in their imitation of various qualities of conversation: they "don't try to emulate talk exactly—just provide a tone and simplicity of vocabulary and syntax that make them as understandable as a clear spoken sentence" (25). Exactly so, and when I teach Dryden's "To the Memory of Mr. Oldham," I begin by reading the first couple of lines and then (since I know the poem by heart) walk away from the lectern and continue reciting it—or, as it were, talking it—to convey a sense of the poem's direct and intimate address to the deceased: "Farewell, too little and too lately known / Whom I began to think and call my own" (*Poems and Fables* 324).[1] In my experience, reciting rather than reading, addressing (with eye contact and, ideally, with movement around the lecture hall) particular student stand-ins for the dead Mr. Oldham, is a revealing way to begin a discussion of how neoclassical English verse often works. Many students are pleasantly puzzled by my performance, intrigued that someone should actually have gone to the trouble of memorizing a poem. That an English professor should like (love!) a poem enough to memorize it may just send an important message about the pleasures and insights that literature can provide.[2]

Recitation or performance can be very useful in teaching most neoclassical English verse, since it communicates the easy interchange between speaker and an implicit interlocutor (and, of course, ultimately a reader) characteristic of some neoclassical English poetic genres. Proper reading or recitation without a book can open up the poem, demystify it, and stage it as the lively and informative conversation that it can be. Although Dryden's poem is written in heroic couplets (except for one triplet near the end), if one reads it properly, the couplets are for the most part productively enjambed, except when periods or semicolons signal a complete stop. Most students, when asked to read poems in class, pause heavily at the end of lines, and these pauses destroy the easy flow and conversational exchange that Dryden in this poem and elsewhere in his work is out to create.

"To the Memory of Mr. Oldham" stages a dialogue with the (necessarily) silent but still present John Oldham, and the intimacy and immediacy Dryden seeks to create can be underlined by quoting the opening of the third line: "For sure our Souls were near ally'd." That "for sure" marks an assurance; he is arguing against what the poem's original audience and, for that matter, the dead Oldham would have said, that the two poets did not know each other very well at all. With that common phrase, Dryden politely insists on an affinity and a sort of easy intimacy; they were, after all, both satirists with the same outlook on the world:

> One common Note on either Lyre did strike,
> And Knaves and Fools we both abhorr'd alike.
> (lines 5–6)

The "we" assumes fellowship: Dryden and Oldham shared a common purpose as satirists. One might pause here to explain to students that this is a tremendous compliment from Dryden, in 1684 the poet laureate of England and the most popular dramatist of the day, to a much lesser and younger poet. The magnitude and grace of that compliment would have been obvious to contemporary readers.

These opening lines are a good place to ask students what it means to address another person, living or recently dead, in a poem. I ask them if they can think of other poems where this happens, and I also ask them that if a poem is not addressed to someone, to whom is it addressed? Of course, I hope that they will see, as the course continues and we read similar poems by Alexander Pope, Jonathan Swift, and others, that Dryden's poem is fairly typical of neoclassical verse in its confident assumption of an audience that shares certain values and that treats poetry as a communicative and informative medium as much as it is a means of self-expression. Much poetry after the Romantics, one can lead students to see, is essentially a matter of soliloquizing; but much neoclassical poetry is dialogical, addressed directly to an audience and engaged with it, committed to communication and not pure self-expression. One point that often enough comes up in discussion is that poems like Dryden's reinforce the values of their intended readers, whereas poetry from later centuries is usually out to revise or reform or reject what readers believe. In this poem and in others, Dryden dramatizes himself as part of a social group, a man talking to others about matters of common concern.

When the class comes to understand differences like these, we can move on to the lesson in genre criticism that Dryden provides. Oldham's untimely death, it turns out, is the occasion for reflection on the nature of satire, since the young poet was known mainly for his work in that genre. This elegy, the students may be surprised to learn, slides easily into an educational opportunity and a discussion of what kind of poetic style is preferable in satire. The death of the young poet in this case involves slightly condescending praise for his slim and narrow output as a satirist and for what Dryden calls his awkward versification.

> O early ripe! to thy abundant store
> What could advancing Age have added more?
> It might (what Nature never gives the young)
> Have taught the numbers of thy native Tongue.
> (11–14)

The parenthetical aside is crucial for the sophisticated tone of this part of the poem and helps establish a confident and unforced digressiveness. One may suggest to students that Dryden is here inserting in the very middle of praise of the precocious Oldham ("O early ripe!") an aside to readers who from experience know that nature doesn't teach young poets versification. The circle of auditors has thus been widened, and the lines that follow, about the requirements for satiric verse, resonate beyond the elegiac praise of Oldham.

To be sure, the criticism is almost immediately modified in the graceful concession that "Satyr needs not those, and Wit will shine / Through the harsh cadence of a rugged line" (15–16)—somewhat rough lines themselves, especially the second, with its initial trochaic substitution and the rolling *r* of "rugged," as it would have been pronounced in 1684. So Dryden can be said to be showing off, making his lines both enunciate and embody the harsh cadence proper to satire. This polite display is part of his concession to Oldham's satirical vigor, a concession that culminates in the triplet in which Dryden compares his own consummate skill at rhyming with Oldham's sharp and forceful verses.

> Thy generous fruits, though gather'd ere their prime
> Still shew'd a quickness; and maturing time
> But mellows what we write to the dull sweets of Rime.
> (19–21)

The sense of that "quickness" is worth dwelling on: as the *OED* reports, the word applies to taste in a now obsolete sense, "sharpness, keenness; pungency or acidity of taste," and this sense derives from a more general primary meaning, "the quality or fact of being alive or living; life, vitality, vital principle." So in this elegant compliment and self-effacing and gently ironic account of what maturity brings to an older, seasoned poet like Dryden, his work is merely a riper and duller sort of poetic fruit—"the dull sweets of Rime." Such modesty is transparent, a mode of politeness in the face of the early death of a young and distinctly minor poet.

Modesty in several senses fades away in the bravura conclusion to the poem, a tour de force of allusive coherence, mournful imagery, and masterful sound effects.

> Once more, hail and farewell; farewell thou young,
> But ah too short, *Marcellus* of our Tongue;
> Thy Brows with Ivy, and with Laurels bound;
> But Fate and gloomy Night encompass thee around.
> (22–25)

The opening "Once more" reminds the speaker that he needs to return from literary criticism to his elegiac business, a stagy reminder that is meant to continue the spontaneity and informality the poem has cultivated. But those qualities give way to the elegiac formality of the concluding lines. The first line echoes the end of a famous Latin poem by Catullus—"hail and farewell" is English for Catullus's "Ave atque vale"—and the last line is an Alexandrine, twelve syllables, with open vowel sounds (*gloomy . . . encompass . . . around*) that suggest a long and mournful organ chord. But it is the second line, with its allusion to Oldham as the "*Marcellus* of our Tongue," that is startling in its implicit, deeply immodest self-dramatization. The first Roman emperor, Caesar Augustus, having no children of his own, named his nephew, Marcellus, as his heir, but the nephew died young. Turning Oldham into Marcellus therefore makes Dryden the Augustus of the English language. More generally, he implies that the political and imperial world of Roman antiquity is parallel to the literary world in which he and Oldham are participants. The poem thus projects a unity of experience, or an ennobling analogy, from imperial Rome to late-seventeenth-century English literature.

Until these last four lines of the poem, the manner is conversational and relaxed, but Dryden's language is throughout deeply metaphoric, although its intimate tone tends to distract readers from that density. For example, in lines 4 and 5 Dryden speaks of Oldham's soul as "cast" like his own in the same "poetic mould," which is a common enough expression, as conventional as the picture in the next line of Oldham and Dryden, poetic singers both, striking their lyres. Running through the middle of the poem (from line 11 to line 21) is the conventional agricultural metaphor in which poems are like fruit. But what are we to make of the (to modern eyes) strange metaphoric development in lines 7–10?

> To the same Goal did both our Studies drive,
> The last set out the soonest did arrive.
> Thus Nisus fell upon the slippery place,
> While his young Friend perform'd and won the Race.

Those in the class who have read the *Aeneid* may recognize the allusion to the footrace in the funeral games to mark the death of Aeneas's father, Anchises. The race features two close Trojan friends, the younger Euryalus and his mentor, Nisus. Dryden is Nisus, of course, and Euryalus is Oldham; so the younger man in the metaphor has won the race of life by dying first. How odd, you will want to say to your students, to liken victory in a footrace to dying early! It's a purely Christian moment, illustrated by a scene from classical antiquity, in which dying young is seen as a victory. Even odder is the presence of such a sentiment in an otherwise secular and straightforward poem of mourning. I have no explanation except to suggest that perhaps Dryden's Christian values are competing for a moment with classical elegiac sentiments. An issue like this can add to the poem, for all its easy lucidity, a slight opacity or ambiguity, which may be to the good when talking about a poet like Dryden. Despite the serene urbanity on display in this poem, Dryden was a Catholic convert who refused to give up his allegiances when a Protestant king, William III, arrived in 1688.

The Oldham poem is occasional, provoked by a particular event, and so too is "To the Pious Memory of the Accomplisht Young Lady Mrs Anne Killigrew, Excellent in the Two Sister-Arts of Poesie and Painting: An Ode" (1686; *Works* 3: 109–15). I have assigned the Oldham poem and the Killigrew ode to graduate students in a course titled Generic Change in Neoclassical Poetry, since the ode strikes me as a generic hybrid: ode, elegy, and even at times a verse letter to the dead Mrs. Anne Killigrew. Despite the odd dwelling in the Oldham poem on early death as in some sense a victory, there is in the poem no hint of the Christian consolation for death, whereas the Killigrew ode is overtly Christian as it addresses the recently deceased Anne in her heavenly home. At the beginning, the address is wonderfully offhand. Wherever you are in heaven, says Dryden, singing with the angels—"call'd to more Superior Bliss, / Thou tread'st, with Seraphims, the vast Abyss" (lines 10–11):

> Cease thy Celestial Song a little space;
> (Thou wilt have time enough for Hymns Divine,
>   Since Heav'n's Eternal Year is thine.)
> Hear then a Mortal Muse thy Praise rehearse,
>   In no ignoble Verse; . . . (13–17)

"Ode" in the title sets the reader up for something rather more exalted than this easy exchange between earth and heaven, and "no ignoble Verse" is modest enough when you begin to read the poem and see just how noble Dryden aspires to be. The poem opens in stately fashion:

> Thou Youngest Virgin-Daughter of the Skies,
>   Made in the last Promotion of the Blest;
> Whose Palmes, new pluckt from Paradise,
> In spreading Branches more sublimely rise,
> Rich with Immortal Green above the rest. . . . (1–5)

Except for the casual and chatty request that she suspend her heavenly hymns for a bit and listen to John Dryden's praise (a frankly earthbound way to speak to one of the blessed in heaven), the first three stanzas and the fifth through the eighth are intensely and, for a modern reader, almost comically panegyrical, installing Anne Killigrew as the reincarnation of the great poets of antiquity. Her "Præexisting Soul / . . . / did through all the Mighty Poets roul / . . . / And was that *Sappho* last, which once it was before" (29–33).

The generic thrust of the ode as an exalting form impels Dryden toward increasingly intense panegyric but with a paradoxical edge, as he spins out ever more fantastic and inventive praise for the dead Anne. For example, in stanza 5 he evokes her natural talent—"Art she had none, yet wanted none: / For Nature did that Want supply" (71–72)—and as he celebrates the chaste maid's love poetry, he invents a baroque tableau in which Cupid and Diana are reconciled by Killigrew's verses:

> Ev'n Love (for Love sometimes her Muse exprest)
> Was but a *Lambent-flame* which play'd about her Breast:
> Light as the Vapours of a Morning Dream,
> So cold herself, whilst she such Warmth exprest,
> 'Twas *Cupid* bathing in *Diana's* Stream. (83–87)

One can argue that gender plays a key role in these paradoxical panegyrics, and students will surely want to discuss the condescension of Dryden's fantastic celebrations of the dead young poet and usefully compare this overheated praise with the judicious celebration of the achievements of Oldham. In the most notorious phrases at the beginning of stanza 5, she is treated as purely (and merely) a force of nature. If the "noble Vigour" of her verses "seem'd borrow'd," Dryden gallantly implies, that was because it was in fact "only born" with her (75–76), not achieved by hard poetic work.

But just as in the Oldham poem, where mourning is an opportunity for literary-critical discourse and self-mythologizing, the praise of Anne Killigrew provides an occasion for instruction, for moral and literary dialogue. Panegyric is balanced by confession, and in stanza 4 Dryden uses the saintly Anne to highlight the moral corruption of the Restoration stage and his own shameful participation in it:

> O wretched We! Why were we hurry'd down
> This lubrique and adult'rate age,
> (Nay, added fat Pollutions of our own)
> T'increase the steaming Ordures of the Stage?
> (62–65)

The choice of diction ("steaming Ordures"!) in these lines is striking when juxtaposed with the luscious artifice of the scenes in which Dryden places Anne, although it may be that one extreme creates the other. The language after this outburst turns both classical and Christian as she serves in this drama as a sacrificial vestal: "What can we say t'excuse our *Second Fall*? / Let this thy Vestal, Heav'n, attone for all!" (66–67).

Perhaps the most suggestive stanza in the poem, the most intensely and overtly pictorial in a series of verbal vignettes starring Anne, is the sixth, where Dryden celebrates her talent as a painter as well as a poet. He arranges the scene in mock-heroic fashion as he wonders why she was not content to rule "the Spacious Empire of the *Nine*" (88)—that is, the nine Muses. But like other ambitious sovereigns—"As Conquerors will never want Pretence, / When arm'd, to justifie the Offence" (96–97)—she claims an undefended territory and by unopposed conquest brings the sister arts together. Killigrew was in fact a painter as well as a poet, and in the rest of this long stanza Dryden evokes her rendering of pastoral and classic scenes: "Her Pencil drew, what e're her Soul design'd, / And oft the happy Draught surpass'd the Image in her Mind" (106–07). Such are her powers of pictorial representation, the stanza ends by saying, that "What Nature, Art, bold Fiction e're durst frame, / Her forming Hand gave Feature to the Name" (123–24). In this stanza and the next, where Dryden evokes Killigrew's portrait of James II and his queen, Mary of Modena, the hyperbole just grows and grows, and the sheer (almost silly) inventiveness of it all needs to be stressed. One might suggest to the students that in a panegyric like this poem there is pressure to turn up the temperature as the poem progresses, that imaginative excess has a cumulative drive. Forthright about the need for that excess, Dryden will allow no compromise in his panegyric, and the brilliant image of a ball of fire in these lines turns Killigrew's genius into a kind of fireworks show:

> Thus nothing to her *Genius* was deny'd,
> But like a Ball of Fire the further thrown,
> Still with a greater Blaze she shone,
> And her bright Soul broke out on ev'ry side.
> What next she had design'd, Heaven only knows,
> To such Immod'rate Growth her Conquest rose,
> That Fate alone its Progress could oppose.
> (142–48)

The repeated intensification of such celebration removes the poem from reality, makes sure that readers know that a gorgeous artifice rules in this genre; it turns the poem into a self-expressive exercise, deliberately and productively excessive, the purest of panegyrics that calls attention to its own fantastic formulations. Yet stanza 8 descends to elegiac actuality from this panegyric altitude, and the language and imagery grow decidedly simpler in the face of the fact that Anne Killigrew died of smallpox:

> Now all those Charmes, that blooming Grace,
> The well-proportion'd Shape, and beauteous Face,
> Shall never more be seen by Mortal Eyes;
> In Earth the much lamented Virgin lies! (149–52)

One way to approach the poem is to place this penultimate stanza (and a few other moments scattered through the ode) as a temporary breather from the unrelenting extravagance of the rest of the poem, which continues to some extent in stanza 9 as Dryden evokes her naval officer brother, at sea when she died, not knowing that she was dead. Look aloft, the poet says to the brother, and you'll see her "[a]mong the Pleiad's a New-kindl'd Star" (175), the brightest of them all!

One should remember that tongue-in-cheek moment in the opening stanza when Dryden asks Anne to pause from heavenly hymning to hear some mortal praise "in no ignoble Verse"—the understatement of the year, as it turns out. Something similar occurs in the final, tenth stanza of the poem. The apocalyptic tableau of the end of days is both sublime and comically realistic, jaunty in its little jokes about reconstituted bodies leaping back into corporeality for the Last Judgment, establishing at the very end of the poem the generic mixture that is the secret, in a sense, of Dryden's ode. Indeed, to call the Last Judgment "the last Assizes" (182) is to bring it down to English earth. This last stanza begins without a transition from the praise of Anne, which has been front and center from the beginning, and at first the abrupt turn to the end of days is puzzling. Dryden suddenly asks readers to imagine "[w]hen in mid-Aire, the Golden Trump shall sound," but he quickly turns from the "Aire" to "the Nations under ground" (178, 179), those untold dead millions who will somehow leap back into their flesh, their "ratling Bones" (184) making a tremendous clatter as they burst from the ground. Next to this grotesque and essentially unvisualizable scene, more aural than visual—an image of what is unimaginable—Dryden focuses on one group of the dead, "the Sacred Poets," who will be the first to hear the trumpet call and "formost from the Tomb shall bound" (187, 189), a comic moment in the midst of the grotesque spectacle as these poets literally jump out of their graves like jack-in-the-boxes and fly up to the sky. In the midst of apocalyptic spectacle, Dryden inserts a combination of worldly comedy and lyric grace to conclude the poem:

> The Sacred Poets first shall hear the Sound,
> And formost from the Tomb shall bound:
> For they are cover'd with the lightest Ground
> And straight, with in-born Vigour, on the Wing,
> Like mounting Larkes, to the New Morning sing.
> There Thou, Sweet Saint, before the Quire shalt go,
> As Harbinger of Heav'n, the Way to show,
> The Way which thou so well hast learn'd below.
> (188–95)

Despite the baroque imaginings and fantastic inventions of his panegyric, Dryden manages to preserve the restrained and earthbound voice we heard in the Oldham elegy, to let readers hear him talking at the edges of the elaborate praise of Anne Killigrew. At the end of the poem, that voice and presence are as clear and forthright as they were in the first stanza, when he cautioned the young Anne to take a break from celestial hymning—"Thou wilt have Time enough for Hymns Divine" (14)—and, in the fourth stanza, when he digressed to frame his mea culpa for his scabrous comedies. There is a light lyric touch in the image of the bodies of these newly resurrected poets singing and soaring "like mounting Larkes" in the "New Morning," a natural and human modulation of the terrific spectacle of the Last Judgment that we are being treated to. The Killigrew ode, in short, is a wonder of tonal balance in which extravagant panegyric and baroque sublimity interact productively with neoclassical clarity and conversational ease. This last stanza brings us full circle, back to the Oldham poem and to Dryden's characteristic urbanity and superb control.

NOTES

[1]I have on occasion modernized the spelling slightly; thus "farewel" becomes "farewell."

[2]To listen to my reading of "To the Memory of Mr. Oldham" (and other Dryden poems, including the Killigrew ode), visit the *Penn Sound* Web site: http://writing.upenn.edu/pennsound/x/Richetti.html.

Dryden's Sweet Saint: The Killigrew Ode in the Survey Course

Deborah Kennedy

For all its impressive grandeur, Dryden's ode to Anne Killigrew (who lived from 1660 to 1685) is still one of his most accessible poems (*Works* 3: 109–15). It is rightly a staple of undergraduate survey courses on Restoration and eighteenth-century literature. When I teach the poem, I concentrate on three topics: the poetic genres of the elegy and the ode, Killigrew herself, and the poem's religious character. But to start, I cite Samuel Johnson's judgment that it is "undoubtedly the noblest ode that our language ever has produced" ("Dryden" 137–38). Once students hear Dr. Johnson's high praise, their curiosity will be piqued.

An initial analysis of the key terms in the poem's long title indicates what the poem is about: "To the Pious Memory of the Accomplisht Young Lady Mrs. Anne Killigrew, Excellent in the Two Sister-Arts of Poësie, and Painting: An Ode." I explain that the poem is an elegy for this young woman, then discuss the classical requirements of an elegy: to praise, to lament, and to console. As we move through the poem, students can see how these three different functions are being fulfilled. They can identify the many compliments paid to Killigrew, the expressions of sorrow over her loss, and the efforts to console the members of her family. I review the historical origins of the ode and its use and development by Dryden and other writers of the seventeenth and eighteenth centuries. This background helps students understand the style of Dryden's poem. With its ornate form, the Pindaric ode was used for special occasions, when, in classical times, people performed and sang different parts of the ode. The word is derived from the Greek *aeidein*, "to sing." I ask students to look at the poem in the textbook and notice how the stanzas are of different lengths, and the line lengths and rhymes are varied. This fluid structure gives the poet a great deal of creative freedom despite the formality of the ode. Finally, I refer to E. M. W. Tillyard's explanation that Dryden's extravagant praise of Killigrew is perfectly normal for a poem of this kind. This knowledge helps to acclimatize students to the elevated tone, imagery, and language.

The stanzaic structure of the ode adds to its teachability. Quite simply, students find the poem accessible because they can study it a stanza at a time. The poem's stately and inherent organization guides them in their reading, since Dryden develops his topic progressively through the stanzas. Moreover, since each of the ten stanzas deals with a specific topic (Killigrew's accomplishments, her family life, her death from smallpox), the class can summarize the stanzas and then compare their summaries as a group exercise. In today's world of text messages and tweets, students know how to summarize, and they can put that skill to use in their academic studies. The ode's stanzaic structure also lends itself to informal writing assignments. I often ask students to select a stanza or a portion of one and write a paragraph about it, reflecting on the content of the passage and also identifying interesting literary elements such as figures of speech and imagery. Again, thanks to the stanzaic structure, this is a manageable task, which allows students to practice their analytic skills and to develop confidence in themselves as readers and writers. It is important to give them the chance to choose a part of the text that interests them in some way instead of requiring them to write about a section that I have chosen. While I do select specific passages for questions on tests, in this paragraph assignment they gain a sense of ownership over the literary work by finding a passage of their own to analyze, a place in the text that they can home in on themselves.

When the structure of the poem has been established, one can turn to Killigrew herself. Students have not heard of many women from the Restoration period. She was not a queen like Catherine of Braganza, not a royal mistress like Nell Gwyn, not a scandalous author like Aphra Behn. But neither was she a typical woman of her time, for she was a poet, a painter, a maid of honor, and the daughter of an influential family. Yet, dying at the age of twenty-five, she might have slipped into obscurity, but for being the subject of "the noblest ode" in the English language. The title of Dryden's poem immediately puts her name in neon lights. But who was she? In its elaborate way, the entire poem tells us, and the notes in the class textbook will undoubtedly help, but the teacher needs to add more. To see Killigrew in the poem, we have to see her outside of the poem.

At my university, wired classrooms allow us to show students material on the Internet. Our library subscribes to a number of databases and electronic resources, so one can access these while teaching. I encourage students to look up authors and personages in the new *Oxford Dictionary of National Biography* and show them how to do that using the projector and screen. We can call up the entry for Anne Killigrew and some of her relatives, like her playwright uncles, Thomas Killigrew and William Killigrew, and her royal chaplain father, the Reverend Dr. Henry Killigrew, pointing out her family's literary and court connections.

In the title of his ode, Dryden emphasizes both Killigrew's Christian piety and her accomplishments. He addresses her as "Thou Youngest Virgin-Daughter of the Skies" (line 1) and asks her to listen to his elegy:

> Cease thy Celestial Song a little space;
> (Thou wilt have Time enough for Hymns Divine,
> Since Heav'ns Eternal Year is thine.)
> Hear then a Mortal Muse thy Praise rehearse,
> In no ignoble Verse;
> But such as thy own voice did practise here,
> When thy first Fruits of Poesie were giv'n. (13–19)

It is useful to highlight this passage, in which the older, successful author addresses the young woman and puts them on the same footing as poets. Dryden is exaggerating, but, although it is in keeping with the conventions of the elegiac ode to speak of the deceased in elevated language, at the same time he conveys an air of humility that adds to the religious texture. This humility is reinforced by his later reflections on the "Heav'nly Gift of Poesy" (57). It was important for the advancement of the reputation of women writers to have someone of the stature of the poet laureate praising a woman's talents and viewing them as God-given. Killigrew's reputation can be contrasted with that of the rakish earl of Rochester (Dryden's early patron), and her work can be compared with that of well-known female poets like Katherine Philips (Orinda) and Anne Finch.

Since Killigrew's poetry is readily available now in anthologies and through electronic sources such as *Literature Online*, one can devote a class period to its study. I recommend the well-known "Upon the Saying That My Verses Were Made by Another," which presents a very human Killigrew expressing her frustrations as a poet. Her defiant tone will surprise students who might expect her to be less assertive. But to be pious does not mean one has to be passive, and I use two of Killigrew's religious poems to exemplify this. In the short but powerful "Herodias's Daughter Presenting to Her Mother St. John's Head in a Charger, Also Painted by Her Self," she conveys the horrors of the death of John the Baptist in a dramatic rendering of the biblical story (Matt. 14.1–12). In "An Invective against Gold," she castigates the greedy: "Mens Faith betray'd, their Prince and Country Sold, / Their God deny'd, all for the Idol Gold" (lines 17–18). In these bold denunciations of evil, she shows that a woman revered for her piety can also be possessed of a strong and valiant voice.

Perhaps the most striking lines in Dryden's tribute to Killigrew are those that compliment her as a poet: that "all the People of the Skie / Might know a Poetess was born" (46–47). His proclamation that the birth of a female poet is cause for celebration implies that the art of poetry can be integral to a woman's identity. Dryden treats it not as a mere whim or pastime but as a vital part of what a woman brings to the world. These lines give teachers an opportunity to address the question of the status of women writers of the period and their relation to canonical male authors. Dryden was praising Killigrew in a hyperbolic manner in keeping with the elevated discourse of the ode, but he clearly thought highly of her and respected her work. It is significant that the one poem he alludes to is that in which Killigrew reflects on the difficulty of being a woman poet. In "Upon the Saying," she complains about those who say she must have plagiarized. Dryden defends her and chivalrously turns the controversy into praise for her talent: "Such Noble Vigour did her Verse adorn, / That it seem'd borrow'd, where 'twas only born" (75–76)—acknowledging the prejudice that women writers faced. When she thought of how she wished to be remembered, Killigrew wrote the following comment in her two-line poem "An Epitaph on Her Self": "When I am Dead, few Friends attend my Hearse, / And for a Monument, I leave my VERSE." Dryden clearly understood that being a poet was central to Anne Killigrew's sense of identity.

At this point it is valuable to expand the class discussion on the Dryden-Killigrew relationship by turning the tables and considering how women poets viewed Dryden. Because of his high reputation and stature as a great English writer, he was a hero to many women, but he may have owed some of their adulation to his Killigrew ode in particular, which was published with her posthumous *Poems* in 1686. After his death in 1700, a group of women joined together to publish a book celebrating Dryden in laudatory verse. While such poetic tributes were common among male poets, this was the first time in literary history that women produced an all-female-authored collection. Even in its title this book heralds a female bonding: *The Nine Muses; or, Poems Written by Nine Several Ladies upon the Death of the Late Famous John Dryden, Esq*. Using the names of the muses as pseudonyms (e.g., Melpomene, Erato, Thalia), the authors present themselves as a sisterhood writing in praise of the late British poet laureate.

To return to his ode, one can see why its stanzas created a type of safe haven for a woman's gaze. In the ode, Dryden devotes considerable attention not only to Killigrew's poetry but also to her work as a painter, especially in stanzas 6 and 7. Since women artists then were few and far between, teaching the poem provides an opportunity to give a brief introduction to the art history of the period. Fortunately, several of Killigrew's paintings survive, including her self-portrait, and one can show the class the paintings that are described in Dryden's poem, such as Killigrew's portrait *James II as Duke of York*, the "Martial King" (line 128). Held in the Royal Collection, this portrait is well known and was used as the frontispiece for volume 3 of the University of California Press Dryden edition, in which the ode appears. Dryden also refers to her landscape paintings, remarking that "Her Pencil drew, what e're her Soul design'd" (106). An oil painting by Killigrew entitled *Venus Attired by the Graces* was available for sale at a London art gallery in 2009, a portrait of her by Sir Peter Lely was on auction at Sotheby's a few years earlier, and in 2012 a mezzotint copy of her self-portrait was for sale in London. Discussing the provenance of these paintings and prints and their value to collectors today is yet another way to raise students' interest in the work of Dryden, Killigrew, and the "Sister-Arts."

Stanza 9 is particularly meaningful to students because it concentrates on a personal sense of loss that they can relate to their own experiences. The elegiac tone is keenest here as Dryden describes the grief of Anne's brother, Henry. A naval officer who later rose to the rank of admiral, Henry Killigrew was away at the time of his sister's death and did not know that when he said good-bye to her, he would never see her again:

> Slack all thy Sailes, and fear to come,
> Alas, thou know'st not, Thou art wreck'd at home!
> No more shalt thou behold thy Sisters Face,
> Thou hast already had her last Embrace.
>
> (170–73)

The picture of the closeness between brother and sister humanizes Anne Killigrew, and more than any other place in the poem she seems here like a real person. Dryden achieves a pathos that enables students to feel they can understand her brother Henry's grief, and they can understand what it means to feel this familial loss. In this stanza, he is a brother and she is a sister, and it does not matter how many centuries ago they lived.

Throughout his poem, Dryden repeatedly alludes to the piety acknowledged in the phrase from his title, "to the pious memory" of Anne Killigrew. But it is the last stanza that most powerfully puts forward the religious context in which her life is to be finally understood. The poem's rich imagery continues in the first line of the stanza: "When in mid-Aire, the Golden Trump shall sound" (178). Students can be asked to identify the religious imagery and to compare the passages from the Bible to which Dryden alludes. For general background, they will find John Spurr's "The Piety of John Dryden" a useful guide. The golden trumpet and the baroque pictures of the resurrection of believers provide the concluding Christian context:

> The Sacred Poets first shall hear the Sound,
>   And formost from the Tomb shall bound:
> . . . .
> There Thou, Sweet Saint, before the Quire shalt go,
> As Harbinger of Heav'n, the Way to show,
> The Way which thou so well hast learn'd below.
> (188–89, 193–95)

Dryden's poetic rhetoric not only returns us to the invocation at the beginning of the ode but also instructs readers of the fate of a faithful Christian. Killigrew is more than daughter of an eminent family, a talented poet and painter. She is now the "sweet saint." In this alliterative phrase Dryden conveys an almost paternal tenderness. Providing this context enhances an awareness of the respect that he pays to Killigrew and brings out the full range of the powerful moods and images that are contained in the ten stanzas of his ode.

A King and No King: How to Use Dryden's Engagement of the Reader in *Absalom and Achitophel*

Christopher D. Johnson

Teaching *Absalom and Achitophel* (*Works* 2: 3–37) to undergraduates is difficult for at least two reasons. First, there is so much context to learn that we have little time to consider the work as poetry. Second, Dryden wrote a type of verse—public and transactional—that remains unfamiliar to students who associate poetry with self-expression. For students in my 400-level satire class, who are far more attuned to the pleasures of Romanticism than to those of neoclassicism, Dryden is little more than an ingenious craftsman who promotes an unappealing political agenda. Hoping to offer them a rewarding understanding of England's first poet laureate, I explain that Dryden's world was in many ways similar to ours: his readers were saturated with misleading information from media that were both partisan and ruthless. I also suggest that the poem is more subversive than it at first appears. Dryden, I explain, challenges biblical authority, reduces the very ideas he appears to defend to little more than rhetorical devices, and encourages a skepticism that sees beyond ideological claims and toward practical solutions. To help students discover these dimensions of his work, I use excerpts from important critical statements as a starting point for a close reading of the poem itself. This approach helps students avoid misunderstandings that would otherwise hinder their appreciation of the poem.

Knowing that Dryden wrote in support of a monarch during a time of crisis, students assume the poem lacks humor and subtlety. Unfortunately, many of the critical statements they encounter reinforce this impression. The editors of the *Norton Anthology of English Literature*, for example, state that "only a heroic style and manner were appropriate to [the poem's] weighty material" (Greenblatt et al. 1: 2088). In the Twayne book on Dryden, George Wasserman notes that *Absalom and Achitophel*'s "final lines echo the triumphant mood of *Astreaea Redux* and *Annus Mirabilis*" (104). J. Douglas Canfield, writing for the *Dictionary of Literary Biography*, states that "Dryden endows his vision of events with sacred authority" ("John Dryden"). Readers of *The Longman Anthology of British Literature* are better served: "Dryden discovered a way of portraying monarchy in a spirit at once appreciative, ironic, and delicately abrasive. In the poem's mischievous opening lines we hear all these possibilities fully orchestrated" (Damrosch et al. 1: 2160). This statement is especially useful, not only because it calls attention to Dryden's nuanced tone but also because it reminds readers of the importance of the poem's aural and performative qualities.

To discover these dynamics, we discuss the ways effective rhetoricians—politicians, commentators, and ministers—present themselves when offering controversial ideas. We then examine Dryden's use of sound, rhythm, and cadence, not as they might work in a purely belletristic poem but rather as they function in a piece of public rhetoric designed to convince a reluctant audience. I ask students to listen to the opening lines of *Astraea Redux*, *Religio Laici*, and *Britannia Rediviva*. With the sounds of these poems in our ears, we consider the first lines of *Absalom and Achitophel*, which, students report, are more musical and far less stately. As we examine the lines, they notice that in *Absalom and Achitophel* Dryden compels the reader to pay attention to rhythm and rhyme. The lines scan clearly as iambic pentameter, and Dryden uses little internal punctuation and enjambment. Each of the first five constitutes a dependent adverb clause, which in conjunction with the use of masculine rhyme emphasizes the poem's meter. Perceptive readers notice how the repetition of sounds contributes to the less than magisterial tone. Others, especially if they have read Pope's *Essay on Criticism*, note the indecorous use of the stressed *did* in the first line, something Dryden repeats with equal clumsiness in lines 8, 11, and 15. These features deprive the poem of the gravitas found elsewhere in his work.

Once students recognize the playfulness of the lines' sounds, they can identify the speaker's irony. "Pious" becomes incongruously associated with "promiscuous." Marriage is presented as a cursed confinement, and David's sexual license captures "Heaven's own heart" (7). When we list the adjectives in the first twenty lines, we notice not only that is David "godlike" for his infidelities but also that his faithful though barren wife is "ungrateful," and Absalom's virtues are attributed to his father's "diviner lust." I ask students to pay particular attention to the use of oxymoron, which will later uncomfortably associate the speaker with the deceptive Achitophel. "How," I ask, "are we to read these lines?" Using a handout of selected quotations, we consider several options from insightful critics. James Winn, for example, reads the lines without irony: "Dryden insists that Charles's scattering of 'his Maker's image' is an essential and defining part of his kingship" (*John Dryden* 351). Heidi Kelchner, in contrast, notes that "diviner lust" is "nearly blasphemous" and argues that the lines are "intended to be comical" (219). Anne Krook agrees: "With the opening, David is partly praised, in locker-room fashion, and partly satirized" (344). These critics help us explore the range of interpretive possibilities in the opening lines and the degree to which Dryden's initial tone defines our subsequent understanding of the poem.

I also remind students that the speaker is not Dryden but a persona he has created, and we discuss Dryden's ability to make fun of himself. Although we do not have time to read his *Marriage à-la-Mode*, I describe the character Melantha, whose "fashionable language" and "courtly ambitions" represent the author to "hilarious and humiliating effect" (Zwicker, "Dryden and the Invention" 77). Perhaps the speaker in *Absalom and Achitophel* is similar to Melantha, or to the narrator of Chaucer's General Prologue, an everyman figure ("*homo*, not very *sapiens*," E. Talbot Donaldson noted [933]) who allows us the pleasure of recognizing hypocrisy he cannot see. Perhaps the speaker is closer to the modern public relations professional—someone who puts unfortunate circumstances in the best light, even to the point of silliness. We go back to our modern performers, the politician, the minister, and the commentator. "Who's speaking," I ask, "Barack Obama, Franklin Graham, or Keith Olbermann?" Students most often align the speaker with the commentator or political comedian who uses self-effacing humor to deflect criticism and who introduces his audience to uncomfortable ideas by first making them laugh.

We then consider the coarser sexual aspects of Dryden's lines, which students miss, perhaps because they seem out of place in a heroic poem. Being something of a prude, I let Winn do the dirty work by way of a handout:

> The brilliant style of this justly famous passage helps make the argument: the emphatic placement of the wonderful verb "Scatter'd" suggests the force of Charles's orgasm, and the teeming alliteration . . . displays an equivalent poetic fecundity. The opening also establishes the voice of the narrator, who shares some opinions with the monarch. When the narrator mutters "cursedly" while describing the confinement of monogamy, he endorses the king's polygamous behavior and implies that he wishes to emulate it. (*John Dryden* 351–52)

Other critics read the lines differently. Kelchner suggests that the sexual imagery, especially David's "greater gust" in siring Absalom, "echoes years of specious reasoning" (219). Keeping in mind that *Absalom and Achitophel* is a rhetorically sophisticated argument, we consider Dryden's purpose. "Is he using humor to humanize Charles and Monmouth? Is he making jokes to calm his readers during a time of widespread anxiety? Is he presenting flawed arguments in such a way that he implies more reasonable arguments for readers to discover on their own?

In exploring these issues, I show that *Absalom and Achitophel* was, as Harold Love demonstrates, published in "the impressive folio format that had been exploited for the Popish Plot narratives it criticizes" ("Fixity" 151–52). These other narratives claimed to be reliable accounts of recent historical events. Dryden imitates their form but uses his subtitle, "A Poem," to remind his reader that his is an imaginative work, a fiction, in this way encouraging suspicion not of plots but of reports of plots. He seems to have designed his work to instruct naive readers. We discuss how the narrator of *Absalom and Achitophel* contributes to this process, not only through his claims but also through his use of either-or constructions, which suggest the boundaries of his understanding and provide a space for the reader's discernment. As the poem progresses, I note, the narrator's arguments become more cogent and reasonable, but because of the poem's beginning, we remain alert and questioning.

We now consider Dryden's use of biblical narrative. Students initially assume that Dryden uses the Old Testament story to give his argument a "seemingly divine sanction unavailable to other analogies" (Miner, *Dryden's Poetry* 109). The second book of Samuel, however, is an imperfect narrative for this purpose. Not only does the biblical Absalom reject Achitophel's council but also David seems at times both too cowardly and too bloodthirsty to be an ideal English monarch. As Winn notes, "the dangers of this story would seem to outweigh its advantages" (*John Dryden* 350). In addition to the infamous story of David and Bathsheba, the second book of Samuel includes Nathan's prophecy to David that "the sword shall never depart from thine house" (12.10 [King James Vers.]), suggesting exactly the sort of civil strife England feared in the late seventeenth century. Dryden manipulates the biblical material to fit his purpose. He often goes well beyond Samuel and calls attention to the limitations of his typology. In line 34, for example, he unnecessarily mentions Monmouth's wife, Annabel, who has no equivalent in the biblical narrative. Five lines later, he references Amnon's murder, which has no Stuart parallel and which problematically associates royal sexual aggression with rape and fratricide. One must wonder why Dryden included these details and placed them closely together early in the poem. Instead of drawing neat parallels, he creates (deliberately, it appears) what Michael J. Conlon has called a "queasy, imbalanced, almost parodic conflation of English and Jewish history" (88).

Michael McKeon states the case more generously but offers a similar assessment: Dryden "insists that Israel is one thing and England quite another" ("Historicizing" 27). For McKeon, Dryden's artfully contrived poem "achieves a self-conscious *aestheticization* of typology" (28). In exploring the significance of this claim, we discuss how aestheticization often works to remove political significance. For example, protest songs become something else when they gain aesthetic value in popular culture, and the political content of the legacy of Martin Luther King, Jr., is compromised, even erased, when his image is used in advertisements. Dryden does something similar, in that by drawing from various biblical narratives, he calls attention to his role in creating the work. This recognition diminishes the authority of the typological argument, which depends, at least in part, on the appearance of artlessness: a typological argument purports to be the manifestation of a providentially controlled universe, something the poet discovers rather than devises. As we consider these ideas, students are surprised to learn that Dryden was not the first to draw parallels between Absalom and Monmouth (Winn, *John Dryden* 350) and that he was part of a culture in which typological interpretation had become "plural and competitive" (McKeon, "Historicizing" 27). This context helps students see how Dryden's appropriation of biblical texts serves as disruptive a purpose as his use of the folio format and his subtitle. In each case, he seems to encourage skepticism, teaching his readers to resist exactly the sorts of arguments he presents.

With this understanding, we examine the poem's temptation scene, where Dryden imitates Milton's Latinate diction in lines such as "Him staggering so when Hell's dire agent found" (line 373) and "Though now his mighty soul its grief contains" (445). My students, who have read *Paradise Lost* in a 300-level survey, recognize that Milton's poem is a fictionalization of biblical narrative and to that degree is similar to *Absalom and Achitophel*. By referencing Milton's work, Dryden creates a fiction of a fiction, reminding readers, once again, that his work is not truthful but contrived. That Milton's political convictions were different from Dryden's makes the use of Milton's poetry all the more revealing, as it suggests the malleability of the biblical texts on which both works are based and the speciousness of biblically based argument.

Earl Miner and others have noted that Achitophel's first speech alludes to the temptation of Christ in *Paradise Regained*, while the second suggests the temptation of Eve in *Paradise Lost* (Miner, *Dryden's Poetry* 133). These contradictory allusions render even the identity of Absalom unstable, as he simultaneously represents a divine character who resists Satan's temptation and an all-too-human character who succumbs to it. The issue becomes even more confusing when he echoes Satan's soliloquy from book 4 (lines 363–66; cf. *Paradise Lost*, 4.58–61). Absalom is at once Christ, Eve, Satan, and Monmouth, an indeterminacy that reinforces the idea that authoritative texts can be used to say anything and as a result say nothing. In the catalogs of conspirators and worthies, students can now find not only depth and complexity but also thematic consistency. For example, in paraphrasing the Gospel of Matthew in his depiction of Shimei (600–03; Matt. 28.20), Dryden does more than turn "the Dissenting habit of quoting Scripture against a prominent Dissenter" (Winn, *John Dryden* 357). He also casts further doubt on the applicability of sacred texts to contemporary politics.

As we read Dryden's statement about government, we discuss McKeon's claim that Dryden's "stance on questions of political sovereignty approximates that of his opponent, Achitophel" ("Historicizing" 31, 30). Paying attention to the narrator's questions—"What prudent man a settled throne would shake?" (line 796)—we explore McKeon's claim that the value Dryden places on the principle of succession is based not on "essential authority" but on "synonymity with what is stable and 'settled'" (32). The differences between the positions of the narrator and Achitophel are practical, not ideological. Achitophel is dangerous because his plans would risk unnecessary strife. The narrator's position is better because it would prevent such unfortunate occurrences. Dryden's conservatism, I suggest, is pragmatic, and his targets are those who use rhetoric to mislead and those who place a greater value on ideological purity than on what is genuinely beneficial. With these ideas in mind, we consider the lines that introduce David's first words (933–38). Students now identify "Heav'n inspir'd" and "godlike" as ironic reminders of David's failings and the speaker's cunning. They also note that David's words recall the poem's opening lines. Far from royal, David appears to be trying too hard, and his lines take on an unappealing cadence. Finally, we consider the poem's closing lines, which, as readers since Samuel Johnson have noted, are both abrupt and unsatisfactory. David sounds unconvincing, and Dryden's use of trite poetic convention (especially the thunder as David speaks) rings hollow. The ending, I suggest, may be a corollary to the ironic elevation of David's sexual potency in the opening lines—it reminds us that some things exist only as rhetorical constructions and are true only in poetry. In this way, the ending is Dryden's final attempt to engage readers in a kind of scrutiny that reveals the tricks of political writing. Like his contemporaries, Dryden offers arguments about the way things ought to be, yet he shows that these ideas are disingenuous and sometimes dangerous. The poem's ending, like its beginning, is contrived, because a contrived ending is the only sort the speaker can make. The real meaning is far more prosaic and awaits discovery by thoughtful readers.

Absalom and Achitophel in an Eighteenth-Century Survey Course

Kirstin R. Wilcox

John Dryden's *Absalom and Achitophel* (*Works* 2: 3–37) confronts students with an unfamiliar literary world where mellifluous metered verse is the medium for vitriolic politics, where the immediacy and topicality of a present-day op-ed page coexists with the allusive grace and wit of high literary forms, where celebrity culture and political theory mingle harmoniously in rhythmic couplets. Getting students to enter that world is difficult. Long Latinate sentences, formidable vocabulary, and a dense weave of unfamiliar allusions nudge students away from the poem itself and toward a careful reading of the modern edition's footnotes and paratexts. Moreover, the history recounted in the poem all too easily swamps the literary dimensions of this important text. Students can come away with a rich understanding of the poem's historical context—the crisis of succession, the persistence of monarchical ideology, the continuing conflict between Catholics and Protestants—but little sense of the poem's aesthetic power.

The goal, then, is to draw students into *Absalom and Achitophel* so that they actively experience its political significance from inside the poem rather than through an external recital of the events that prompted it. To that end, I use the poem early on in the course to introduce the interpretive challenges presented by Restoration and eighteenth-century literature. Only after students have grappled with its surface-level meanings do I introduce the historical background that they will need for this poem (and that will prove useful for subsequent readings). The effort to make sense of Dryden's poem on their own will draw out and unsettle their unspoken assumptions about Restoration and eighteenth-century literature, teach the interpretive skills that they will apply to other long poems we will read in this course, and reveal experientially how poetry was at this time deeply entwined with politics.

Absalom and Achitophel is one of the first readings on the syllabus for the sophomore-level English survey of Restoration and eighteenth-century literature that I teach, which attracts a mixture of majors and nonmajors, many of the nonmajors from outside the liberal arts. *Absalom and Achitophel* usefully complicates the Whiggish model of historical change onto which students in this course tend to map their assumptions about the period. To elicit some of these tacit beliefs, I begin on the first day of class, before assigning any reading, by asking them three questions: When does the Restoration and eighteenth century begin and end? What major events does it encompass? What ideas are associated with it? Among the terms that emerge in this exercise, students invariably mention the American War of Independence, the French Revolution, and changing ideas about equality and political authority.

At the close of the exercise, I point to this cluster of concepts (which will yield a handlist of key words that we return to throughout the semester) and tell students that we are starting the course with a long political poem that predates these seminal events by a hundred some years but still falls within the period known as the Enlightenment (another key term from our discussion). Rather than divulge further information about *Absalom and Achitophel*, I close with three tips for reading the poem, which, I stress, differs from the lyric poetry they're familiar with: read sentence by sentence, making sure to take into account all the ideas that lie between one period and the next before moving on; read, at least at first, for surface meaning only, as if this were an essay or historical narrative, not a poem; and ignore the preface to the poem and the footnotes supplied in the textbook. Not that this information won't eventually be relevant, I assure them! But I hold up my own copy of the course anthology, in which I have covered up all paratexts with sticky notes, to show that one can read this poem initially without any historical apparatus.

Informal online writing helps reinforce this emphasis on careful, close surface reading. In advance of the first class meeting on *Absalom and Achitophel*, I explain what a paraphrase is and request that students post to the course blog a prose paraphrase of a single complete sentence of their choosing from the poem. I find a course blog a comfortable and user-friendly format for such assignments, but there are other ways to require timely and informal advance writing: the online discussion boards available on course management software like *WebCT* or *Moodle*, an e-mail discussion list, or even short in-class responsive writing. For our first class, I photocopy a few of these paraphrases. Examples that are mostly, but not entirely, accurate work best. A precise and graceful sample paraphrase can make this poem seem inaccessible to all but the most gifted and well-informed readers, while less successful efforts illuminate and give students room to overcome the difficulties of the poem. As they identify places where a subordinate clause, omitted word, or peculiar sentence structure has interfered with comprehension, I define the obstacle and write the terms *hypotaxis*, *elision*, and *inversion* on the board, terms I apply to subsequent passages that we discuss. *Heroic couplet* also gets written on the board and defined—later on the blog, students will have the opportunity to write heroic couplets of their own. I stress the classical origins of this form, which Dryden, like many poets of the period, emulates without the benefit of Latin declensions to anchor the grammar. We conclude by examining couplets in which the form justifies the challenges it presents by giving a sentiment epigrammatic punch. We may cover fewer than twenty lines of the poem in this class, but the students' initial bewilderment will have become an avenue for recognizing key features of eighteenth-century poetics. Students emerge with some confidence that they can overcome the particular difficulties of the poem to find higher-order levels of meaning in it.

In preparation for our next meeting, where we will broach the broader meanings of *Absalom and Achitophel*, I post a question on the course blog inviting students to identify and paraphrase a short passage that intimates that something more is going on than a retelling of the first book of Samuel. To reinforce the lessons of the first class, I award extra points for correctly identified instances of hypotaxis, elision, and inversion. Responses to this assignment lay bare extensive confusion about Dryden's agenda, a confusion that may already have surfaced in class discussion. Just whose side is Dryden on? Those inclined to believe that any writer encountered in a class on literature from the 1700s will affirm principles of liberty and equality as conceived in American Revolutionary terms misread him to fit that paradigm. Others by now have peeked at the footnotes and paratexts and found their impression confirmed that Dryden is supporting the monarchy against some kind of threat, though they may not be sure what that threat is.

I begin the second class with a handout of particularly factious short passages from the poem. The choices vary, depending on what passages have already come up for discussion, but I look for lines invoking key terms—*court*, *state*, *democracy*, *property*—that resonate differently in Dryden's political world and in our own. Possibilities are "that Golden Calf, a State" (line 66), "[d]rawn to the dregs of a Democracy" (227), and "the herd of such / Who . . . / Adored their fathers God and property" (533–36). Students examine these passages in small groups and look for answers to the following questions: What is being discussed in the passage? What is the context for the passage? What does the passage convey about Dryden's political views?

The answers will show that, although students have grasped, with one another's help, the outlines of the main characters, the narrative arc, and Dryden's monarchist sympathies, they remain puzzled about the motivations circulating in the poem. Their mounting frustration may dismay them but is pedagogically useful. While the small groups are working, I draw two columns on the board. Under the column labeled "Crown," I write "David/Charles II," and under "Parliament," "Achitophel/Shaftesbury." I also draw a heart around "Absalom/Monmouth" between the two columns. As the groups share answers and try to explain to one another how democracy can have "dregs" and why Dryden scoffs at those who worship "property," I add terms to the two columns: "Jews/English," "Jebusite/Catholic," "enthusiasm," "democracy," "Whigs," "Tories," and so on. The discussion gradually segues into a five- to ten-minute lecture in which I describe how the "Restoration" in the title of their textbook means the restoration of a monarch, which quickly led to events that made the succession of James II a political pressure point. There are audible sighs of relief as students reach for their notebooks. By now they have some investment in the poem, so this information strikes them as necessary to fill a gap in their understanding. A one-page handout with a time line, glossary of names (with their biblical referents), and quick rundown of the binary terms associated with the Crown-Parliament divide helps reinforce this necessarily sketchy account.

With one more class on the poem left, however, I don't want to leave students with the impression either that their firsthand work on the poem is done or that the poem is reducible to the historical events that it interprets. The two blog posts for our final class elicit a different set of responses to the poem, which I will use to connect students' newfound awareness of the poem's context with their direct engagement with the poem. My first post asks students to identify lines in the poem where Dryden represents a more complicated political world than that depicted in our Whigs versus Tories chart. (I give them explicit permission at this point to use the footnotes and read Dryden's preface to the poem, though by now many have already done so.) My second asks them to analyze two to six lines that strike them as particularly effective and pleasing—not because they're right or say something important but because they say it beautifully. The intention here is to get them to view the factual, historical background as a necessary tool for engaging with the intersection of literature and politics in this poem.

Our final session begins with the preface. I point out Dryden's role as poet laureate and ask whether Dryden does indeed "affect to be thought more Impartial than [he is]" and whether his implied audience is in fact "the more Moderate sort" (pp. 3–4). As students discuss his rhetorical skill in presenting partisan political views as candid evenhandedness, it is easy to prompt the question of why this text, centered as it is on a largely forgotten political crisis, warrants attention in the early twenty-first century. As soon as this question is articulated, I ask the students to pair up and discuss it for a few minutes, then randomly canvass their responses. Some students will wait to hear what others say, some will simply affirm that it is a Great Poem, but some will see the parallel between Restoration politics and that of our own day. Some will mention how informative it is to read a text that explains why, in the century before the famous revolutions, people thought monarchy was a good form of government, and some will suggest that the poem illuminates an important and resonant chapter in British history.

As students talk, I write a brief version of their answers on the board, numbering them under the heading "Reasons for Reading This Poem Now." When a range of answers has been suggested, I circulate a handout that contains the responses to the most recent blog question, about particularly beautiful or expressive passages in the poem. I ask students to quietly read over their classmates' selection of passages and determine whether any of the reasons for reading this poem now can be applied to them. If so, which ones and why? Whether the selected passages match beautifully with the reasons for reading or involve a stretch, the exercise pushes students to connect the aesthetic pleasures of the poem with justifications for the poem's canonization. The result is a variety of good-faith efforts to articulate how Dryden's verse is a supple and expressive medium for both unambiguous partisanship and fine political distinctions.

This kind of teaching entails some painful trade-offs. First, the student-driven nature of my approach means bracketing vast chunks of the poem. The passages students identify on the blog and in small-group discussion rarely include, for example, Dryden's deft and biting verse portraits of the friends and foes of

Charles II (lines 491–680, 811–913). The wit of these passages is lost on undergraduates, for whom the principal characters of the poem are arcane figures, and when I assume the job of identifying relevant passages, I need to focus on more thematically important material. Second, because I encourage students to begin reading Dryden's masterpiece without any explanatory background, they can become overconfident. They may not recognize that their interpretive powers are not always adequate (despite my efforts!) to parse passages that we did not discuss in class or on the blog. Finally, a certain amount of misinformation and bafflement percolates through the class before they get authoritative information about the poem, so the danger exists that they will fail to correct themselves or that they will become so frustrated that they cease to put effort into the class. The reward for courting these pedagogical risks is that students get invested in the poem. The understanding that they bring away from it may be spotty and incomplete, but it is theirs, won by their efforts to wrestle with a dense and complicated text. Moreover, because they have acquired their understanding in the process of gaining skills and information that they will apply to later texts in the course, I will have opportunities to correct their misreadings and fill in gaps in their knowledge.

Most significant, however, is the stance toward the literature of the past that they acquire by reading this text early in their study of Restoration and eighteenth-century literature. After all, those Whiggish supporters of parliamentary intervention who "think too little, and who talk too much," in the opinion of Dryden (534), were on the right side of history—or at least on the right side of the assumption students bring to the poem, that early modern history is a steady march toward democracy. Yet this textually centered approach causes many students to deplore Shaftesbury's perfidy and champion Charles II's statesmanlike qualities as they lock on to ideas and emotions circulating in the poem before they gain a clear sense of its politics. The reversal of their expectations is the beginning of intellectual humility and openness to what texts of the past actually say as opposed to what students expect them to say. As a result, *Absalom and Achitophel* makes them aware of the blind spots of the present, the limits of the authority conferred by the canon, and the complexity of the past. Moreover, students gain this disciplinary insight while learning to overcome one of their own blind spots: their deep and unspoken conviction that partisan politics and aesthetically important poetry necessarily occupy two separate and nonintersecting cultural planes.

Restoring Dryden to the Core Curriculum: Groups, Crowds, and the Poetry of Public Occasion

Ann A. Huse

Resistance to Dryden extends beyond the Restoration coterie. The satirists of a later age, the mid–twentieth century, also sharpened their wit at the expense of the professional writer who had risen from the ranks of the lesser gentry to assume the roles of poet laureate (1668) and historiographer royal (1670), offices gained in large part through his shrewdness as court propagandist. In a letter of 26 March 1947, Kingsley Amis proposed to Philip Larkin a new metric for determining literary value:

> I think "one dryden" ought to be a sort of unit of hate for a writer—only D. achieves 1.00, elsewhere the figure is always less than one, e.g.—
>
> | | | | |
> |---|---|---|---|
> | Johnson | .5 dryden | Jonson | .85 dryden |
> | Keats | .5 dryden | Shelley | .85 dryden |
> | Milton | .9 dryden | Chaucer | .9 dryden |
> | | | (i.e. "tends to" 1 dryd.) | |
>
> (qtd. in Leader 193)

In becoming the gold standard only by seeming most deserving of derision, the master ironist would still likely have enjoyed surpassing "our old English poet" (553), Chaucer, selections from whose tales he modernized in the 1690s.[1] Yet some of the remarks made at the tercentenary celebration of Dryden's death, held at Yale University in October 2000, might have tested the poet's equanimity. Although the critic William H. Pritchard is undoubtedly correct in asserting that "Dryden has fared well at the hands of the professoriat" (6), the two-day conference included enough negative comments to prompt an undergraduate to ask that, if Dryden could be an indifferent translator (as Emrys Jones said of Dryden's rendering of Persius) and if he failed to produce a masterpiece (as Barbara Everett asserted in her assessment of the oeuvre), "Then what's the point of studying this writer at all?"

It is a question that deserves an answer, especially in a volume on pedagogy, since teaching requires that we provide students with a rationale for the subject of study. This essay situates the response to the student's query in the context of the core curriculum, a mandated sequence of classes also referred to as general education or liberal studies. These sets of common courses have recently been much under attack or revision, with the University of Chicago scaling back its requirements in 1999 and Harvard refocusing its general education program in 2007. But my hope is that the approaches offered here will help incorporate Dryden's writings into whatever iteration of the humanities core becomes the primary preoccupation of a considerable number of faculty members teaching undergraduates. In any case, the challenge that general education poses—the coverage of (an admittedly broad range of) canonical texts in widely divergent learning environments—is no doubt familiar to most college instructors.[2]

Dryden's relevance to courses providing the intellectual foundation to an undergraduate education springs from three interrelated qualities of his work. The first is that, over his long career as a poet of public occasion, Dryden marked transitions in authority with shifts in idiom, and this practice corresponds to the humanities survey's attention to form's relation to historical or political change. Second, that he did so without the protective entitlement of his aristocratic rivals, such as the earl of Rochester, allows students to be exposed to a professional writer's maneuvers to capture the tenor of the times while retaining the favor of the powerful. Third, not merely a historiographer and poet in title, Dryden provides compelling material for the increasing number of interdisciplinary classes that combine literature, history, and political philosophy under the banner of the humanities. For instance, the tension between him and the coterie poets—"Sydley, Shadwell, Shepheard, Wicherley / Godolphin, Butler, Buckhurst, Buckinghame," to quote from Rochester's "Allusion to Horace" (Wilmot, lines 121–22)—is vividly illustrative of early modern concerns about status or position. This is not to pit Dryden against the Cabal as a working-class hero. Still, I have found that these three reasons for studying this writer, explicitly stated, capture the attention of general education students not previously interested in literature—or, for that matter, in the liberal arts.[3]

Dryden makes his appearance in this context as part of the study of medieval and early modern literature. Choosing a relevant theme is one way to motivate students to advance into such unfamiliar territory, where Dryden keeps company with Marie de France, Malory, Chaucer, Erasmus, Shakespeare, and Aphra Behn. Since my home institution, John Jay College of Criminal Justice, has a mission implicit in its name, I selected "Groups and Crowds" as a theme for students interested in issues of public order if not directly involved in some form of policing. The syllabus explains that we will study the ways that groups affect the behavior of individuals and that crowds take on identities of their own. How do these authors suggest that a crowd can become a source of power or a threat to authority? How do they treat their readers as groups that can be manipulated? Students will trace the stages and define the key terms of this premodern European conversation about group behavior and identity.

Students are told that they will be expected to write clearly and perceptively on these issues, to recognize continuities in the Western cultural tradition while also acknowledging historical change as represented in literature. The tale of the shift from corporate to individual identity is shopworn, but the professor may invoke it to qualify, criticize, or substantiate this teleological sweep. Selections from each author should allow the class to grapple with the topic in all its complexity and contradictions. But the approach should remain flexible, enabling broad temporal, cultural, and generic coverage without reducing the literary works to installments in an overarching narrative.

In the seventeenth century, Behn's *Oroonoko* (1688) is bracketed by two of Dryden's poems honoring momentous transitions, "To His Sacred Majesty" (1661) and "The Secular Masque" (1700). The masque serves us as a coda; we read it out loud on the last day of class. How do Dryden's maskers' descriptions of the "old age" that is "out"—"Thy wars brought nothing about; / Thy lovers were all untrue" (lines 94–95)—differ from Behn's (and the younger Dryden's) conceptions of Restoration political and literary culture? What does the difference in tone between works from the two periods, luxurious jubilation giving way to moral exhaustion, say about our own perspective on the past and, in particular, on the medieval and early modern writers we have encountered this semester? The role of the panegyric in the course is more substantive and goes beyond preparing students for Behn's recuperative royalist fantasy, though it fulfills that purpose as well. We begin by exploring the biblical imagery of the opening lines, which cast the "wild deluge" (1) of the Interregnum as an era of dangerous and slippery commingling—"When life and sin one common tomb had found" (2)—that drowned the distinctions necessary for social order. The rest of the class session is devoted to exploring how Dryden establishes himself as the poet most attentive to the forms of hierarchy and authority emerging in this postdiluvian England.

The poem's first crowd scene bears close reading, since it describes the character of Restoration coteries, groups seeking the higher ground beyond the "small prospect of a rising hill" (3), a first signaling of the reappearance of social stratification. The syntactical inversion in the first line of a key sentence makes it difficult to discern the precise identity and interests of the witnesses to the regal procession that will culminate in the coronation:

> Your cavalcade the fair spectators view
> From their high standings, yet look up to you.
> From your brave train each singles out a prey,
> And longs to date a conquest from your day.
> (37–40)

The apostrophe is, of course, to the man who would be king, but the rest of the figures are hazier. Stressing that this is a poem about locating and describing social positions after a period of (supposed) leveling, I identify the place of the viewers: they are in the balcony of Westminster Abbey, looking down at the royal train though looking up to Charles in that they will emulate him. It takes longer for students to recognize that these "fair spectators" are selecting from the king's attendants a potential partner and hoping to honor the return of the monarchy with a sexual triumph—a libertine version of the Norman Conquest. My students do not realize at first that the spectators are fair in that they are lovely women engaging in the sexual predation that would distinguish Charles's court circles. (Although I often pair this Dryden poem with another on the event, Katherine Philips's "On the Fair Weather Just at the Coronation," this juncture is also an apposite one for bringing in Behn.) Charles himself enters next and at the center of the spectacle attracts women's erotic attention. Yet Dryden ushers in his reign with an account of a recumbent and strangely passive figure who responds to the ceremony by succumbing to "[o]fficious slumbers" peopled with "pleasing shapes" (42, 44). To discover why Dryden represented a potential royal patron in this way, as a dreamer being led to "the sacred temple" to receive his crown (45), we require some familiarity with the political and personal challenges that met the restored monarch.

To this end, I assign Samuel Pepys's diary entry from 23 April 1661 and the chapter on the Restoration in the new Oxford World Classics edition of *History of the Rebellion*, by Edward Hyde, earl of Clarendon (395–424), instructing students to take notes on the problems confronting the returning Crown. In the next class, as we collate the vexations Charles faced, I quote Clarendon's acerbic portrait of the suitors mobbing the heir to the throne in the last days of his exile, in Flanders:

> In the mean time Breda swarmed with English, a multitude repairing thither from all other places as well as London, with presents, and protestations how much they had longed and prayed for this blessed change, and magnifying their sufferings under the late tyrannical government, when many of them had been zealous ministers and promoters of it. (419)

Another crowd presents itself here, a throng seeking preferment and absolution, pressing Charles to recognize them as innocent of rebellion. The Act of Indemnity and Oblivion of 1660, which Clarendon brokered, spared Charles this impossible task of national sorting, because the act, a keystone piece of Restoration legislation, restricted prosecution to those who were directly involved with his father's trial and beheading. Students can now appreciate the political payoff to Dryden's representation of the king's oblivious, sensual ease in "To His Sacred Majesty": "Among our crimes oblivion may be set, / But 'tis our king's perfection to forget" (87–88). The king is forgetful, or at least willing to appear so, about the troubled times that saw revolution and regicide.

I add other background information in a brief lecture. Not just the British subjects but time itself needed to be divided into spans of guilt and innocence: the coronation was delayed until Saint George's Day in 1661 so that two months of Charles's exile would not be included in his coronation year, as it was calculated according to the Julian calendar. In response, Dryden anxiously resets England's clock, excluding the "guilty months" of Charles's forced residence on the Continent from the "untainted year" that dated from the king's coronation rather than from his return to native soil (18–19). The Stuart court's exile had implications not only for those Lisideius refers to in Dryden's *Essay of Dramatick Poesie* (1668) as "bad Englishmen" (94) but also for the reputation of the restored monarch. Charles had spent nearly three years of his exile in France, frequently repairing to his mother's court there even after settling with his retinue at Cologne or Bruges. While in residence at Henrietta Maria's court, he considered marriage with her niece, mademoiselle de Montpensier, and toward the end of 1659 he sought the hand of Cardinal Mazarin's niece (Patterson 212). By the time he acted out his romance of the happy return, his attraction to foreign women (and, it was feared, to their absolutism and idolatry) was well known in England. My class probes how Dryden minimizes the dangers posed by a monarch enamored of pleasures, especially those that were foreign imports. Most notably, Dryden bathes the scene of the coronation in gorgeous sensory impressions: the tactile warmth of the repetition of the king's name, which smells like incense, the "melting strains" of music that taste like honey ("To His Sacred Majesty," line 55). The synesthesia that dignifies Charles's reputation for sensuousness by placing it in a context of royal pomp, making his appetites seem aesthetic rather than religious or political, also introduces students to the part of the poet's career spent recasting Charles's liabilities as assets. It affords, for instance, an easy segue to the depiction of King David's "vigorous warmth" in *Absalom and Achitophel* (1681; line 8).

This discussion of the generous languor that would set the Restoration rakes apart from those seemingly less refined dovetails nicely with a secondary source relevant to the theme of groups and crowds, Maximillian Novak's "John Dryden's Politics: The Rabble and Sovereignty." Introductory general education classes tend to restrict the reading list to primary sources, but I often include one carefully selected article at the end of the semester to prepare students for higher-level, research-oriented classes. Bearing in mind that most students in this literature core class will not go on to major in English, I ease them into the critical language of the discipline, asking them to prepare a handout on the essay. They summarize it, critique the argument, pull out two important quotations and respond to them, ask two analytic questions, and draw two connections to the literary works—whether to Dryden or other writers accompanying him on the syllabus. Before moving on to Behn and concluding with Dryden's world-weary maskers, we place the former laureate in this briefest of critical contexts so students can get a sense of the position his singular talent currently occupies in that most changeable of groups, the canon.

NOTES

[1]All references to Dryden in this essay come from *The Major Works*, edited by Keith Walker.

[2]Because of the unfortunate disjunction between postsecondary education and the schooling that precedes it in this country, and the relative lack of training in pedagogy

available to graduate students, most college professors have never received formal guidance in shaping a class session. The five-step lesson plan that public school teachers are required to use demands that educators state an objective for the lesson as part of the "anticipatory set" that focuses and motivates their students. Although these rubrics (available online at sites such as HotChalk *Lesson Plans Page*) can be restrictive and artificial, they nevertheless help provide structure and purpose.

[3]Without reigniting the culture wars of the late 1980s that oversimplified the positions of both sides, I mention in passing that students seem most thirsty for what used to be called, somewhat condescendingly, "cultural literacy" when they have had little previous exposure to canonical texts or historical frameworks.

Forward from "Mac Flecknoe": British Literature, 1660 to the Present

Scott R. MacKenzie

Despite its oddness and its haughty esoterica, I find Dryden's "Mac Flecknoe" (*Works* 2: 54–60) a thoroughly practical work for an introductory undergraduate survey class (the class discussed in this essay covers British literature from 1660 to the present, has forty to forty-five students, and combines lecture with open discussion). Few widely anthologized literary works outside the English neoclassical tradition present such direct and unleavened invective, particularly toward rival poets. "Mac Flecknoe" offers the opportunity to trace the outlines of English Augustan satire and some of its classical antecedents and to differentiate key elements of the early part of the survey from ones that emerge later. If any portion of Byron's *Don Juan*, particularly the dedication, features in a later part of the syllabus, so much the better.

Dryden's poem allows the instructor to assemble a kind of manifesto for the rich neoclassical conception of wit, a nexus of ideas that we need not fear exhausting in a survey course. Some or many of the interpretive gestures I describe may be too obvious to require inclusion, but I think it prudent to retrace all my steps. One fifty-minute class session is unlikely to be long enough for the outline I am offering, but selective use can be made of it. The themes and interpretations detailed here are also adaptable for more advanced classes. I have used, and supplemented, the materials I discuss here in 300- and 400-level undergraduate classes.

To begin, providing the class a brief overview of the poem's context is essential: I identify Dryden, Richard Flecknoe, Thomas Shadwell, their relationships and rivalries, the poem's private distribution, its first publication without the author's consent. Most editions provide some degree of annotation, but a professorial recap will orient the discussion that follows. I also emphasize the speculative nature of accounts of the animus between Dryden and Shadwell. Richard L. Oden's introduction to *Dryden and Shadwell, the Literary Controversy and* Mac Flecknoe offers a useful analytic grounding. As an alternative, instructors may find it rewarding to preface their introductory sketch with a brief appeal to the class for uncoached responses: Does this poem seem weird? Why? Have you encountered other examples of such fierce denigration in verse or in other situations? What do you imagine could put Dryden in such a fury? Versions of those questions can also be provided to students in advance for preclass preparation and for submission as part of a reading journal. More strictly critical reading questions might focus on what Dryden means by wit or dullness.

I then parse fairly rapidly the voices, allusions, and events of the poem, ensuring that students are as clear as possible about the speakers who divide it among them, about the mock-heroic mode of satire, and about the geographic features of Dryden's London (with its palimpsestic echoes of the medieval town, the Roman Augusta, and Rome itself). I draw to students' attention the frequency with which Dryden uses images that suggest

absence or emptiness: "full stupidity" (line 18), "Sh——— never deviates into sense" (20), "thoughtless majesty" (26), "Of all the pile an empty name remains" (69), "this monument of vanisht minds" (82), "from Ireland let him Reign / To farr Barbadoes on the Western Main" (139–40), "Pangs without birth and fruitless Industry" (148), "Thou art my blood where Johnson hath no part" (176), "What share have we in Nature or in Art?" (177), "a tympany of Sense" (194)

negation: "Sh———'s genuine night admits no ray, / His rising Fogs prevail upon the day" (24–25), "Born for a scourge of Wit, and Flayle of Sense" (89), "His Brows thick fogs, instead of glories, grace" (110), "damps of oblivion" (135), "Thy Tragick Muse gives smiles, thy Comick sleep / . . . / Thy inoffensive Satyrs never bite" (198–200)

waste or filth: "Pissing-Alley" (47), "Morning Toast that Floats along" (50), "Scenes of lewd loves, and of polluted joys" (71), "Martyrs of Pies, and Reliques of the Bum" (101), "loads of Sh——— almost Choakt the way" (103)

heaviness: "his goodly Fabrick fills the eye" (25), "[Jonson's muse] always floats above, thine sinks below" (186), "Sinking he left his Drugget robe behind" (214)

slavish copying or plagiarism: "He / Should onely rule, who most resembles me" (13–14), "Let 'em be all of thy own model made" (157), "let thy men of wit too be the same, / All full of thee, and differing but in Name" (161–62), "When did [Jonson's] Muse from Fletcher Scenes purloin, / As thou whole Eth'ridg dost transfuse to thine?" (183–84)

tautology: 30, 56

It should be possible to develop a discussion with students about what ties those categories together and how they serve Dryden's poetic purposes. Connecting absence and emptiness to negation presents no great challenge, but connecting them also to heaviness, filth, and plagiarism may take more work. Emphasizing and reemphasizing the incongruity between Dryden's elevated poetic perspective and his mean, dirty, and cheap irreverence can direct students to think carefully about the principles that inform the portrait of dullness. Beginning the semester with a few books from *Paradise Lost* enables me to refer students to Miltonic negation—"darkness visible" (1.63) and "shape, / If shape it might be called that shape hath none / . . . / Or substance might be call'd that shadow seem'd" (2.666–69)—and to suggest that Dryden's characterization of Shadwell with "genuine night" (23), "thick fogs" (110), and so on borrows Milton's tactic of figuring absence as a paradoxical presence, emptiness as a paradoxical weighty bulk. Alexander Pope recognizes and reiterates this parallel in *The Dunciad*: "Indulge, dread Chaos, and eternal Night! / Of darkness visible so much be lent" (4.2–3), and his goddess Dulness is "the seed of Chaos, and of Night" (4.13).

Excrement functions as a kind of governing trope for this metaphysic; it is a substance devoid of form, value, or distinguishable quality. I point out that the little fishes that throng about Shadwell's boat take the same interest in Shadwell as in the turds ("morning toast") with which they all share the river. The California edition of "Mac Flecknoe" retains the orthography that elides Shadwell's name as *Sh*———, a lacuna that allows one to read *Shit* or *Shitwell* in its place, though *Shit* does not fit the iambic pentameter. The phrase from line 103, "Loads of *Sh*——— almost Choakt the way," makes the conflation quite convincing. I also propose to students that, although I cannot find authoritative record of an idiomatic usage equivalent to *cack hand* or the French *main de merde*, the line "Thou wield'st thy Papers in thy threshing-hand" (52) in such proximity to "morning toast" calls us to imagine what else one may do (besides conducting a "harmonious band") with paper in one's hand and whether "reliques of the bum" may result. I think it equally plausible that *threshing hand* implies left-handedness and the deep symbolic resonance that has accumulated around it. Dullness, in short, is essentially shit.

It is a small step from there to account for plagiarism, slavish imitation, and tautology as further variations on the concept of waste products, or wasteful productions, yielding nothing but empty matter or insubstantial volume. That which refers to or partakes of nothing beyond itself cannot, for Dryden, have value; it implies only solipsism and unmeaning. A hollow echo—a sound simply reverberating or an imitation that copies an imitation—is dullness and falsehood just as much as a word that refers to nothing or to nothing in nature. Which brings us to the anagrams, acrostics, puns, and emblem poems of the conclusion to "Mac Flecknoe." These figures, which "torture one poor word Ten thousand ways" (208), readily exemplify a central principle of neoclassical poetics: the imperative that form be authorized by substantial precedent or legitimate referent.

To flesh out this principle, and perhaps carry it through later class discussions of texts from the same period and on into the eighteenth century, one may draw attention to its application in Pope, particularly the *Essay on Criticism* ("Those Rules of old discovered, not devis'd, / Are Nature still, but Nature Methodiz'd" [lines 88–89]; "The sound must seem an eccho to the sense" [365]), *The Dunciad*, or *Scriblerus*. It also informs neoclassicist critics' reconstruction of the Aristotelian distinction between the probable and the marvelous, Henry Fielding's prefatory definition of affectation and the ridiculous in *Joseph Andrews* (itself based on an Aristotelian distinction between burlesque and "just imitation of nature" [4]), and can readily support an examination of Jonathan Swift's "The Lady's Dressing Room" as well as Mary Wortley Montagu's response, "The Reasons That Induced Dr. S. to Write a Poem Called *The Lady's Dressing Room*," both of which are even more scatologically frank than "Mac Flecknoe."

Where time permits and as inclination leads, instructors may also link Dryden's principle to social anxieties of the period—for instance, concern about the rise of credit and mobile property, which looked suspiciously evanescent next to gold and other kinds of fixed or landed property and provoked fears about class transgression or disaffection with aristocratic title and monarchic succession. The South Sea Bubble episode makes an ideal example of empty signifiers escaping the poet's page and creating genuine public peril. And the opposition of dullness and wit lends itself well to an explanation of what the foundational distinction between art and nature meant to seventeenth- and eighteenth-century English readers.

All these oppositions and anxieties can be found in the *Spectator*. Erin Mackie argues that Joseph Addison feels "a distaste for forms of verbal manipulation that call attention to the body of language, to the material word, to the autonomy of the signifier," seeing in them "a disregard for sense and a cultivation of features of language that have little to do with verbal stability, permanence, reason, and easy communication" (226). For instructors who include the *Spectator* on their syllabi, I recommend numbers 1, 3 (the dream of Lady Credit), 35 (false and true humor), 50 (the Indian kings in London), and 61 through 63 (on wit). The "Pleasures of the Imagination" sequence needs no extra endorsement from me.

While teaching "Mac Flecknoe," I make use of excerpts from *Spectator* 62, in which Addison addresses both Dryden's definition of wit (from his "Apology for Heroic Poetry and Heroic Licence") and the more famous one by John Locke, from his *Essay concerning Human Understanding*. Locke's definition is limited to cognitive psychology, where wit names the function of "putting [ideas] together . . . wherein can be found any resemblance or congruity" in contradistinction to judgment, which operates by "separating carefully, one from another, ideas wherein can be found the least difference" (qtd. in Addison and Steele 1: 263–64). That elementary definition leads readily into a classroom discussion of what else goes to define wit. Students can be expected to come up with plenty of answers: quickness, intelligence, insight, humor, irony, and so forth. It is also not difficult to establish to their satisfaction that even the broadest application of concepts of wit based on Locke and on current usage seems narrow compared with the consequence and prestige with which Dryden endows his concept. Dryden says—and Addison paraphrases in *Spectator* 62—"The definition of wit (which has been so often attempted, and ever unsuccessfully by many poets) is only this; that it is a propriety of thoughts and words; or, in other terms, thoughts and words elegantly adapted to the subject" (*Works* 12: 97 ["Author's Apology"]). Addison's dry response, "with all the deference that is due to the judgment of so great a man," underscores the breadth of implication in Dryden's characterization: it "is not so properly a definition of wit, as of good writing in general" (Addison and Steele 1: 267). While Addison finds such an encompassing conception unsuited to his argument, we can pursue its implications for Dryden's poetics and politics as far as we like. Again, citing Pope may be helpful: "True Wit is Nature to Advantage drest, / What oft was Thought, but ne'er so well Exprest" (*Essay*, lines 297–98).

Propriety is the term we want to investigate most carefully in this part of the discussion. Students may or may not produce sophisticated responses to the question, "What does Dryden mean by propriety, and what are its implications?" To stimulate deliberations, I introduce a citation, usually attributed to the anthropologist Mary Douglas: "[D]irt is matter out of its proper place."[1] Inventive students will come up with a bigger range of responses to this juxtaposition than I can cover here. The principle can be illustrated by any number of examples or anecdotes. I sometimes provide audiovisual examples, which help make sense of complex classroom issues. To demonstrate Douglas's thesis I have screened a brief excerpt from an episode of *Seinfeld*, "The Gymnast" (season 6, episode 6), in which the character George Costanza eats a chocolate éclair that he finds in a trash can and gets caught (Berg and Schaffer). The clip requires one to investigate whether dirt is simply a matter of contact with matter out of place or whether a witnessing other, real or imaginary, is essential for dirt to be the cause of revulsion and humiliation.

Further conversation can address the relation between literal and figural notions of place: How does being at or near or simply associated with Pissing Alley, Barbican, Bunhill to Watling Street, or Ireland make one dirty or abject? How does Dryden treat social place—with what kinds of distinction and conflation (Augustus; the queens, infant punks, and little Maximins of the mother-strumpets' vast courts; Flecknoe, the type of Elijah and of Shadwell, who sinks downward rather than being borne aloft)? What makes "morning toast" and "the scattered limbs of mangled poets" detritus rather than proper matter belonging naturally to humanity?

Prepositional relations are clearly crucial: what is *within* differs from what is *without*, what is *above* from what is *below*, and so forth. Dryden invokes modes of categorization and bounding to associate persons and things with dirt, exclusion, and wickedness. Instructors may take the opportunity here to discuss the workings of metonymy and synecdoche. Both associative and comparative tropes perform Dryden's categorizations in "Mac Flecknoe." Students may be asked how the simile "Fleckno . . . like Augustus, young" (3) compares with a metaphor like "thou art my blood, where Johnson has no part" (175). It might be pointed out that dullness is defined overwhelmingly by what it is not; it is not heroic or imperial (4, 139–42), not lucid (22), not productive of sense (20), not tuneful (44–46), not sober (121, 126), not substantial (196), not continent (103), not generous (174), not decorous (147), not knowledgeable (147), and not technically adept (197–202).

So is more at stake for Dryden than a spiteful desire to denigrate a rival poet? Why does the course of empire, the portent of Old Testament prophecy, and fear of Catholic insurgency trouble this poem? Why should a punning hack threaten the heritage and succession of English letters? Let students consider why this arsenal of poetic weaponry and virtuosity needs deployment against the tottering fortifications of the theater district and printers' row. Return to these same topics if the syllabus later comes to *An Essay on Criticism* or *The Dunciad*. Ask also, If dullness is something close to pure negation, what is wit? Does Dryden allow us to define wit more positively and clearly than simply as the opposite of dullness? Samuel Johnson's assessment might be cited: "What was said of Rome, adorned by Augustus, may be applied by an easy metaphor to English poetry embellished by Dryden, *lateritiam invenit, marmoream reliquit*, he found it brick, and he left it marble" ("Dryden" 155). From what sources did Dryden quarry the stone for his noble pile?

NOTE

[1] Douglas's actual phrase does not contain the word *proper*: "If we can abstract pathogenicity and hygiene from our notion of dirt, we are left with the old definition of dirt as matter out of place" (44), but nor does Douglas claim it as her own. The origin of this idea tends to be attributed to Viscount Palmerston, twice prime minister of Britain in the mid–nineteenth century (see, e.g., Leckie 40). Douglas is, in any case, frequently paraphrased with *proper* included, and I think the example not inappropriate for the undergraduate classroom.

Introducing John Dryden the Dramatic

Margaret Anne Doody

"Dryden and Pope." That was the phrase that once—but no more—sprang automatically to the lips of college teachers. Or, "the age of Dryden and Pope." They remained uncomfortably and unsuitably forced into Siamese twinhood until the blunt knife of time at last sundered them. When I went to college (sometime before the Flood), we still had an age of Dryden and Pope. We were trained to regard the work of the English Romantics as real poetry and most of what came before as mere prologue. But times were altering—not to say a-changing. Both at Dalhousie University and at Oxford, I was taught to prize some medieval lyric and to develop, along with a certain solemn reverence for Milton, a high regard for the English metaphysicals. Donne and Marvell were the real thing, apparently, the last real poetic thing before Wordsworth and Coleridge. I was not singular in coming to regard the Restoration and eighteenth century as a level if well-tilled plain between two ranges of visionary mountain peaks.

Yet Pope was quite enjoyable. Pope is vivid, brightly colored, and his verse is alive with the lively sensuousness of things. "And all *Arabia* breathes from yonder box" (*Rape* 222). The attractive details, the colors, the iridescence, and sensuousness made Pope attractive. So too did the comic punch lines: "And lo! two puddings smoked upon the board" ("To Allen Lord Bathurst" 585). Dryden suffered from being set beside him; he had fewer revelings in description, fewer appeals to the senses, and he did not seem to have nearly as many punch lines. Like Pope, he wrote in the iambic couplets—the "rocking horse" of which Keats was—rightly, we felt—to complain (77 ["Sleep and Poetry"]). But Dryden's couplets felt different, were not usually as emphatic. Dryden always suffered by our placing his work beside that of Pope.

It is true; there are difficulties in introducing Dryden's major—or standard—poems. They require the instructor to supply a considerable amount of background as to the English Civil War and Restoration politics at precise historical moments. The subject matter should be interesting—the events and conflicts Dryden is dealing with are at the root of our political parties and two-party system in the English-speaking world. But they are likely to seem a bit bizarre, like old newspapers. Even the teacher can get tired of supplying answers to this—and biblical history as well. Who was King David? Who was Absalom? Who was the Duke of York? What was the Popish Plot—and what does *Popish* mean?

The reading becomes hampered by so much background information, and the poems are likely to seem not quite to justify the effort. Placed beside the work of Pope, the work of Dryden may seem to unenlightened readers to offer a kind of pallor of generality, and a certain loose carelessness. There is admittedly the occasional aphoristic couplet, oft quoted and quotable. In *Absalom and Achitophel* (*Works* 2: 3–37), "Great Wits are sure to madness near ally'd; / And thin Partitions do their bounds divide" (lines 163–64). But in general Dryden doesn't seem to pay too much attention to his couplet. He is not tidy; the ideas run over the lines.

Over time, it has come to seem to me that the best answer to the problems of introducing Dryden is not to stick him in with Pope. The two poets should be kept well apart. If Pope is a noun, Dryden is a verb. What drives him fundamentally is an interest in action, including interior, psychic action. Let Dryden keep company with the epic poets Vergil and Milton, who taught him so much. Exhibit some examples of the sort of description he admired, using his translation of the sections on burning Troy in the *Aeneid*, which to him is obviously an action poem. But above all, even before talking about Dryden the epic poet, introduce the dramatic poet. Start with the plays.

I have tried this (though admittedly with graduate students only). And in this endeavor I am repeating my own experience. I could have written a very passable essay on Dryden's poems, true, and received good grades for acceptable comments written with the passion of an icicle. For I rather disliked Dryden. I personally did not come to like Dryden—really *like* him as a poet—until I started work on my dissertation on Richardson, and read through all of Dryden's plays while I was tracking down the quotations from Restoration drama in *Clarissa*. In reading his plays it burst upon me who Dryden really was—a dramatist at heart, a playwright, and no mean songwriter. (This last fact alone might win him some support among students in our song-mad era—if I were advertising a course featuring Dryden, I would describe him as dramatist, poet, and songwriter.)

In saying "start with the plays," I most empathically do not mean that warhorse of the anthologies, *All for Love*. That is an anomaly among Dryden's own works; it doesn't show him at his best or most characteristic—and of course

Shakespeare's *Antony and Cleopatra* is bound to come off superior. Avoid *All for Love*, by all means. Get into the heroic tragedies, especially *The Conquest of Granada* and *Aureng-Zebe*. For contrast and complement, if time allows, choose one of his best comedies, like *Marriage à-la-Mode*. After a brief discussion of the theater of Dryden's time and the dominant acting styles (perhaps with some help from excerpts from *The Rehearsal*), get the students stuck into one actual play. It should be "acted" not just read aloud while sitting down. Let individuals take different roles (and actors can vary from scene to scene) and though each actor may have the text in one hand, let them be encouraged to engage in expressive heroic gesture with the other. Speaking Dryden is a surprisingly different experience from reading him cold on the page. Conflict becomes more evident, and we will also stumble into certain moments of absurdist comedy.

In the plays we can observe Dryden's representations of power and the search for it. We see his people and ideas in contestation, driven by desire for power, and the search for it. And not only a search for a power external to the individual—Dryden understands that power is made. It is there, up for grabs as we say—but it is to be made or transformed rather than merely grabbed. In depicting the conflict of characters and ideas, Dryden is a predecessor of Scott (who edited him and loved him), and Scott is the predecessor of Hegel in noting the clash of thesis and antithesis at a given historical moment. Dryden knows firsthand what it is like to be caught up in such struggles—and he has a comic sense about the nature of what we call an ideology when it is sited in a particular individual. The individual is always inadequate, and the ideology imperfectly expressed or understood.

Dryden's dramatic characters can seem at first glance alien to us because they articulate political ideas. But that very fact can also make them congenial. Almost all of his characters are organized around a degree of self-centeredness, even if they have a relatively poor comprehension of who the self is. Such characters are ever aware of the wider world of which they are a part, because they usually want to make an impression on that wider world. They sense, if awkwardly, the larger nature of the principles for which they contend—even if the contention is in part absurd, as Dryden always shows it to be. His favorite plots and settings engage us in struggles at a moment of historical change. Dryden's themes involve what we have learned to call "the clash of civilizations"—but he knows that civilization is a dubious matter, born out of conflict and never complete.

In the first act of part 1 of *Conquest of Granada*, Almanzor, who has been fighting as a free lance in the civil war in Moorish Spain, is captured by the angry Moorish King Boabdelin, who threatens him with death. Almanzor denies that this or any king has rights over him:

> No Man has more Contempt than I of breath
> But whence hast thou the Right to give me Death?
> Obey'd as Sovraign by thy Subjects be,
> But know, that I alone am King of me.

I am as free as Nature first made Man,
E'er the base Laws of Servitude began,
When wild in woods the noble Savage ran.
(1.1.201–09)

Boabdelin retorts that in that case "mankind shou'd use you like a common Foe" (211), that a man outside all law and loyalty is an absolute outlaw. Almanzor argues that he makes laws only for himself. Theirs is a central and enduring argument, picking up the puzzle of the relation of freedom to power. How, if at all, can Liberty possibly coexist with Authority? Almanzor sees, as Hobbes does, an original state of Nature in which there is as yet no ruler, state, or communal authority. To Hobbes, this condition is horrible—proverbially "nasty, brutish, and short" (57). But to Almanzor, a predecessor of Ayn Rand, Liberty is so self-evidently desirable that he must logically deny Authority—not of a king but of any society or community. For Almanzor, civilized society depends on "base Laws of Servitude." A savage thus becomes paradoxically noble because he is not enslaved or subordinate to anyone; the savage in the wilds retains that ineffable treasure, his own liberty. The project of civilizing the world, whether undertaken by Muslims or Christians, is a project of enslavement. Dryden gave us a remarkable phrase in "noble Savage," a phrase to be repeated in the century that follows. But in Almanzor's ideal of himself, his idealization of heroic individualism, he prophetically hits on a permanent element in American thought. "Give me Liberty, or give me Death," says Patrick Henry. "Sic semper tyrannus," says Booth, firing on Lincoln. The noble frontiersman preferring liberty above all else, the American mythical man, is a figure very much in line with Almanzor's idea, as is the notion that the state is always bad and government can do nothing good.

Of course Dryden does not let Almanzor rest with that ideology. In the course of the play he does reluctantly get tamed by love and society. His heroic stance is a precondition for individualism, but Dryden's characters are never able to stop at individualism. Even the greatest egotists are thinking of their social role, and present abstractions in terms of their own (real or imagined) social persona.

In *The Conquest of Granada* the villain, Zulema, argues contemptuously with Abdullah against the concept and authority of virtue:

If, when a Crown and Mistress are in place,
Vertue intrudes, with her lean holy Face;
Vertues then mine, and not I vertues Foe:
Why does she come where she has nought to do?
(2.1.208–11)

Virtue is comically personified as a haglike figure in an allegorical painting, an undesirable presence—like a cross between a nun and a mother-in-law—poking in where she doesn't belong. Virtue on the move is just intrusive, a nag, and Zulema himself, the straightforward Zulema, is the victim of inappropriate and comic nagging. This speech of jocular contempt is designed mainly to enhance the speaker's persona, including its masculinity.

The search for power is visible in almost every character (to that extent Dryden is true to Hobbes). But Dryden underlines the absurdity of the search for power by creating some characters who are overtly comic in their simple quest for power. *The Conquest of Granada* has Lyndaraxa, a woman who is searching for the right man. Her right man is the one who will succeed in becoming king (presumably by bumping off his rivals). She finds her men defective, and they judge her fickle. This verdict exasperates her, as her desire seems to herself perfectly reasonable:

> O could I read the dark Decrees of Fate,
> That I might once know whom to love or hate!
>   For I my self, scarce my own thoughts can ghess,
>   So much I find 'em varied by success.
>   As in some wether-glass my Love I hold;
>   Which falls or rises with the heat or cold.
>   I will be constant yet, if Fortune can;
>   I love the king, let her but name the Man.
> (4.2.71–78)

Lyndaraxa is constant; she loves "the King"—whoever that turns out to be. Emotions in her view should be fastened not to the stability of the person feeling, but the stability of an object defined as point of power. An individual man is to Lyndaraxa not at all concrete, a mere secondary and shadowy half personage less real than the abstraction. In a kind of strange feminism, Lyndaraxa, a staunch egotist like so many of Dryden's characters, unmasks the personal as secondary to the political. The political creates—or recreates the personal. As usual in Dryden the action takes place at a time of political upheaval and uncertainty; nothing is any more stable than Lyndaraxa's "wether-glass." We see how swelling pressures, confusions, and incessant change shape what we know as personality. Lyndaraxa's fickle fascinations enchant her lover, Abdalla, even when he thinks that his pursuit is useless. He enjoys the peculiar position of being passively active, helpless to resist; he compares himself to a man in a nightmare struggling to run. To the urging of Abdelmelech that he should stop, he responds with another simile of motion:

>   Like him who on the ice—
> Slides swiftly on, and sees the water near,
> Yet cannot stop himself in his Carrear,
> So am I carry'd. (3.1.90–93)

Abdalla expresses a certain satisfaction in contemplation of his own passivity—for he is passivity on the motion, the victim of a motion and yet the subject of his own momentum. He expresses a craving for swift if deleterious movement, and in expressing the craving, embodying a verb form in himself, he seduces himself satisfactorily.

Dryden's characters, like the actors who portray them, speak and act with an eye to an immediate audience. This fact renders them, among all dramatic characters, uniquely susceptible to seduction. Seduction need not necessarily be sexual—though an element of sexual seduction inheres at the center of every political and moral seduction, regardless of the gender or age of the players. Almanzor, apparently so confident, is asking for approval, which is almost the same thing as asking to be seduced. Almahide, presenting herself as equally strong, gains power over him once she engages him in conversation.

Almanzor is one of Dryden's attempts at the archetypal. And Dryden always presents archetypes as in part absurd. Almanzor is not meant to be a total success. All of Dryden's major characters have an absurd side, and are colored by a certain degree of failure. The characters' arguments with each other about worldviews are likely to become misshapen or strained, or to result in some unexpected upshot. In Dryden's world, political actions are not completed, ideologies are not yet formed, events are continually demanding reactions, and nobody is in control of what is tumultuously happening.

In Dryden's dramas, everything is in movement. Rhyme, rhythm, and images are designed to create that perception. We begin to notice that his iambic pentameter and rhymed lines are really geared to allow characters maximum expressiveness and emotional point. Dryden rarely fully end-stops a line—you cannot readily divide his two lines into four neat parts, as is so often and so pleasurably the case with Pope. There are indeed connections and antitheses, but they work very differently. Dryden carries his lines across a bigger space; his unit is the verse paragraph, the speech outburst, rather than the couplet. He shares with the metaphysicals an interest in the telling image, but Dryden is not interested in remaining at the level of conceit. Neither will he rest with description—even after all that Vergil taught him in the *Eclogues* and the *Georgics*. Dryden's metaphors and similes are all active. Most involve movement, sometimes disastrous, sometimes comically awkward:

> Still they write on, and like great Authors show;
> But 'tis as Rowlers in wet gardens grow
> Heavy with dirt, and gathering as they go.
> (lines 29–31 [prologue])

We focus here not on objects merely (rollers and dirt) but also on the heavy, obsessive motion of the implement rolling relentlessly on through mud. In embodying its own movement, the authorial mind, like the roller, participates with Abdalla in an egotistic if hapless delight in its own momentum.

Once the class has had the pleasure of experiencing part 1 of *The Conquest of Granada*, we can turn with new eyes to *Absalom and Achitophel.* We now may find familiar elements, recognizing even in the narrative authorial voice the fascination with power and passivity, an understanding of the paradoxical engagement of movement that might prove fatal: "But wilde Ambition loves to slide, not stand: / And Fortunes ice prefers to Vertues Land" (lines 198–99). The delicious active helplessness of Abdalla is repeated with variation in Achitophel's lust after the long slide.

Absalom and Achitophel should be treated as one of Dryden's greatest dramas, I would suggest. One way of achieving this might be to approach each segment first with several students standing up and reading short passages. To an ear and eye trained on the drama of *The Conquest of Granada*, the dramatic nature of *Absalom* will become obvious. The narrative third-person passages employ a good deal of the sort of language we are used to in personages' descriptions of themselves and others in the plays. Almanzor's ideology is visible and audible again in the portrait of "the Jews" (the English people, more particularly the disaffected and dissenting Protestants):

> These Adam-wits, too fortunately free,
> Began to dream they wanted libertie;
> And when no rule, no president was found
> Of men, by Laws less circumscribed and bound,
> They led their wild desires to Woods and caves,
> And thought that all but Savages were Slaves.
> (51–56)

A nascent ideology which we heard in an Almanzor objectively is now being described subjectively by a narrator who wants us to see it as an absurd ideology. This will undoubtedly stir some classroom debate; we are now having a view forced on us. What was sympathetic in Almanzor is not allowed to be sympathetic here. But resemblances in dramatic situation will be clear. We can certainly ask if Charles-David is not dangerously near being another Boabdelin, if his Monmouth-Absalom is really like Almanzor or merely persuades himself that he could take on such heroic grandeur. Once Dryden has worked on his extensive set-up we get into the drama proper: "*Achitophel* still wants a Chief, and none / was found so fit as Warlike *Absalon* . . ." (221–22). The immediate objective of this complex and active personality is clear. We are now free to enjoy the lengthy process of dramatic seduction which is the center of the poem. Achitophel works at changing Absalom's "mind"—that is, his perceptions, with plausible if contradictory statements. The son will be like (wishes to be like) his father David in being strong; on the other hand, David is weak, and dotes on his son. If Absalom's title by law is illegitimate, his title is by blood unmistakable. So Achitophel teaches the youth, allowing us to wonder whether the blood is not emerging in a certain likeness in indolence and fantasy. It is necessary for Achitophel to hitch Absalom to his own action. Absalom, a feeble noun, must be made into a verb. The older man teases the younger with the notion that he will be seen as passive and timid, "Content ingloriously to pass thy days / Like one of Vertues Fools that feeds on Praise" (246–47). Achitophel molds the illicit prince into a kind of Zulema, proud of his resistance to conventional virtue and seeking heroic stances and deeds. As the narrator notes, the seducer knows what means to employ: "What cannot Praise effect in Mighty Minds, / When Flattery Sooths and when Ambition blinds?" (303–04). The pretended defense of Absalom shows him ironically as weak—the narrative point of view reflecting the way Achitophel sees him: "Made Drunk with Honour, and debauch'd with Praise" (312). The reader is offered the fascinating if morally uneasy spectacle of a man deteriorating while he thinks he is rising. This is a dramatic story. Absalom is a tragic figure in the way that Dryden's dramatic figures are tragic—that is, tragic-comic, and absurd. Without self-knowledge, let alone humility, he is anxious to be remolded as a self—an important self—and his attempts at strength and action complete his antagonist's work, turning him into somebody else's puppet. Achitophel himself is the central tragic figure. He is rational—if impatiently rational—and he is anxious to exert himself, to play, to hazard all. A number of readers have noticed his resemblance to Milton's Satan. As a seducer Achitophel evidently feels some impatience with the youth he is seducing, who becomes the more contemptible as the more susceptible. But both men are caught up in the turmoil of the moment, of unfulfilled political action and ends—a world of change and possibility. Achitophel is really as drunk on the possibility of change and power as he makes Absalom—he just (as we say) holds his liquor better. Dryden understands that diabolical attraction in Achitophel, and needs to play with it while damping it down a trifle. He creates an authoritative figure contemptuous of stasis, and ruthless without being exactly cruel. This power must be met by the less visible authority if legitimate figure, David-Charles. He must be roused from stasis and, without being cruel, gives some impression of banked energies: "Beware the Fury of a patient Man" (104). But David never really captures the centre of the action. The heart of the story is the rapid assemblage of a dangerous political coalition, doomed to burst apart again. At the heart of that drama is the forged relationship between the older statesman and the young bastard.

Without much overt criticism of the darling young man on the narrator's part, we are made privy to his weakness and self-delusion, and the effect on him of fear as well as of the divine discontent that Absalom claims (or is taught to claim) for himself:

> Why am I scanted by a Niggard Birth?
> My Soul Disclaims the Kindred of her Earth:
> And made for Empire, Whispers me within;
> Desire of greatness is a Godlike Sin. (369–72)

At one level, this statement is almost purely comic, dramatically so, for we can see that rather than being "made for Empire" Absalom seems best suited to doing what he is told. Like other dramatic characters in Dryden's works, he performs for his audience, and the audience always includes the mobile self as well as the objective auditor. He satisfies himself for a while by fabricating an interesting persona, and doesn't realize he is doing so under detailed competent instruction. As with many of Dryden's dramatic characters, Absalom would be capable of assuming another pose and another direction, if he were removed from this particular pressure, to be jostled by other events. Absalom is not loyal to action, to the verb; he has a secret default position of passiveness. "I cannot help it" can be—and is—the secret or open motif of many of Dryden's characters.

The study of one heroic tragedy by Dryden will teach us—teacher as well as students—how to interpret and enjoy the political mock epic, or poetic narrative drama. We will develop an appreciation of the use of images of stress, energy, and motion. Together we can work out the depths and the range of playfulness. And seeing what Dryden thinks of human characters will give us keys to his poetic expressiveness as well as to his understanding of the tragic-comic dynamic of political affairs. At least, at the end of our reading, it is unlikely that anyone will confuse Dryden with Pope.

Teaching *Marriage à-la-Mode* in a Course on Restoration Comedy

Will Pritchard

John Dryden's *Marriage à-la-Mode* (*Works* 11: 219–316) has long been seen to represent Restoration comedy at its best or worst. Bonamy Dobrée observed in 1924 that "the whole idea of Restoration comedy is summed up" in the play's opening song (106), and L. C. Knights, in condemning the genre as "trivial, gross, and dull," concurred: "Restoration comedy nowhere provides us with much more of the essential stuff of human experience than we have here" (578). Despite its representative qualities, however, the play is seldom anthologized; Norton, Penguin, Oxford, Riverside, and Blackwell all omit it from their collections of Restoration drama. (It is included in *The Broadview Anthology of Restoration and Early Eighteenth-Century Drama*, however, and there are excellent solo editions of the play in the New Mermaids and Regents Restoration Drama series.) But if anthologists have not favored the play, critics have. It has received the sustained attention of numerous prominent scholars,[1] whose shared task has been to grapple with the double or divided plot of *Marriage à-la-Mode*—perhaps to render it coherent—and to consider the political valence of the play. These critics have tried to explain how the play's heroic and comic plots work together and what their ideological implications might be.

This essay focuses not on the play's double plot but on its title, which is so good that William Hogarth and Katherine Mansfield each recycled it. What is "marriage à la mode," and what is the play saying about it? In the classroom, I approach these questions in three stages. We begin with nondramatic texts that show how marriage and mode were being portrayed and contested in the 1670s. Then we turn to the play itself (published in 1673 but first performed in late 1671) and see what it does with the terms and arguments put forth in the polemical texts of the day. Finally we examine contemporary comments on *Marriage à-la-Mode* to see how it was interpreted in its day. This approach helps refute Charles Lamb's claim that Restoration comedies "are a world of themselves, which has no reference whatever to the world that is" (568).

"Marriage" and "À la Mode"

The years 1670–75 witnessed a lively debate in print on the topic of marriage. Texts that launched a skeptical, libertine assault on marriage were countered by ones energetically defending the institution.[2] The antimarriage texts portray matrimony as slavery and tedium, with meager pleasures that are soon exhausted. Marital sex is drudgery, merely "the Eccho of forgotten Joyes" (*Broadside*, line 30); a husband must "Repeat [his] Loath'd embraces ev'ry Night, / Prompted to act by Duty, not delight" (7–8). Would-be husbands risk cuckoldry and are advised to choose a mistress, a prostitute, or "a Glass of Claret" instead (*Poor Anthony's Complaint*, line 80). A strong streak of misogyny underwrites all this misogamy. "If *Women*, then, in general, be so bad," asks one text rhetorically, "*what an hazard is it then to Marry*?" (Seymar 83).

In response, the promarriage authors deploy religious and civic arguments, depicting marriage as divinely ordained ("It is not good that the man should be alone" [Gen. 2.18]) and as fundamentally human ("Marriage laid the foundation and first principle of civil society" [*Essays* 38]). It is praised as the proper means "to quench the lust of youth" (Hodges 34), and "the comfortable and constant warmth of a well-grounded *Love*" is preferred to "the Feaverish heats of never-satisfied *Lust*" (*Maid's Complaint* 7). The defenders of marriage scorn the alternatives, arguing for instance that "the embraces of a *modest* Wife are not only more *cheap* and *wholesome*, but much more *pleasant* than the treacherous Dalliances of a wanton *Miss*" (7). Husbands are commended for producing heirs, unlike modish bachelors who "leave the next generation nothing but sorrowes, distempers, and French consumptions" (*Account* 59).

Appended to this essay is a table of excerpts recommended for classroom use; they can all be found using the *Early English Books Online* database. However, the marriage debate can also be effectively encapsulated in the following pair of acrostics, one of which answers the other:

W *is Double Woe,*
I *Naught else but Jealousie,*
F *is fained, flattering, fraud*
E *is naught but Enmity*. (Seymar 12)

W *Wealth is which the Wife doth bring*:
I *Ioys without repentance loud can sing*:
F *Friendships sacred league does signifie*:
E *Entertains you with eternity*. (*Marriage* 12)

It pays to spend time in class on this pair, asking not only where they disagree but also what assumptions they share. Both concern themselves solely with what the husband gets in marriage; both presume a single, monolithic thing called WIFE, capable of being summed up and properly valued or devalued; both strike an extreme, controversial position. There were also more moderate voices in the marriage debate, such as Thomas Hodge's *Treatise of Marriage* (1673), which defended marriage but warned against love that was merely "Syllogistical" (e.g., "Every man must love his wife: . . . this woman is my wife; Therefore I ought to love her" [30]). Even *Marriage Asserted* (1674), in vindicating the married state, acknowledges the imperfection of all sublunary existence: the problem is not in "the condition of this or that sort of life, but life it self" (10). The pro- and antimarriage authors, despite their exaggerated polarization, occasionally found common ground.

Determining what *à la mode* meant is a little trickier. *Mode* is a more elusive topic than *marriage*, and it did not undergo the same sort of systematic analysis.[3] The phrase means literally "in the fashion" or "after the fashion," and it reinforces that meaning through its Frenchness (think of *soup du jour* vs. *today's soup*). On title pages it generally promised the latest and the finest: a cookbook contained "À la Mode Curiousities," a self-help book showed how to write "Letters à la Mode," an anthology featured "New Songs and Poems à-la-Mode," and a grammar book billed itself as "The High Dutch Minerva à-la-Mode." But the phrase was also frequently satirical, evoking fashion that tried too hard or went too far. The word *modish* too, like *trendy* today, was almost always pejorative: "modish Vices," "modish nonsense," and so on.

Once they have got acquainted with marriage and mode in the 1670s, I ask my students what they expect from a play called *Marriage à-la-Mode*. Will it offer a happy, progressive alternative to marriage, as *The New Way of Marriage* (1680?) purports to do: "We will the modish way / of love pursue, / Love and lye without a tye, / yet still be true" (49–52)? Or does the title introduce a satirical attack on the present, modish corruption of marriage and "the incivility of those times that forbear to respect it" (*Essays* 38)?

Marriage à-la-Mode

When we turn to Dryden's play, students recognize much in it. The celebrated opening song sets forth the now familiar critique of marriage, maintaining that "a foolish Marriage Vow" has no force once "Passion is decay'd" and that, indeed, a "Marriage is dead, when the Pleasure is fled" (1.1.3, 6, 9). These claims open the door to adultery, since "he whose joys did end / And who cou'd give no more" cannot be wronged by his wife's having "Pleasures for a Friend" (13–14, 11). These abstract sentiments are tested in the play's comic plot, which features two couples on the brink of adultery. Rhodophil and Doralice, who sings the opening song, have been married a year, and their marriage has grown stale; Palamede and Melantha are soon to embark on a marriage arranged by their fathers. Rhodophil and Palamede are friends, but soon each is attempting secretly to seduce the other's partner. The women encourage the men's attention but remain elusive.

This comic setup affords many opportunities for characters to disparage "the Banes of Matrimony" (3.1.63). Rhodophil, for instance, offers this whimsical but poignant account of the progress of his feelings for his wife:

> All that I know of her perfections now, is only by memory; I remember, indeed, that about two years ago I lov'd her passionately; but those golden days are gone, *Palamede*: Yet I lov'd her a whole half year, double the natural term of any Mistress, and think in my conscience I could have held out another quarter; but then the World began to laugh at me, and a

> certain shame of being out of fashion seiz'd me: At last, we arrived at that point, that there was nothing left in us to make us new to one another: yet still I set a good face upon the matter, and am infinite fond of her before company; but, when we are alone, we walk like Lions in a room, she one way and I another: and we lie with our backs to each other so far distant, as if the fashion of great Beds was onely invented to keep Husband and Wife sufficiently asunder. (1.1.144–57)

This short speech gives a subtler, more nuanced view of marriage than one finds in the polemical texts. Rhodophil does not hate his wife, though he no longer loves her; they have grown distant, but the distance troubles him. He acknowledges that some of his dislike of marriage is purely modish (loving one's wife is "out of fashion"), but he also identifies the real challenge lovers face in making themselves perpetually "new to one another." In this passage, and in the play as a whole, Dryden transforms the stark oppositions of the marriage debate into something more comic and more complex.

Unlike the polemicists, Dryden also gives a voice to women's dissatisfaction with marriage. The dullness and dumpishness of husbands is a recurrent topic, as is their sexual neglect of their wives. As Doralice exclaims after Rhodophil exits:

> Well, since thou art a Husband, and wilt be a Husband, I'll try if I can find out another! 'Tis a pretty time we Women have on't, to be made Widows, while we are marry'd. Our Husbands think it reasonable to complain, that we are the same, and the same to them, when we have more reason to complain, that they are not the same to us. Because they cannot feed on one dish, therefore we must be starv'd. (3.1.85–91)

This is not exactly a feminist manifesto, but it moves beyond the androcentric perspective of the marriage debate. Dramatic form permits (or requires) Dryden to give vent to a woman's marital discontents and her need for pleasure.

Marriage à la mode, then, seems to have two key features in *Marriage à-la-Mode*. First, the modish husband and wife are estranged, either publicly (Melantha plans never to be seen with her husband [2.1.72–75]) or privately (Doralice and Rhodophil pretend to be in love when others are watching [3.1.1–35]). Second, the husband has a mistress, and the wife may have a gallant. Palamede observes that "all mankind set up for [i.e., hire, employ] Mistresses" (1.1.175–76), and he plans to enjoy both wife and mistress "as a reasonable man ought to do" (2.1.103–04). The play satirizes the insatiably modish Melantha for "run[ning] mad in new *French* words" (2.1.47–48) but it seems hardly to mind her eagerness to be seduced (3.1.248–58). She is mocked for preferring the word "*amour*" to an "old phrase" such as "intrigue" (2.1.15, 14, 14), but her desire for amorous intrigue itself is tolerated and encouraged almost to the very end.

Almost. The play verges on adultery but backs away at the last minute. As the epilogue puts it, "Though 'twas well offered, there was nothing done" (line 12).

The would-be adulterers reach various epiphanies that deter them. First, the effort of convincing her that he is sufficiently à la mode interests Palamede in Melantha: "with taking all this pains for her, I begin to like her" (5.1.188–89). Next, he and Doralice, having been thwarted by various circumstances, conclude that perhaps unconsummated love is to be preferred. As Doralice puts it, "The only way to keep us new to one another is never to enjoy" (272–73). Finally, jealousy renews Rhodophil's desire for Doralice; he reasons that "if [Palamede] loves you, there's something more in ye then I have found: some rich Mine, for ought I know, that I have not yet discover'd" (324–26). This argument further convinces Palamede of Melantha's worth (327–30), and after toying with the idea of "a blessed community" in which they would share their wives, the two men conclude by "mak[ing] a firm League, not to invade each others propriety [i.e., property]" (359–60). This agreement seems to suffice; Doralice is pleased with the prospect of increased sexual attention from her husband and stipulates only that in case of any future husbandly neglect, "both the Women shall revenge themselves, by the help of the other party" (365–66).

What is the force of this ending? Has Dryden rehabilitated marriage by the play's end? Robert D. Hume argues that no play from this period genuinely "attack[s] marriage as an institution" or "envisage[s] any serious alternative." *Marriage à-la-Mode*, he writes, "comes as close as any, but Dryden's conclusion is uncompromisingly conservative" ("Myth" 29). The play's conclusion may be conservative in comparison with its first four acts, but less so in comparison with hardcore promarriage pamphlets like Z. C.'s *Marriage-Musick; or, Nuptial-Duties* (1670) or William Smith's *Joyfull Tidings . . . with a Few Words of Counsel unto Friends concerning Marriage* (1672). Most of the play's antimarriage barbs are left unanswered, and while the adulterous impulse is curbed, it is hardly cured. Some have argued that the lovers in the heroic plot redeem marriage for all: "[T]he relationship of Palmyra and Leonidas opens the possibility that desire achieved might breed more desire, the possibility that steadily experienced sexual love has deep within it the fount of energetic, striving life. If that is so, then marriage loses its terrors" (Crane ix). I find this reading unconvincing. The idealized sentiments of the heroic scenes (e.g., "Think not that time or fate shall e'er divide / Those hearts, which love and mutual vows have tied" [2.1.486–87]) do not seem to impinge on the real-world concerns of the comic plot. Neither of the comic couples takes heart from the glowing example of Leonidas and Palmyra, and marriage is left more or less to fend for itself. Read in the context of the marriage debate, Dryden's play seems most notable for its refusal to take sides.

Contemporary Responses

Hume's sense of *Marriage à-la-Mode*'s conservatism is both confirmed and undermined by the play's epilogue, which is the first comment on the play that we turn to in class. Here Dryden portrays himself as a satirist who has lashed the faults of the age with "examples drawn . . . / From most of you, who hear, and see the *Play*" (lines 7–8). He backs off from this pose, however, explaining:

> He would not quite the Women's frailty bare,
> But stript 'em to the waste, and left 'em there.
> And the men's faults are less severely shown,
> For he considers that himself is one. (13–16)

He admits that he has taken it easy on the women and even easier on the men and also that he has tempered his satire by forbearing to "lay the Scene at home" (19). Rhodophil, who speaks the epilogue, notes gratefully that the playwright has "spar'd [his] shame" (25), and the play's Sicilian setting does the same for the "*Rhodophils* in this Theatre" (9). The epilogue's claim to have "inform'd the nation" (1) and "led you all the way to Reformation" (2) appears to be largely tongue-in-cheek.

One of the promarriage texts does endorse the play, however. *Marriage Asserted* takes seriously the epilogue's reformation argument and counts the play among its allies:

> What is either wicked or silly in modish colours he has so well painted, as would divert any person that is owner of the least ingenuity, from both: more particularly this of shunning Marriage, and being entred perfidiously to break a vow so easy to be kept, in his Play of *Marriage a-la-Mode*: a more gentile Satyre against this sort of folly, no Pen can write. . . . (75–76)

The play's satire was so gentle (or genteel), however, that the assembled crowds, despite "see[ing] themselves abused," were moved "neither to be angry nor ashamed" (76). Audiences appear to have responded to the play's irreverent wit and disregarded its ostensibly conservative conclusion.

That response and disregard certainly characterize the final contemporary comment on the play, a long satirical poem entitled *Gallantry A-la-mode* (1674). In part 2 of this poem, the speaker begins his seduction of his beloved, Phillis, by taking her to the playhouse, where "'Twas the first *Time* that e're was show'd / That *Play* call'd *Marriage A-la-Mode*" (line 81). The speaker offers another gloss on the play's title, which he takes to mean "that *Marriage* now was made / But *after-Game* to *bankrupt Trade*"—that is, that men do not now marry until they have exhausted themselves with a mistress. He concludes, "If so; I am resolv'd a *Miss* / T' enjoy, before that Destiny / *Condemns* me to such *Drudgery*" (82). He declares his intention to pursue this "*Design*" even though the poets curse him for it, and once the play is over, he seems largely unscathed by its satire. He acknowledges that the playwright has made him look at his "*Coppy*" and that his "self acted was ith' *Play*" (84). However, like the spectators described in *Marriage Asserted* who saw themselves abused by Dryden's satire yet were "moved neither to be angry nor ashamed," the speaker of *Gallantry A-la-mode* is undeterred. He commends the poet "In *Gratitude*" and is particularly thankful that Dryden's satire has worked "at a *distance*" and without "*naming*" (84). He proceeds with his seduction of Phillis, emboldened rather than chastened by the play. Hume claims that *Marriage à-la-Mode* offers "an explicit repudiation of libertine principles on the ground that they are unworkable" ("Myth" 43), but judging by contemporary commentary, few took that repudiation seriously, if they noticed it at all.[4]

The approach I have outlined here pays various dividends in the classroom. It helps students see Restoration comedies not just as isolated texts but also as components of a larger discourse on morals and manners. It allows them to get their hands dirty with obscure texts that have not been modernized and annotated. And it requires them to think about the ways in which works of art, particularly dramatic ones, do or do not take a position in a larger cultural debate. These reasons—not to mention the excellence of the play itself, which Dryden thought his best comedy—argue strongly for adding it to a Restoration comedy course or even for letting it take the place of *The Country Wife* or *The Way of the World* in a larger survey course.

NOTES

[1]See L. Brown; Hughes, "Unity"; McKeon, "Marxist Criticism"; Canfield, "Ideology"; Rothstein and Kavenik; Braverman; Sherman; Kroll; and Rosenthal, "'All Injury's Forgot.'"

[2]For recent treatments of marriage and libertinism in this period, see Spurr, *England* (esp. ch. 7); Novak, "Libertinism"; Webster; D. Turner; and J. Turner. Novak, "Margery Pinchwife's 'London Disease,'" remains a useful overview.

[3]The first twenty pages of *A Protestant Antidote against Popery* (1674) offer a succinct indictment of "the great atheisticalness and vain amours now in fashion."

[4]Hume argues elsewhere that "the play seems to have been misunderstood by the Carolean audience, which took the subplot as nothing more than titillation" ("Marital Discord" 270).

APPENDIX: EXCERPTS FROM THE MARRIAGE DEBATE

	Pro	Con
Poems and Ballads	Z. C., *Marriage-Musick; or, Nuptial Duties* (1670) *A Vindication of a Marriage Life* (1675)	W. H., "A Just, True and Honourable Description of Marriage" (1673) Mr. C.'s "Song: Against Marriage" (1674) *A Broad-side against Marriage* (1675) *The New Way of Marriage* (1680?) *Poor Anthony's Complaint* (1662–88)
Pamphlets and Treatises	*An Account of Marriage* (1672) S[mith], *Joyfull Tidings* (1672), 6–8 Hodges, *A Treatise of Marriage* (1673), 1-7 ("Of Marriage") and 59-64 ("Of Adultery and Fornication") *Remarques on the Humours and Conversations of the Town* (1673), 75-89 *Essays of Love and Marriage* (1673), 35-50 *Marriage Asserted*, 1–26 *The Maid's Complaint against the Batchelors . . .* (1675)	Seymar [Ramsey], *Conjugium Conjurgium* (1673), 1–30 *Hey for Horn Fair . . . a Merry Progress of Nine Several Sorts of Cuckolds* (1674) *The Batchellors Answer to the Maids Complaint . . .* (1675)

Teaching Dryden's Heroic Plays

Daniel Gustafson and Elliott Visconsi

There is no modern equivalent to the rhymed heroic play, the dominant dramatic genre of the new Restoration stage. Then as now, the genre was located in the hazy boundary zone between sententiousness and camp. In the hands of John Dryden, the genre's master practitioner, the rhymed heroic play is an expression of high-serious literary ambition that describes unusually well the social norms and political figures of its moment. It is for the same reason quite teachable today: blending the formal and affective characteristics of French neoclassicism with the energy and spectacle of the English stage, the heroic play is spectacular and outward-looking in ways that appeal to tastes honed on Hollywood special effects. It aims for greatness of impact and depth of emotional expression; it paints world-historical pictures and shrinks from the mundane and the domestic. And because the rhymed heroic play is such an artificial genre, it offers teachers an unusually clear illustration of the ways in which a generation of playwrights (especially Dryden) saw literary form as an efficacious instrument of persuasion and political therapy.

We have found *The Indian Emperour* (*Works* 9: 1–111) to be remarkably successful in a range of upper-division survey courses devoted to seventeenth- and eighteenth-century literature. Like most heroic plays, it is best understood in the broader context of seventeenth-century European drama. When included in a syllabus with writers such as Shakespeare, Marlowe, Jonson, Beaumont and Fletcher, Corneille, Molière, Calderon, and Racine, *The Indian Emperour* seems both familiar and innovative.

It is a good thing for students that Dryden was an eager reporter of his dramatic and literary purposes. Many of his plays are equipped with statements of aims and principles, and reading short sections of these statements can be enormously helpful for discussion. In the California edition of *The Indian Emperour* (which we use as a photocopy or PDF file in lieu of a suitable teaching edition in print), the play is accompanied by an important and easily excerpted essay, Dryden's "Defence of the Essay of Dramatick Poesie" (9: 3–22). There as elsewhere, he outlines his ethical program for the heroic play and expresses his confidence that literary authorship is itself a form of heroic action. In the "Epistle Dedicatory" (13: 3–9) of his *All for Love* (1–111), he posits an alliance between the playwright and the heroic personality; the relation is one of plain subordination, but the bond is nonetheless a bond of nature. While a dramatic poem transmits rather than creates worthy action, the playwright should be the agent of political education for the state. This mission is on display in *The Indian Emperour*, and we have found that the formally elevated (or exaggerated) qualities of the play help students perceive quickly the ethical ambition underwriting Dryden's literary enterprise. Many students encounter Dryden only as the shrill and polemical author of *Absalom and Achitophel* (2: 3–37), but the heroic play, especially *The Indian Emperour*, gives them and instructors a chance to see him in a less strident, more experimental mode, when he is learning his literary craft and taking risks with form and spectacle even while hoping to bind together a recently divided English polity (Visconsi). Because the heroic play is so idiosyncratic and rooted in history, we provide an account of the theatrical and literary context of *The Indian Emperour* before turning to strategies for teaching the play.

The heroic play flourished on the London stage in the 1660s and 1670s but remained part of the repertoire well into the eighteenth century. We have found it useful to mention Sir William Davenant in any study of the English heroic play and especially of *The Indian Emperour*. An exile at the court of Charles II, Davenant absorbed the norms of French neoclassical drama (especially Corneille) and Italian opera, combining these modes with a more "natural" English drama (Waith, *Ideas* 177–93). Davenant offered a theory of literature as political education; his *Proposition for the Advancement of Moralitie* makes a clear and concrete claim for the utility of epic and serious drama. His short essay is provocative and easy to teach, for it offers an unambiguous account of the literary as an instrument of political persuasion and, in so doing, cuts against the grain of our modern post-Romantic aesthetic. Davenant also wrote a short propaganda play called *The Cruelty of the Spaniards in Peru*, which became an important source for Dryden's *Indian Emperour*. The two writers were frequent collaborators until Davenant's death in 1668.

Davenant and Roger Boyle, earl of Orrery, were the English promulgators of the heroic play, but it was Dryden who did the most to define the genre. In his 1672 essay "Of Heroic Plays," he argued that "an Heroick Play ought to be an imitation, in little, of an Heroick Poem" and that "Love and Valour ought to be the Subject of it" (*Works* 11: 10). The plays staged the grandeur often associated with epic poetry, usually through portraying collisions of love and duty through which kings and aristocrats had to navigate. The genre makes few claims to verisimilitude (students will surely notice this) and strives for elevation and idealism (Hughes, "Heroic Drama"; McGirr). The plays represented, as Dryden writes, "all things as far above the ordinary proportion of the Stage as that is beyond the common words and actions of humane life" (*Works* 11: 10).

The genre got within touching distance of epic in a number of ways. The monumental subject matter—kings and princes, clash-of-civilization plots, martyrs and angels—demanded a lofty style, and thus the sentiments, language, settings, and costumes tended toward extravagance. The heroic play was nearly always set in exotic, distant, pseudo-historical locales amid the turbulence of imperial warfare or revolution. The grand scope of its plots was reflected in lavish scenery, elaborate spectacle, choreographed dances and battle scenes, music, stage machinery, and—most notoriously—dialogue in rhyming couplets (Kirsch 19; McGirr 15–16; Nettleton, Case, and Stone 6). The tight alliance with epic is enormously profitable in the classroom; we have found *Paradise Lost* to be an indispensable partner to *The Indian Emperour*. These two works offer starkly divergent views of heroic personality, formal effect, and normative order, yet they share the same ambition. Importing Satan into *The Indian Emperour* thickens any account of heroic personality in the play, and we like to ask students to consider Montezuma, Cortez, and Satan as competing modalities of fallen political passions—including the desire, evident in Cortez and Satan, to conquer new worlds by force of individual will.

The dramatic use of rhyme (that "troublesome and modern bondage" for Milton [*John Milton* 210]) became a major point of contention among contemporary critics, Dryden taking the lead as rhyme's defender. In his *Essay of Dramatick Poesie* (1668; 17: 2–81), he argued that heroic representations required an elevated poetic style and that the rhyming couplet was the most appropriate form with which to express grand principles: "Tragedy we know is wont to image to us the minds and fortunes of noble persons, and to portray these exactly, Heroick Rhime is nearest Nature, as being the noblest kind of modern verse" (74). Rhyme also helped achieve the neoclassical effect of balance, and for Dryden it served as a tool to delight and instruct the audience (Kirsch 8–9). Unlike traditional tragedy, the rhyming plays tried to evoke awe and admiration in the audience rather than fear and pity: the goal was mimetic (the imitation of virtues) rather than cathartic (the purgation of turbulent emotions). This program can be a lot for students to digest, and they usually greet Dryden's rhyming verse with skepticism if not ridicule. We try to move beyond this initial resistance by asking students to think how form might actually work to cause the imitation of virtues. This question is posed with an analogy to architectural form: does monumental architecture (the Lincoln Memorial, for instance) cultivate a sense of coziness and sympathetic identification or a feeling of elevation and awe?

Some attention to the new conditions of the London stage adds to students' experience of the play. On Charles II's restoration, the playhouse changed into a recognizably modern shape. Unlike the platform stage of the Elizabethan era, the Restoration stage had a proscenium that was thrust out well into the audience. The arch on which the curtain hung divided the stage into fore and aft sections; it supplied the performers with a forward area for the declamation of great speeches and offered a recessed area for the spectacular scenes and machines (Langhans). This division added to the dramatic effect of heroic drama and to the illusion of players performing in real towns, gardens, and bedrooms. Doorways on either side of the proscenium permitted the entrance and exit not only of the performers but also of the chariots and horses that heroic plays often required. Finally, the theater managers developed elaborate machinery for shifting the movable flat scenery that helped create many spectacular effects, such as flying spirits and naval battles (Langhans; Nettleton, Case, and Stone).

In contrast to the defense of natural aristocratic virtue and of the restoration of kingship, and in contrast to the successful navigation of extremely difficult moral conflicts that was the standard fare of the heroic play (Hughes, "Heroic Drama"; Kewes; Maguire; McGirr), Dryden's excessive heroes signal a skeptical vision of the regulability of human passions (Staves, *Players' Scepters* 51–73). His *Tyrannick Love* (1669 [*Works* 10: 105–93) and the two-part, ten-act *Conquest of Granada* (1670–71 [11: 1–218]) present characters who make no pretense at being ideal figures of rule. The blustering Almanzor of *Conquest* even is bent on disrupting the social order, telling the play's king, Boabdelin, "Obey'd as Soveraign by thy Subjects be, / But know, that I alone am King of me" (1.1.205–06). Although Dryden does punish his villains and give his heroes glorious deaths or the restitution of their natural rights, these plays remain deeply ambiguous about the role of the heroic in Restoration society. We have found this ambiguity to be one of the most powerful approaches to *The Indian Emperour*, asking students to try to reconcile the formally elevated aims of the play with the unconsoling and often corrosive view of heroic personality evident everywhere in it. Only by reading the play naively as a triumphal celebration of Cortez can readers look past this fundamental tension between form and normative content.

Dryden returned one last time to the genre in his play set in Mogul India, *Aureng-Zebe* (1675; 12: 147–250). It tones down many of his past excesses, and in the prologue he announces an overdue breakup:

> But [the poet] has now another taste of wit;
> And to confess a truth (though out of time)
> Grows weary of his long-loved mistress, Rhyme.
> (lines 6–8)

This was in fact the last play he would write in rhyming verse. After *Aureng-Zebe*, he relinquished the now campy elevation of the heroic play and turned instead to blank-verse Shakespearean tragedy in *All for Love* and *Troilus and Cressida* (1679; 13: 217–355). The change is evident in the very first we see of Antony, the hero of *All for Love*. Instead of declaiming in rhymed couplets and so announcing his suitability for worthy actions, he enters disturbed, wringing his hands over his abdication of the norms of a masculine warrior culture. He throws himself to the ground in a heap and laments his unheroic fate:

> Lye there, thou shadow of an Emperor;
> The place thou pressest on thy Mother Earth
> Is all thy Empire now: now it contains thee;
> Some few dayes hence, and then twill be too large,
> When thou'rt contracted in thy narrow Urn,
> Shrunk to a few cold Ashes. (1.1.216–21)

This short scene is an entertaining and illuminating expression of the end of the line for the heroic play and its ambitions.

Teaching Dryden's heroic plays is a pleasure and should be an essential part of any survey of early modern drama or of a course in seventeenth- and eighteenth-century English literature. These plays are interesting as evidence of the norms of their age, but they also offer an especially visible illustration of his breaking and remaking the English literary tradition. Discussions of his heroic plays are most profitable, in our view, when they turn away from the concrete historical details of English and European political history. Not that many students today know about the economic implications of the Second Anglo-Dutch War or the court politics of Charles II. We focus instead on the ethical, formal, and theoretical issues at the heart of *The Indian Emperour*. The play asks thematically familiar questions in a genre that is unfamiliar and provides students with lively opportunities to perform or create scenes in class. Because *The Indian Emperour* is so over the top, it seems advisable to allow skepticism toward the play's seriousness of purpose without diminishing the play as the primitive expression of an underdeveloped literary culture. It rewards in-class performance; the torture scenes and love-and-duty wrangling are perennially popular with students.

The following questions may be useful in structuring class discussion:

Is the play a history play, or are the vivid historical settings merely meant to raise the stakes for the audience? Does the play use historical materials faithfully? If not, how and why does Dryden manipulate the historical record?

When teaching the play with *Paradise Lost*, we like to juxtapose examples of fallen or compromised personages in history as a pathway to a discussion of political passions. In contrast to Satan, do Dryden's two putatively heroic characters, Montezuma and Cortez, dramatize the need to regulate the excessive and self-consuming ambition of a warrior aristocracy, or do they represent a lost ancient ideal of magnanimity and heroic excellence?

Does *The Indian Emperour* condemn or endorse the Spanish conquest of the New World? Is Cortez a reasonable model of heroic action? Is his virtue, transnational and aristocratic, easily distinguished from the brutal avarice of his Spanish peers? Is the strained love plot between him and Cydaria redemptive or suspect, and to what degree does it intersect with the historical source material or render more durable the familiar romance of the go-between? Is race or ethnicity meant to be an important element in the play?

Does the play promote an idealized vision of pre-Conquest Mexico and present the Conquest as the tragic destruction of a golden age, or does Dryden describe the necessary and inevitable replacement of warrior paganism with European Christianity? The most profitable reading of this question, however, is that the play presents the collision of two equally flawed and violent cultures without endorsing either.

The play contains a set-piece argument between Montezuma (on the rack) and a Jesuit priest, which has long been regarded as marking

Dryden's debt to Montaigne's essays on the New World and describing Dryden's anticlerical bent and philosophical interest in natural religion. This scene (5.2), spectacular, highly wrought in verse, and relying on fantastic stage machinery, is especially well suited to classroom performance.

To what degree does the play fulfill Dryden's theoretical precepts as outlined in the *Essay of Dramatick Poesie* or Davenant's *Proposition for the Advancement of Moralitie*? Does the verse form succeed in elevating the play to epic grandeur? Most readers will say no, but it is important to consider the alternative: What would the play have achieved in prose? A contrast at this point with Milton's politically freighted choice of blank verse for *Paradise Lost* is useful, insofar as Milton repudiates the "troublesome and modern bondage of Riming" as one among many forms of "barbarous dissonance." (210, 346)

The spectacular nature and world-historical sweep of the form invites comparison with popular epic films of the present. James Cameron's *Avatar* (2009) comes most readily to mind, although there are plenty of cinematic options in this idiom. Indeed, although that hypersuccessful and visually spectacular film may not use form to cultivate political virtue, it is nonetheless closely akin to the heroic play, and it pairs especially well with *The Indian Emperour* in thematic and aesthetic terms.

Dryden's heroic plays are carefully wrought dramatic poetry; spectacular but also learned, they are early expressions of a confident model of authorship in which the playwright seeks to direct a turbulent political sphere through the formal and affective tools of a wildly popular literary medium. *The Indian Emperour* is less strange than it seems, and in the classroom we have found it to be remarkably accessible and popular with students. Although there can be an initial resistance in many readers, the play repays students and instructors alike and is well worth a place on the syllabus of any course in early modern literature.

Teaching the Passions in *All for Love*

Blair Hoxby

Some of Dryden's great works reserve their deepest pleasures for readers who have been nursed on the Bible, have supped at the table of Homer and Vergil, and have made a study of politics under the later Stuarts and William and Mary. Few undergraduates fit this description. But *All for Love* (1677; *Works* 13: 1–111) is an exception. It can be readily enjoyed even by students who have scant knowledge of the classics and have never heard of the Second Triumvirate.

What's more, this text can perform vital service in a wide variety of courses. In a history of English literature, it follows naturally from *Paradise Lost* (1667), whose inset tragedy of Adam and Eve might well be subtitled, as *All for Love* is, *The World Well Lost*. In a course on tragedy, it fits nicely into a sequence of love-and-honor tragedies like William Shakespeare's *Antony and Cleopatra* (1607), Pierre Corneille's *Horace* (1640), Jean Racine's *Bérénice* (1670), and Joseph Addison's *Cato* (1712). In a survey of the long eighteenth century, it falls into easy conversation with libertine verse like that of John Wilmot, earl of Rochester, Restoration comedies like Aphra Behn's *The Rover* (1677), and dissenting texts like John Milton's *Samson Agonistes* (1671). And in a course devoted to Dryden, it marks the turning point when Dryden leaves behind many of the opinions he advanced in his *Essay of Dramatick Poesie* (1668; 17: 3–81), reevaluates his relation to Shakespeare, and puts into practice the new principles of tragic dramaturgy that he codifies soon after in his *Grounds of Criticism in Tragedy* (1679; 13: 229–48). If we accept R. J. Kaufman's suggestive account of Dryden's development as a poet, *All for Love* is also an essential stepping stone on Dryden's way to becoming a satirist. Writing in an age too late, when dramatists could no longer yoke heroic memories to the biting analysis of deluded motivation, as Shakespeare and John Webster once had, Dryden brought the double (but indissoluble) vision of Jacobean tragedy to separate perfection in *All for Love* ("a museum of vital feelings" [Kaufman 89]) and *Absalom and Achitophel*, a masterpiece of satire.

How I teach *All for Love* depends on the constellation of texts that I have arranged around it. If I have assigned *Antony and Cleopatra*, I contrast Shakespeare's use of two hundred distinct entrance and exits in forty-two scenes (carefully indicated in Nicholas Rowe's edition of 1709) with Dryden's respect for the Aristotelian unities of time and place, and I ask students to analyze parallel passages in the plays in the light of Dryden's discussion of tragic diction in his *Grounds* (243–47).[1] If I have assigned *Bérénice*, I contrast Dryden's patient, Racinian development of the passions in *All for Love* with his earlier conviction that "Grief and Passion are like floods rais'd in little Brooks by a sudden rain; they are quickly up, and if the concernment be powr'd unexpectedly in upon us, it overflows us: But a long sober shower gives them leisure to run out as they came in" (17: 48). In *All for Love,* Dryden is not just grappling with the legacy of Shakespeare, he is also reckoning with the measured but powerful technique of Racine, his contemporary.

But for the purposes of this essay, I assume that instructors have only two class sessions to devote to the play and are not teaching it in conjunction with any particular text. When I am in that position, I use the first class to introduce students to what Dryden referred to as the "mechanic beauties of the Plot, which are the Observations of the three Unities, Time, Place, and Action" (233–34 [*Grounds*]). I use the second to invite students to consider how Dryden imitates the passions, what it means to purge the passions by example, and what the consequences of a politics based on the affections might be.

For the first session, I assign or present short excerpts from Corneille's *Discourse of the Three Unities* (1660), Thomas Rymer's translation of *Monsieur Rapin's Reflections on Aristotle's Treatise of Poesie* (1674; Rapin), Dryden's *Heads of an Answer to Rymer* (1677; 17: 185–93), and Dryden's *Grounds of Criticism in Tragedy*. (Dryden's *Essay of Dramatick Poesie* records more youthful opinions and is difficult for students because it alludes to so many authors whom they have not read.) With brief excerpts from these essays, it is possible to introduce students to the ideals of verisimilitude (*vraisemblance*), probability (*le nécessaire*), and decorum (*les bienséances*); to explain how these ideals implied a need to respect the unities of action, time, and place; and to make students realize that neoclassical playwrights were not pursuing the ideal of organic form that the Romantics valued in Shakespeare. If the playwrights had been, they would not have filled their treatises with references to the designs, foundations, superstructures, and perspective lines of tragedies.

What saves these essays from appearing like the dead hand of the law is the willingness of their authors to question authority on the basis of experience. Corneille observes that if critics tried writing ten or twelve tragedies, "they perhaps would enlarge the rules still more than I have done as soon as they recognized, by experience, how much restraint there is in abiding by them exactly and how many beautiful things are thereby banished from the theater" (119). Dryden questions whether Aristotle's definition of tragedy is adequate, denies that pity and terror are the only ends of the genre, maintains that plot is the first element of tragedy not because it is its "Master-piece" but because it is its "Foundation," and revises his ideas from one treatise to the next ([*Heads*] 185–86). Such doubts, regrets, and changes of heart make neoclassical criticism seem like a vital field of theoretical inquiry rather than an old prescription past its sell-by date.

Yet however strongly some students may be attracted to such attempts to distill general principles, others will feel no interest in abstract rules like the unity of place unless they see them in action. I therefore ask my students to research the nature of Isis (Plutarch's *Of Isis and Osiris* is the locus classicus), then invite them to discuss the significance of Dryden's decision to set his tragedy in her temple. Does the setting acquire associations as the play unfolds before it?

Does it affect the way we view Cleopatra, a queen who assumed the habiliments of Isis in the marketplace? Does it transform the theater into a sacred space, and, if so, what does Dryden's play hold sacred? Suddenly unity of place is not an arbitrary rule but a formal characteristic inseparable from the themes of the play and from the affective experience of the viewer. Dryden's confined setting won't let us forget that Antony is "Shrunk from the vast extent of all his honors, / And crampt within a corner of the World" (*All for Love* 1.1.176–79). It can be just as rewarding to ask students to consider why the tragedy transpires on Antony's birthday, when all is given over to "Pomp and Triumphs (139) and the priest of Isis orders that the general voice declare to heaven, "Live *Antony*, and *Cleopatra* live" (141).

When encouraging students to analyze how Dryden achieves a unified action, it is useful to focus on smaller units like acts. I ask students to identify the first and last remarkable stage tableau of an act, and then we analyze how Dryden seamlessly transports his characters from one state of fortune (or mind) to the other. In act 1, for example, Antony has scarcely entered the stage before he is lying facedown, weeping, and anticipating his death. But by the end of the act, he and his Roman companion, Ventidius, are marching boldly into battle, ready to begin the noble harvest of the field like Time and Death. How does Dryden bring about this transformation? Does his respect for the *liaison des scènes* make it more compelling?

Because they have been nurtured on a steady diet of novels and Shakespearean drama, students are used to thinking of plot, character, and language as the basic units of literary analysis. But early modern readers of Aristotle knew that the mimetic arts imitated the actions, manners, and passions of men, and I would maintain that the passions were actually the most important unit of meaning in neoclassical tragedy. After all, Aristotle stressed the genre's peculiar power to effect a purgation of the passions through pity and fear, and his Renaissance interpreters also observed that while a tragedy could do without recognitions, reversals, or character development, it could not dispense with pathos (Hoxby, "Passion").

To get students thinking about the passions as dramatic units, I provide descriptions of basic passions like wonder, pity, and terror found in René Descartes's *The Passions of the Soul* (1649). I accompany these with contemporary illustrations (found in Roach; Barnett; and Hoxby, "Dryden's Baroque Dramaturgy"). I produce a page from *The Art of Speaking*, by James Burgh (1761), showing how he uses marginal glosses to teach actors to enact a series of discrete passions such as "remorse, attempt at repentance, obduracy, despair" when they perform the role, say, of *Hamlet*'s Claudius at prayer (213). Then I superimpose a Cartesian grid on a depiction of a stage with a proscenium arch and perspective scenery and ask students to imagine how the four basic emotions of joy, grief, attraction, and repulsion could be expressed against such a grid. Joy and grief are registered on the vertical axis when the spirits are elevated or depressed, while attraction and repulsion are registered on the horizontal axis when characters move toward or away from each other (explained in Hoxby, "Passion"). Dryden's use of this grid is particularly evident in the first act, when the depressed Antony lies facedown on the stage like the mere shadow of an emperor, and in the third act, when Ventidius surprises Antony with Antony's Roman wife, Octavia, and their children: although Antony should feel a natural attraction to his own family, he instead betrays an unconquerable aversion.

Dryden imitates the passions because he believes that they hold the secret of tragedy's power to please and are the key to its capacity to instruct. The passions are a source of pleasure because, as René Rapin explained, "Nothing is more sweet to the Soul than Agitation, and of all Passions Fear and Pity are those that make the strongest Impressions on the Heart of Man" (112; also see Dryden, *Works* 13: 232; E. Wasserman 288–90). They teach because, as Dryden observes, "to purge the passions by Example, is . . . the particular instruction which belongs to Tragedy" (13: 231).

Just what it might mean to purge the passions by example was a vexed question in Dryden's day (as it remains in ours), but I simplify matters by explaining that there were two major lines of interpretation from 1550 to 1750. The first considered catharsis to be a form of training for the passions that refined our ability to judge how we ought to feel even as it instilled a habit of proper feeling. In a passage that Dryden repeats with approval (232), Rapin observes that tragedy cures the two besetting vices of men—pride and hardness of heart—by means of fear and pity: tragedy makes the viewer "modest, by representing the great *Masters of the Earth humbled*; and it makes him tender and merciful, by shewing him on the Theatre the strange Accidents of Life, and the unforeseen disgraces to which the most important persons are subject" (109). Yet tragedy also teaches people not to fear ordinary accidents or to waste their compassion on those who do not deserve it, for "there is an injustice in being mov'd at the Afflications of those who deserve to be miserable" (110). The second line of interpretation emphasized the fact that catharsis is a term drawn from Greek homeopathic medicine. When a hero displayed his passions on stage, the sight and sound agitated the souls of the audience, drawing out and purifying their passions. Whereas the first line of interpretation emphasized the role of judgment, the second emphasized the need for sympathy; whereas the first supposed that tragedies supplied deficits and relieved excesses, the second imagined that tragedies brought patients to a crisis that provided relief. Classical descriptions of purgation by fire and flood suggested that catharsis could be a ravaging experience.[2]

It can be a rewarding exercise to ask students to point to specific passages in which Dryden seems to invite judgment or promise a flood of feeling. They need not look far for the flood, because in his opening speech Serapion reports that the Nile "flow'd ere the wonted Season, with a Torrent, / So unexpected, and so wondrous fierce, / That the wilde Deluge overtook the haste / Ev'n of the Hinds that watch't it" (*All for Love* 1.1.3–6).

How we should interpret Dryden's depiction of Antony and Cleopatra in the political context of the late 1670s remains a matter of debate. Is it a bitter reflection on the merry monarch, who spent more money on his mistress Barbara Palmer, first duchess of Cleveland, than on the Second Anglo-Dutch War and who was now lying in the arms of Louise de Keruoalle, duchess of Portsmouth, a French spy who celebrated her influence with a medal depicting Cupid perched atop the world beneath the motto *omnia vincit* ("love conquers all things")? Or was John Dennis correct to conclude that the *All for Love*'s final line—"No Lovers liv'd so great, or dy'd so well" (5.1.519)—should be read without irony as a defense of Charles II? "Certainly never could the Design of an Author square more exactly with the Design of White-Hall, at the time when it was written, which was by debauching the People absolutely to enslave them" (*Critical Works* 2: 163).

I side with Dennis when I consider Dryden's professed "loathing to that specious name of a *Republick*" (13: 6 [*All for Love*]). Conscious of the efforts of men like Milton to depict monarchs as tyrants because they are slaves to their own passions, Dryden rejects any social contract or calculus of interests as the foundation of civil society and insists, instead, on the value of affective bonds. In doing so, he invokes the terminology of Seneca's *De Beneficiis*, which enjoyed a wide circulation in the seventeenth century in the translations of Arthur Golding (1578) and Thomas Lodge (1620) and the abstract of Roger L'Estrange (1679).[3]

Seneca's treatise teaches that men should enter into relations of mutual obligation in a spirit of generosity and gratitude. They can do this by conferring and accepting benefits. As L'Estrange explains, "The whole business (almost) of Mankind in Society, falls under this Head: The Duties of Kings and Subjects; Husbands and Wives; Parents, and Children; Masters, and Servants. . . ." The "Art, and Skill of conferring Benefits" is "the very Ciment of all Communities, and the Blessing of Particulars" (2–3). L'Estrange decided to publish his abstract in 1679 because he believed the "Unthankfulness of the Times" (vi) needed a remedy lest some of the "very Actors" in the "Tragedy" of Charles I's execution should set a similar "project on foot against the current government" (x).

Although we should not bestow benefits in the sordid expectation of profit, the kindness, pity, friendship, or loyalty that motivates others to bestow benefits on us does deserve a return. In *All for Love*, all these words take on tremendous significance. Variants of the word *kind* alone appear forty times, for kindness is the most important standard by which Antony's relationships with Ventidius, Dollabella, Octavia, and even Cleopatra are judged. Nouns that imply a relationship of mutual obligation, such as *friend*, *lover*, *father*, *husband*, and *emperor*, are also common in the drama. One of the reasons that Dryden wants his characters to shed tears and embrace each other so often is because he wants to emphasize that the economy of benefits is not the mere "driving of a Trade" but the "Cultivating of a generous Commerce" in which it is the affect that counts, not the service rendered or the good bestowed (L'Estrange 86).

What Antony, Cleopatra, and even Ventidius learn during the course of the tragedy is to place less weight on interest and honor than on love. Dryden meant it when he entitled his tragedy *All for Love; or, The World Well Lost*, but the love he had in mind was a great deal more pervasive than Antony and Cleopatra's: it was the cement of a society founded on benefits, a society whose demise men like the earl of Clarendon mourned as they would mourn the dead.[4]

NOTES

[1]For comparisons of the plays, see Hughes, "*Aphrodite katadyomene*"; Novak, "Criticism" and "Commentary"; Muir; and Leavis.

[2]For more on catharsis, see Hathaway 205–300.

[3]On the importance of Seneca's *De Beneficiis* to Dryden's plays, see Wallace; Levine.

[4]Useful critical interpretations of *All for Love* include Canfield, "Jewel"; Hughes, "Art" and "Significance"; Milhous and Hume 107–40.

Multimedia Dryden: *All for Love* and a Performative Baroque Aesthetic

Dianne Dugaw

John Dryden's literary art voices a complex sensibility that engages multiple expressive forms—textual, dramatic, pictorial, musical, and typological. My students at a midsize research university find Dryden exciting, provocative, and relevant. I regularly teach his works in three eleven-week undergraduate courses: a three-hundred-student, lower-division survey of English and American literatures between 1600 and 1800, required for English majors, and two forty-student, upper-division courses that satisfy a history requirement for majors. When they arrive, my students have not heard of Dryden and know practically nothing of his conflicted context or of the baroque style that offers a way into his art. But given their *YouTube* videos, cell phone photography, and tweets, these young people are perhaps more receptive to Dryden's multimedia art than any generation since 1800.

My lectures set Dryden against the backdrop of a complicated and unstable political and religious environment in late-seventeenth-century Britain, presenting the religiopolitical and vitally philosophical divide of Anglican, Dissenter, and Catholic. Dryden's conversion to Catholicism—the most mystical and supernaturally attuned of these three Christianities—gives an avenue for understanding that world, his work, and the choices faced by the man himself. His aesthetic, especially as it develops from *All for Love* (1677; *Works* 13: 1–111) through the 1690s, represents the baroque sensibility of Catholic Continental Europe, especially in the last half of his career (Dugaw 271–73). My students engage this supratextual literary art through pertinent paintings, visual images, and musical performances and through the concept of the baroque.

M. H. Abrams defines the baroque as a style that "employs the classical forms of the *Renaissance*, but breaks them up and intermingles them to achieve elaborate, grandiose, energetic, and highly dramatic effects" (Abrams and Harpham 23). Relevant analytic concepts provide touchstones for the study of Dryden: the dynamics of order and chaos, regularity and irregularity; the play of contrasts (chiaroscuro, verbal antithesis, etc.); aesthetic surprise; sweeping expansion; the dialectic of reason and passion; exploration of complexity, hybridity, and paradox; the interplay of materiality and immateriality; the tension between private and public experience; and, finally, an underlying architecture that enlists echoing hypertexts of typology and allegory.

At the outset of each class, we hear seventeenth-century instrumental music for several minutes while the students write on a topic central to the day's discussion. For example, on the first day I ask about their intellectual background and what the word *baroque* brings to mind. Later, when we consider *All for Love*, they write about a scene we will discuss: the opening entrance of Antony, an encounter between the two main characters, the interiority of a character in a first-person voice, and so on. Filling the room with baroque music creates an experiential context for ideas, readings, and discussions.

We next consider the visual baroque in Dryden's England. *The Allegory of Peace and the Arts*, by Orazio Gentileschi and Artemisia Gentileschi, painted for the ceiling of the Queen's House in Greenwich (late 1630s), presents idealized female figures that demonstrate how larger-than-life, mythological allusion and emblem functioned (the ceiling may be viewed at www.artemisia-gentileschi.com/ceiling1.html). Such images posit a Platonic realm of art, thought, and rule that is mirrored in the courtly sphere below. The world of the Carolinian court and these specific figures were known to Dryden, who in turn created lyric and theatrical works that evoke just such emblems and allusions.

Iconically, *All for Love* and other works of Dryden supply artistic focus, both satiric and expressive, to highly individualized experience. A painting that demonstrates similar qualities is Artemisia Gentileschi's *Allegory of Painting* (1638–39), a self-portrait (done in England) that applies the generalized allegory of the arts in a notably individual way. The woman painter leans into her task with a muscular focus and determination, unidealized despite the allegorizing intent (fig. 1). The woman artist is depicted in an earthy, realistic, present moment that applies the lofty realm of "peace and the arts" to this particular painter in this particular act of painting.

Moving between levels of intimate and public signifying, *All for Love* translates the often told story of love's undoing of the imperial power of Antony and Cleopatra into a personal tragedy. Dryden's dual protagonists play out their destruction amid the emotional twists of all-too-human relations, with flaws seen up close, against the backdrop of their well-known political history. The interplay of earthly and mythic, individual and collective, interpersonal and imperial creates a baroque realism—like the sinews in a Caravaggio painting—new to the English stage. The play's tension is like that between the two Gentileschi baroque paintings: the one mythic, typological, and lofty, the other localized, individual, and material.

All for Love places the Antony and Cleopatra story in the context of a cavalcade of earlier versions from the theatrical, literary, and visual arts. The tragedy is a rerendering of Shakespeare's *Antony and Cleopatra* and of other sources. Dryden's foregrounding of individuality becomes apparent in a contrast of the descriptions of Cleopatra in her galley from the two plays. In Shakespeare's speech, Enobarbus looks on from afar and conjures a wide-angle view, a historic and myth-inflected panorama that features objects of power, wealth, and grandeur:

> The barge she sat in, like a burnished throne
> Burned on the water. The poop was beaten gold;
> Purple the sails. . . .
> . . . .

Fig. 1. *Allegory of Painting* (1630s), by Artemisia Gentileschi. Royal Collection, Kensington Palace, London

For her own person,
It beggared all description . . .
. . . .
and Antony,
Enthroned i'th' marketplace, did sit alone. . . .
(2.2.200–25)

Dryden reworks this speech into an exchange of inflamed remembrance between Antony and Dolabella. Antony recalls for Dolabella the sight that the two men viewed together, and each re-creates his own feelings of seduction. The passage zooms in on Cleopatra:

> She lay, and leant her cheek upon her hand,
> And cast a look so languishingly sweet,
> As if, secure of all beholders' hearts. . . .
> (3.1.168–70)

The contrasting descriptions strongly suggest paintings. Shakespeare gives a triumphalist Renaissance view of the entire scene, with Antony gazing from the frame; Dryden gives a baroque close-up.

With the introduction of Octavia, Dryden explicitly positions Antony between passion for his Egyptian mistress and obligation to his Roman wife. This division formulates the tragedy in sharp emotional chiaroscuro and echoes the dilemma of Hercules. That classical story, told by Prodicus, teacher of Socrates, describes the young Hercules perplexed as to which road to follow and visited by two persuading women, the one Vice or Pleasure, the other Virtue (Xenophon 38–42). The hero chooses the high road of virtue, supplying a didactic model that *All for Love* echoes but complicates.

The Herculean dilemma appeared in numerous textual and visual versions (paintings, sculptures, tapestries, and prints). A vivid example, *The Choice of Hercules* (1596), by Annibale Carracci (1560–1609), is in the baroque style (fig. 2). Dynamic curving lines, asymmetry, contrasting colors, and binary design set up the hero's choice between duty and pleasure. Virtue in a frontal view points upward, dressed in discreet and ordered garb, her face lucid and intent, at her feet a book representing reason and thought. It is easy to trace the kindredness of Dryden's Octavia and her call to matrimonial, rational, civic, and military obligation. By contrast, in Carracci's depiction the voluptuous and revealing backside of Vice offers her seductive invitation into the gnarly forest of pleasure, with musical instruments and masks of theatrical artifice and sensuality at her feet. Dryden's Cleopatra among the siren calls of Egypt forms an easy parallel.

Having posed this emblematic choice, *All for Love* undermines its simplicity: Octavia, Ventidius, and the ostensibly high road of Roman power are compromised through the cold manipulations of Octavia and the falsity of Ventidius. Caesar himself is brought low in Antony's demeaning criticism: "Fate mistook him; / For Nature meant him for an Usurer; / He's fit indeed to buy, not conquer, Kingdoms" (3.1.213–15). The lofty public realm of virtue and reasoned Roman rule is implicitly likened by Dryden, the inveterate satirist, to an increasingly capitalizing and finance-dominated Restoration England.

In turn, the sexily orientalized Cleopatra, originally cast as suspect by identification with the pleasurable vice of the Herculean paradigm, is vindicated in *All for Love*. She proves loyal and unable to deceive. True nobility of heart in this non-Roman, nonmale character reverses the cultural sanctions and imperatives of the Herculean dilemma. Tragedy resides in the lack of either passion or truth that triumphs in a Rome of such calculating wives as Octavia, such mercantile emperors as Octavius Caesar: a "world well lost" for the nobler Cleopatra and Antony.

Fig. 2. *The Choice of Hercules* (1596), by Annibale Carracci. Capodimonte Gallery, Naples

The multimedia masque that opens act 3 invokes myth to accentuate the public, larger-than-life realm against which the play's catastrophe of private life plays out. A moment of ceremony unites the lovers:

> At one door, Enter Cleopatra, Charmion, Iras, and Alexas, a Train of Ægyptians: at the other, Antony and Romans. The entrance on both sides is prepar'd by Musick; the Trumpets first sounding on Antony's part: then answer'd by timbrels, &c. on Cleopatra's. Charmion and Iras hold a Laurel Wreath betwixt them. A Dance of Ægyptians. After the Ceremony, Cleopatra Crowns Antony. (p. 55)

A profusion of media and sensory elements abounds: music prepares the masquing scene as an exotic play of Egyptian timbrels answers the announcing blast of Roman trumpets; in visual spectacle, richly costumed and contrasting entrants move across the stage to enact the cross-cultural union—Egypt from one side, Rome from the other; an "Ægyptian" dance, with more music, follows the procession with symbolic laurel; and private love and public pomp join for a moment in the ceremonial crowning. Following this tableau, the ruling couple greet each other and embrace with another mythological as well as astronomical allusion: "My Brighter *Venus!*" Antony exclaims. "O my greater *Mars!*" Cleopatra replies (3.1.11–12). The storied pair of the classical (and planetary) pantheon, emblematic warrior and emblematic lover, express exactly the interplay of allegory and individual experience noted in the Gentileschi paintings.

The play concludes with the lovers positioned in death, in a fashion reminiscent of a baroque canvas. Serapion, priest of Isis, enters to find the two deceased, enthroned, with Cleopatra's servants dead at their feet:

> See, see how the Lovers sit in State together,
> As they were giving Laws to half Mankind.
> Th' impression of a smile left in her face
> Shows she died pleased with him for whom she lived,
> And went to charm him in another World.
> . . . .
> Sleep, blessed Pair,
> Secure from human chance, long Ages out,
> While all the Storms of Fate fly o'er your Tomb;
> No Lovers lived so great, or dy'd so well. (5.2.507–18)

The final emphasis on Cleopatra and on the lovers' relationship as coded by personal feeling—the "smile left in her face," her pleasure to die "with him for whom she lived"—frames a painterly scene whose catharsis exalts individual experience and the passions of private life, securing these tragic lovers from "human chance" and "the Storms of Fate."

Study of Dryden's transmutation of prototypes found across baroque media can set the stage, as it were, for mimetic work by students. Indeed, Dryden supplies a model in his translations, saying of his *Aeneis*, "Taking all the Materials of this divine Author, I have endeavour'd to make *Virgil* speak such *English*, as he wou'd himself have spoken, if he had been born in *England*, and in this present Age" (*Works* 5: 330–31 [dedication of the *Aeneis*]). Some assignments in my classes proceed from this aesthetic of imitation. One essay option prompts students to imitate, in one to two pages, a work we have read; to consult several relevant critical discussions; and to write an analysis of the stylistic features they have mirrored with consideration of what this process of imitation has taught them about Dryden and his literary voice.[1] Engaging Dryden's art through the mimesis crucial to his own process, students develop and formulate their critical understanding from the inside out. I read and often admire their imitations, but the graded evaluation is based on their analytic report on what they have learned and observed about Dryden's style and sensibility.

In response to this assignment, students write short play scenes, lyric poetry, odes, satires, prose narratives and essays, and so on. One example is Jonathan Stark's cinematic reformulation of a scene from *All for Love*. *All Is Loveless* is a seven-minute film noir translation of the confrontation between Cleopatra and Octavia in act 3 (2.390–470).[2] This film enactment of Dryden's text explores the play's focus on gender and private life. "Dryden is modern," Stark observes,

"That's what struck me most when reading him in class. . . . I wanted to transpose Dryden's script, as brazenly as possible, into a modern setting and see if it made sense" ("Re: All Is Loveless"). The scene's insightful reading, adapted in a manner analogous to Dryden's resetting of classics, now features in my teaching of *All for Love*.

Stark writes that he wanted a scene that was "self-contained enough to be emotionally powerful," and his selection was further determined by his sense that "the true focus of the play is on the women," a view supported by Dryden's introduction of Octavia and the Herculean echo ("Re: All Is Loveless"). Stark's noir queens encounter each other in the sultry Egypt Club of the businesswoman Cleopatra, with Alexas as bartender. Dryden's lines are reincarnated in video close-ups that emphasize the play's sexy, conflicted intimacies. A cogent and nuanced reading of Dryden's original results from the transposition to cinema.

The confrontation of aggrieved wife and femme fatale in *All Is Loveless* reaches a climax that conveys both the erotic intimacy in Dryden's translation of earlier models and the undermining of the Herculean morality in the complex figure of Cleopatra. The blocking design reflects Stark's analysis of the play:

> The two women get closer and closer until Octavia interrupts Cleopatra's speech with a slap, probably the largest change I made to the original play. This closeness represents the growing tension between the women. . . . That Octavia is the first to break and lose her temper says something. . . . Rigidity is often useless against pressure and force. . . . I wanted this Cleopatra to be a woman who keeps moving on.
>
> ("Re: All Is Loveless")

A consistently careful interpretation of the play guided the project, which opened to view, in a contemporary idiom, the tragedy's spirit and meaning.

Through their imitation assignments, students frequently engage Dryden's mentality, discourse, and craft in a way that stretches their own concepts and writing—sometimes with an ironic self-reflection that Dryden would have appreciated. In a final paper for another class, Lily Maher performed a close reading of Dryden's "To the Memory of Mr. Oldham" through her imitation and analysis. An excerpt from "To the Memory of Mr. Dryden" reveals her admiration for the poet, along with deft management of pentameter couplets and triplets:

> As Mr. Oldham was a muse for thee,
> You now, in turn, inspire a poem from me. . . .
> If to our modern age you now could speak,
> And add to wit and heart thy tongue in cheek,
> How we are in need of such critique![3]

The concluding remarks of Maher's accompanying analysis bring together her consciousness of period lyric style and a witty stance in relation to her model:

> Though Dryden does not deviate from a flawless rhyme scheme in this elegy, I incorporate a slant rhyme on "maker" and "paper" . . . to break the symmetry between my poem and the original. Dryden . . . depict[s] a perfect harmony and resemblance between the two subjects of the poem, Oldham and himself. I use a disruption of the rhyme scheme to reveal, however, that I am not really a poet or a true disciple of Dryden. . . . My slant rhyme breaks the perfection of the heroic couplet and the symmetry of the parallel between Oldham, Dryden, and myself. I finally reveal that this poem is not really a lofty elegy but a final paper assignment and that I am not a poet, but merely a student sitting in the library trying to focus on my work amidst the commotion of dead week. (5)

Our twenty-first-century students grasp and appreciate Dryden's art, especially its satirical indeterminacy and its echoing and pansensory hypertextuality. Theirs is a mimetic and multimedia imagination, and they respond to Dryden's kindred sensibility.

NOTES

[1]The text of the assignment is: "Write a short episode of your own (1–2 pages) in close imitation of some part of one of the works we have read—poem, prose, of play. Consult at least three additional critical sources that discuss the style of the work of Dryden. Then write a four- to-six-page discussion of how your imitation is stylistically and thematically like your model. Point to precise features of the original that you imitate. Use your additional sources to shape your ideas, and use at least three critical terms—in boldface—from the syllabus (tragedy, figurative language, dramatic irony, etc.). Include your bibliography."

[2]Stark graduated with a BA in English from the University of Oregon in 2008. He took my course Major British Writers: Milton, Dryden, and Behn in 2008, when he created *All Is Loveless* together with other students in the University Film Organization. The film, now available on *YouTube*, was written and produced by Stark with direction by Abby Iverson; production design, editing, and effects by Mandi Vernoy; sound editing by Dylan Leeds; and lighting by Emily Tennis. In the cast are Stark as Alexas, Amanda Levie as Cleopatra, Miranda Schmidt as Octavia, and John Roesch as Ventidius. Stark discussed the film in an e-mail message to me ("Re: All Is Loveless").

[3]Maher graduated with a BA in English from the University of Oregon in 2009. She took my course Restoration and Early Eighteenth-Century British Literature in 2008, when she wrote "To the Memory of Mr. Dryden."

A Potion for *Secret Love*

Thomas F. Bonnell and Katie Sullivan

In the late 1990s, a long-anticipated chance arose for us to collaborate on staging a period drama at Saint Mary's College, Indiana. In the fall of 1997 we settled on Dryden's *Secret Love; or, The Maiden-Queen* and put it on the syllabus of Script and Stage, 1660–1790, a 400-level seminar offered for the first time in the spring of 1998. That summer, with in-house funding (hereby gratefully acknowledged), we labored over the script, located costumes, worked on the music, discussed design, and otherwise prepared for auditions, casting, and rehearsals for October performances. By describing aspects of that process here, we hope that a wider audience will be encouraged to experience this extraordinary play. As Dryden's work will be read at different times for various purposes, we have suited our comments to the following occasions: a seminar in Restoration and eighteenth-century drama; a survey course, either general or period-specific; and a campus-wide project leading to a stage production.

For those unfamiliar with *Secret Love* (*Works* 9: 113–203), a synopsis of its intertwining plots (one heroic, one comic) is in order. The Queen of Sicily is under pressure to settle the issue of succession. Hoping to marry her is Lysimantes ("first Prince o' th' Blood," being her cousin [1.3.28]), but she has fallen in love with Philocles, a subject raised to prominence by her choice of him as adviser. Philocles loves Candiope (sister of Lysimantes) but admires the Queen so unboundedly that when he discovers she loves him, he no longer knows his own heart. The Queen's confidante is Asteria, whose brother, Celadon, a courtier, catches the eye of Florimell, a fresh beauty at court. As the Queen struggles to remain true to her "glory" without giving up her incorrect passion (1.3.38, 260), Florimell aims to cure Celadon of his rakish ways, getting him to focus on their mutual infatuation as they head toward a radically experimental form of marriage.

Theater Seminar

When first taught, Script and Stage, 1660–1790, was limited to fifteen students, mostly juniors and seniors; since then, it has been a 300-level English class, cross-listed with the theater program and capped at twenty-five. For English majors it counts as a period course; for theater majors it fulfills the dramatic literature requirement for a course focusing on an era, a genre, playwright or group of playwrights. In 1998, Katie (in the theater program) read all fourteen plays and attended every session, becoming a virtual coleader of the seminar with Tom (in English) as she steeped herself in the period.

Our seminar centered on student involvement. Each session began with a forum, segued into a discussion, and ended with a subset of students outlining a production concept for that week's play. During the forum, as students voiced their responses to the play, we did not utter a word. This silence was a novelty for them, because too often students are conditioned to be consumers of education rather than value-adding producers. For us, the trick was not to jump in and assert professorial control. To our surprise, since we had not tried this approach previously, the students raised most of the issues we otherwise would have addressed. In the discussion, we revisited the insights emerging from the forum, pressed the students to consider certain questions in greater depth than they had managed on their own, and noted other key concerns. The group work on production concepts was challenging. However firmly students may grasp a play intellectually and intuitively, it is harder for them to conceptualize a "producible interpretation" or "critical reading that a director could communicate to an audience in performance" (Milhous and Hume 3). Such a unified, overarching concept depends on a fuller mastery of the script than a single reading will give.

Our own production concept for *Secret Love* took into account its setting in Sicily and a conceit expressed early in the play. "In all this Labyrinth," Asteria tells the Queen, "I find one path conducing to your quiet" (1.3.263–64). Several characters, not just the Queen, face labyrinthine choices that involve hazard. The idea of looming danger formed the literal backdrop for our stage: a depiction of Mount Ætna, the quasi-mythic topographic feature that Sicily inevitably brought to mind. Dryden did not name the volcano explicitly in *Secret Love,* but he relied on its trembling terrors as an everyday metaphor in *All for Love*: ". . . shook his Fabrick like an Earthquake; / He heav'd for vent, and burst like bellowing *Ætna*" (4.161–62).

The Queen and Florimell, by our concept, owned the play; their characters set the terms of the drama. We rejected the idea that the Queen "identifies more readily with conventional roles corresponding to her gender and social status than with the unusual role and power of the monarch" (Flores 181). To the contrary, the "glory" of her position is the nonnegotiable bedrock of her psyche. Likewise, our Florimell did not view Celadon's "pre-nuptial infidelity [as] his most seductive attribute" per se (186); rather, she loved his energy as a "high Flier" and his disposition to be "bounteous of himself" (3.1.301). The Queen and Florimell were the all-determining roles in Dryden's original production as well, judging from Samuel Pepys, who thought *Secret Love* "one of the best plays I ever saw" and "certainly the best acted of anything ever" at the King's Theatre. One night the finest of the best was Rebecca Marshall as Queen ("particularly, Becke Marshall to admiration" [9: 37]); another night it was Nell Gwyn as Florimell ("there is a comical part done by Nell . . . that I never can hope ever to see the like done again by man or woman" [8: 91]).

A weekly assignment that engaged students with each new play was a short report, limited to half a page single-spaced (or to a note card). Concise summaries of an article or a chapter in a book or an Internet resource, these reports tasked students with learning something extra about the play, whether that extra involved literary interpretation or an aspect of its performance history, including reviews of revivals that reflected practical decisions regarding set design, costumes, character analysis, and so forth. Casual enough not to become too onerous, these reports successfully reinforced the habit of thinking theatrically about each script.

Survey Course

Two concerns (one general, one specific) require attention when *Secret Love* is taught in a survey course: the challenge of reading plays, and particular features of Restoration drama.

Poems and novels embody print culture; hearing them aloud enhances pleasure and understanding, yet a student with book in hand holds the thing itself. Drama is a performing art; a script in hand is not the thing itself. The term *playwright*, as opposed to *poet* or *novelist* or *dramatist*, reveals that making is essential to the craft: actors, costumes, sets, lighting, sound, blocking, movement, and other elements must be physically realized in three-dimensional space on stage. Reading with all this in mind requires leaps of imagination.

Students encountering *Secret Love* in a survey course should appreciate what sets the Restoration apart from other periods and how its distinctive energies were abetted by the playing of female roles by women. Capitalizing on this opportunity, playwrights explored with unprecedented candor and irreverence the dynamics of sexual dalliance, courtship, marriage, and adultery. The ethos of Restoration comedy owed as much to the "thrill" women yielded as "eroticised object[s]" (Findlay 140) as it did to the randy behavior of Charles II and his court. Both factors are perfectly conveyed by *Secret Love* through biographical details: Nell Gwyn and Charles Hart not only exemplified the sexual entanglements entered into by players, courtiers, and the king, but, by originating the roles of Florimell and Celadon, they also were instrumental in defining the kind of witty couple (or "gay couple," in John Harrington Smith's classic phrase) perfected in the Restoration—ironic, scheming, erotically powerful, and verbally brilliant.

We devised an easy in-class assignment that is invaluable for prompting students to conceive of the play on stage. In small groups, they list responses to the script under four headings: crucial scenes, opportunities, challenges, and puzzles. The first heading gets them to consider the play's structure; the second, its happiest or most memorable moments; the third, things that might pose difficulties in performance; and the fourth, whatever they failed to grasp. After ten minutes, the students air their results. The crucial scenes they identify are tellingly various; the intricacy with which the actions of the play unfold is immediately evident. The list of puzzles usually involves misconceptions that are easily cleared up or playhouse conventions (students know what asides are, for example, but wonder how such utterances can be performed credibly when other actors stand within earshot).

Under the second and third headings, students recognize at once that opportunities and challenges are interrelated. Without fail, they marvel at the feat of Florimell, who, dressed in breeches to impersonate a man, outtalks and outdances Celadon to draw off the amorous attention of two young flirts—the scene of Gwyn's that most enraptured Pepys: "best of all, when she comes in like a young gallant; and hath the motions and carriage of a spark the most that ever I saw any man have. It makes me, I confess, admire her" (8: 91).

A short out-of-class assignment gets students to connect with the play. Asked to ponder an aspect of the drama that reflects something in their own lives, they find similarities that make the Restoration world seem less remote. The actual parallels are peripheral to the insights they produce into the characters of *Secret Love*. Here, for example, are some recent thoughts on Florimell: "She knows her desires, but she is more careful than rash when going after them"; "She even says that while Celadon is not the ideal man, she wants a man with his kind of flaws." On the Queen: "She hated the fact that she had to choose between her life as she had always known it, and her heart"; her discovery that Philocles loves Candiope is "almost more than she can bear." On Philocles: "He is a man who has made a commitment to a woman, and then falls for the Queen, who comes with 'a Crown too.'" On Asteria: "Is telling Philocles the Queen's secret the right thing to do, or by telling him, is she abdicating her duty as secret-keeper, an encumbrance that is by no means an enjoyable one?"; "Does her telling relieve the Queen of a burden that weighs so heavily on her heart?"

Campus Production

In academic programs there is a mandate, not always mirrored in professional theater, to produce a broad representation of genres and periods. This diversity provides training for young practitioners of the theater (whether graduate students or undergraduates) and also educates the campus community. Too often, however, when the time arrives for a Restoration or eighteenth-century play, an old standby is chosen: *She Stoops to Conquer, The School for Scandal* (or *The Rivals*), *The Country Wife*, or *The Way of the World*. We sought an alternative to such predictable favorites.

Hunting through scores of works for a new play, we were drawn to Dryden's *Secret Love* initially by its modest cast size and its ratio of eight female roles to three male roles. Close to magic at an all-women's college like Saint Mary's, numbers like these may equally charm coeducational institutions where women actors outnumber men and where *Secret Love* would bring another kind of balance to a theater season.

This practical consideration is outweighed, of course, by the primary appeal of the play: its rich, complex characters. In both plots, up and down the social order, Dryden confronts his characters with tough choices over whom to love, how (or whether) to disclose their amorous desires, how (or whether) to conquer jealousy, and how (or whether) to persevere in quest of fulfillment. With such issues ever present, the tension between the comic and serious scenes serves the play well: truly funny at one moment and genuinely moving at the next, humor and seriousness "coexist harmoniously and in fact complement each other in producing the distinctive tone of the play" (Loftis 335). Coming to terms with the affinity between the two plots, their "natural compatibility" (336), and emphasizing the mutual dilemmas that perplex the characters onstage is a fruitful process.

Working with the cast on character analysis was highly satisfying. The Queen offers a wonderful study of the divide between personal yearnings and official duty: can she enjoy a private life, one in which she is intimate and vulnerable, without compromising her regal authority? As Asteria worries, stress has changed her: "You are of late so alter'd I scarce know you. / You were gay humour'd, and you now are pensive, / Once calm, and now unquiet" (1.3.194–96). To play her in a manner that reveals her natural ebullience and centeredness, while portraying the emotional distraction that preoccupies her presently, is a tall order that any actor would relish.

The Queen's dilemma resonates down the social order and across the seriocomic divide, as the pursuit of love (for various reasons) enjoins some form of secrecy on other characters also. Suffering a kind of emotional bewilderment, Philocles begins the play unaware of the full nature of his attachment to the Queen, and he ends it hiding his inner turmoil from Candiope. Might Candiope share a modicum of her brother's guile? In quizzing Philocles (before an intended elopement) to determine whether he will be able to thrive away from the court, does she betray a secret relish of her own nearness to power? Does she detect jealousy when the Queen humiliates her? Lysimantes, otherwise consumed by self-interest, unburdens himself in a final speech that astonishes (5.1.568–74): once the Queen has decided to remain unmarried, he vows a single life, declaring that his passion was for her "person, not [her] Crown" (570). To treat the disclosure as inauthentic robs the role of its potential pathos; to treat it as a cynical pose, one last indication of inveterate craftiness, limits the role to cartoonish dimensions. Celadon's need for subterfuge arises from his chasing after Olinda and Sabina in violation of his promise of fidelity to Florimell. The proviso scene stipulates that Florimell may one day pay Celadon back in kind, codifying her hidden plan, hatched earlier in a fit of pique, to marry and then cuckold him, yet the very openness of the agreement diminishes the chance that any secret reservation destructive to their contract lurks in the mind of either party.

In terms of the physical portrayal of character, actors learn much about the period through costume and gesture. Their bearing will be influenced by the line or silhouette of their clothing, along with accessories like fans, masks, wigs, and shoes. If these elements can be incorporated into rehearsals, the actors will grow more comfortable with them. Because such intricate garments are expensive to create, many costume shops might make a few pieces but rent most of them from a large university or commercial renting agency. The costume shop will become a microcosm of the Restoration for nonacting theater students; working with a faculty adviser, they will get an education in the design and construction of Restoration dress even if they merely take in and let out rented costumes or trim them in the show's color palette.

Stylized movements requiring attention range from the coded language of fans to the dancing of a "Jigg" (5.1.73). Choreography for the scene where Florimell outcapers Celadon to distract his love-struck admirers (68–83) was created and rehearsed by a dance major, while music for the gigue (scored for flute, violin, cello, and harpsichord from late-seventeenth-century figured bass) was provided by costumed musicians. Chamber pieces were performed also before the opening curtain and at intermission.

Another crucial musical moment comes when Asteria asks the Queen, "Shall I sing the Song you made of *Philocles*, / And call'd it *Secret-love*?" (4.2.19–20). Pointing to the title of the play, the song captures the definitive throughline of the drama. Having written it herself—unlike the Queen in *The Spanish Fryar*, who, wanting solace, desires her maid to sing from Ariosto—the Queen in our production, gradually reanimating the joy and anguish expressed in her verses, joined in with Asteria, thus turning the song (in a musical setting, with harpsichord accompaniment, composed by Tom) into a duet.

For our acting script, though some may deem it heresy, we adapted Dryden's text in two ways. With proper vocal coaching, students will rise to the demands of the heroic verse and the colloquial prose, but wherever archaic phrasing or convoluted syntax might have left the audience momentarily puzzled, Tom altered the script, though as little as possible. Also, in line with Katie's convictions regarding pace and playing time, we kept our performance to two hours and fifteen minutes through careful cutting.

Prescription

At the regular dosage, *Secret Love* will engage students in any classroom where it is taught. We urge teachers, however, at a propitious time, to try the maximum dose: to propose the play to their theater program and underscore its enticements for dance and music majors as well. Bringing it to life on stage—and living with Dryden for weeks on end—could become one of the most compelling experiences of their teaching career.

"Hither This Way": Musical Dryden for Nonmusician Students (and Nonmusician Teachers)

Amanda Eubanks Winkler and Kathryn Lowerre

Dryden was profoundly interested in music and its effects, as demonstrated in his prefaces to *Albion and Albanius* (1685), *Dioclesian* (1690), and *King Arthur* (1691); his "Song for Saint Cecilia's Day" (1687); and several other sources. In all these writings he presents fascinating and often contradictory statements about the relation between poetry and music. Sometimes, as in the "Song for Saint Cecilia's Day," he praises music as a representation of celestial harmony. But in *King Arthur*, he complains to the marquis of Halifax that he had to "cramp my Verses, and make them rugged to the Reader, that they may be harmonious to the Hearer" (*Works* 16: 6). His views regarding the respective claims of sound and sense were constantly shifting; even though he appreciated music, he sometimes resented or was suspicious of its power.

Despite his conflicted views, Dryden was interested not only in the theoretical and philosophical qualities of music but also in practical music making, and he took great care in crafting lines intended for musical setting. As James Anderson Winn notes, he had "considerable professional experience with music . . . [was] attentive to vowel color and metrical variety, he made his lyrics musical before he passed them along to the composer" (*When Beauty* 21). Talented composers, most notably Henry Purcell (1659–95), rose to the occasion.

The music composed for Dryden's lyrics rewards attentive listening regardless of one's knowledge of classical music. Even those who say they know nothing about music will recognize, from modern film, television, or theater, many musical techniques used to convey meaning. Dryden's composers wrote for less than attentive playhouse audiences, employing a musical language that was rarely subtle. For instance, Purcell's duet "Two Daughters of This Aged Stream," sung by sirens in act 4 of *King Arthur*, leaves little to the imagination. The singers' voices weave sinuously around each other (a musical analogue to copulation), enticing Arthur to "come, come bathe with us" (2.39).

In this essay we present some approaches we have used in teaching Dryden's musical works to students who are not musicians. As our title, drawn from Dryden's "dramatick opera" *King Arthur*, suggests, we particularly encourage the use of this work in the classroom.[1] Specific resources and recommendations for other musical selections can be found below. In our final section, we include suggestions for teachers and students who have musical training and interests. Assuming that Dryden's musical works will constitute only a portion of the courses designed and taught by most readers of this volume, we have provided options suited for adaptation into various course types.

Use of Music in Specific Course Types

For a standard survey of Restoration literature or Restoration drama, Dryden's musical works can be used in historical frameworks organized either by chronology or topic.

Dryden's early musical works from the 1660s, such as his and William Davenant's revised version of *The Tempest*, adapt Renaissance musical conventions to fit Restoration tastes. *King Arthur* was meant to be performed in the mid-1680s with *Albion and Albanius*, but this never came to pass; Dryden later revised it to suit the new post–Glorious Revolution political reality. Because of this fractured genesis, *King Arthur* provides an ideal case study for exploring the relation between the intertwining of court and popular culture, perceived high and low styles, patriotism and English legends, political allegory before and after the Glorious Revolution, depictions of magic and the supernatural, and constructions of gender. In the 1690s, Purcell's association with Dryden's dramatic works developed further as the composer set many songs for new and revived plays and transformed others into operatic spectacles (e.g., *The Indian Queen*). After Purcell's death, the family association with Dryden continued; Purcell's relative Daniel wrote music for *The Secular Masque*.

In designing a course organized by genre rather than by chronology or topic, the teacher should consider including examples of Dryden's works that involve music. The following works have available recordings:

Opera

King Arthur, music by Henry Purcell (many recordings available, including John Eliot Gardiner's and William Christie's)

Albion and Albanius, music by Louis Grabu (an excerpt, "Concert of Venus," is performed on the CD *Baroque Music for the Restoration Violin Band*)

Ode

"Ode on the Death of Mr. Henry Purcell," music by John Blow (available on *Countertenor Duets*, by Purcell and Blow, directed by Robert King and in a video performed by the Yorkshire Baroque Soloists on *YouTube*)

"Song for Saint Cecilia's Day," music by Giovanni Battista Draghi (on *Odes to St. Cecilia*, by Playford Consort and the Parley of Instruments)

Plays with music (*Amphitryon*, *Indian Emperour*, *Tyrannick Love*) with surviving music by Purcell (available on *Purcell Songs and Dialogues* and on *Theatre Music*)

A course specifically on Dryden could explore all these works or one work in depth.

Incorporating Music: General Class Activities

We suggest starting a music-related class on Dryden by discussing the ways music can shape the understanding and reception of a poetic text or dramatic performance. To stimulate discussion, students and teachers can share their listening experiences. What are Western expectations about the meaning and context of a song accompanied by electric guitar versus piano? by steel drums? How does our perception change if the music played for the entrance of a character or the appearance of a new scene is a fast dance track or a slow ballad? What, besides repetition, either localized or in larger structural units (i.e., refrains or choruses), makes sung words memorable?

On the basis of assigned secondary reading (teachers might use Roger Savage's "Theater Music" or excerpts from Curtis Price's *Henry Purcell and the London Stage*), seventeenth-century conventions for dramatic operas like *King Arthur* and for other types of plays can be discussed. What kinds of scenes feature music? Who sings (and who doesn't) and why? Reading aloud highlights language (vocabulary, rhythms, sounds) that could be musical. Dryden's stated views on dramatic music require "double Rhymes, and ordering of the Words and Numbers for the Sweetness of the Voice" (15: 9 [preface to *Albion and Albanius*]). What might Dryden's dictate mean in practical musical-poetic terms?

Turning to performance, teachers should discuss the effects of the music in transmitting Dryden's words. How does the musical setting affect the shape, sense, and sound of his verse? With focused listening (two or three times at least), students will be able to distinguish

- the speed or pace of the music (the tempo): Is it fast or slow?
- the rhythm (regular or irregular) and meter (duple or triple): How does rhythm relate to poetic meter?
- whether (and when) the music is loud or soft (the dynamics, usually the performers' decision)
- whether it's a solo singer, small group, or big chorus; whether it's one instrument, a few instruments, or a larger ensemble
- if the music emphasizes certain parts of the text through rhythmic accents, pitch, duration, or ornamentation: Is there more than one note per syllable?
- repetition of or changes to Dryden's text—for particularly complex or interesting examples, a side-by-side comparison may be presented on a *PowerPoint* slide or a handout
- musical repetition: Where does the music repeat, and how does this repetition relate to the poetic form?

We urge that the listening be done through good-quality speakers, not built-in laptop ones, if at all possible. This will make it easier to hear the musical features listed above.

King Arthur: *Three Focus Areas Incorporating Primary Sources*

Many colleges and universities now offer the possibility of streaming music through a course Web site. *Blackboard* and similar software packages make it easy to upload MP3s and even musical scores. We recommend *Oxford Music Online* (specifically *Grove Music Online*) for general musical information and biographical information on Purcell.

The 1691 text of *King Arthur* is available at *Early English Books Online*, allowing students to experience the work unmediated by a modern editor. Modern editions include H. Neville Davies's edition in Michael Burden's *Henry Purcell's Operas: The Complete Texts* and Vinton A. Dearing's edition in the California Dryden. For pedagogical purposes, one may be more appropriate than the other, or teachers may wish to compare them and discuss editorial practices. Differences between the printed texts, musical texts (in Purcell's *Works* [1968–2007] [2008–]), and recorded performances demonstrate *King Arthur*'s status as a living work; the dramatic opera appeared in several different versions in the long eighteenth century alone.

We appreciate Dearing's effort to include Purcell's *King Arthur* music in a descriptive appendix, though it is not likely to be of much use to readers who do not know a fair amount about music. We do not recommend it for students, but it may be helpful to teachers regarding poetic and musical meters and rhythms. As an introduction to the music, we suggest Price's *Henry Purcell and the London Stage*. Although Price's political interpretation has been questioned (Hume, "Politics"), his discussions of the work's protracted genesis and its music are invaluable.

King Arthur is available in several fine recordings. Three are recent historically informed performances (i.e., performances that use instruments or reproductions of instruments from the era as well as a playing and singing style derived from seventeenth-century practices and techniques), directed by William Christie, John Eliot Gardiner, and Trevor Pinnock. There are also significantly older recordings by the countertenor Alfred Deller and others.

Teachers may wish to explore the differences between the newer and older recordings in connection with the implied goals of modern performances of Dryden's stage works. How can we know what is authentic or appropriate historical performance practice? What evidence do we have? Bruce Haynes's recent *The End of Early Music* provides an excellent introduction to the musical side of these questions. Streaming audio examples (through the Oxford University Press Web site) make Haynes's points accessible to those who do not read music.

The DVD recording of the Salzburg Festival performance of *King Arthur* (2004), conducted by the early music pioneer Nikolaus Harnoncourt and directed by Jürgen Flimm, should be used with caution. Intended for a German-speaking audience, Flimm's production translates much of Dryden's text into German, adding lines referring to Salzburg Festival politics, road construction, and the conductor (among other things) that can be confusing to students. There is no coherent production concept: a pseudo-punk Philidel hobnobs with a windsurfing Merlin, and a Monty Pythonesque Arthur wars with an Oswald who resembles Kelsey Grammar. Also complicating matters is the choice to double-cast characters who both sing and speak. Thus we sometimes see two Philidels and Grimbalds. Despite these significant drawbacks, the lyrics of the sung portions are in the original English, and selected segments can be used effectively in class.

We suggest three foci for class assignments, concentrating on primary sources. These can be supplemented with secondary-source readings. For a brief introduction to Dryden's ideas about and use of music, James Anderson Winn's *"When Beauty Fires the Blood"* (esp. 20–28) is valuable. Winn's third chapter, "'To Please the Hearing': Dryden on Poetry and Music," provides background on Dryden's musical odes. For classes focused on opera, Burden's "Aspects of Purcell's Operas" or Winn's chapter 5, "'Beauty like Yours Commands': Dryden and the Sexual Politics of Opera," may be assigned. Essays by Winn ("Dryden's Songs") and by Dianne Dugaw from Jayne Lewis and Maximillian Novak's edited volume *The Enchanted Ground* (which includes a CD of musical examples) are appropriate supplementary material.

Our first option, which briefly explores theatrical depictions of gender through music, is suitable for a single day in a survey course on Restoration literature or drama. Students should read the pastoral interlude in act 2, scene 2, of *King Arthur* and listen to "How Blest Are Shepherds" and "Shepherd, Leave Decoying." In the first song, the overall affect is languid seduction. A shepherd (tenor voice) praises pastoral, erotic pleasures in the lilting rhythms of a minuet, a dance type drawn from the French court. Aggressively masculine pursuits, celebrated earlier in act 1 with the martial song "Come If You Dare," are alluded to by the fanfare figures Purcell assigns to the text "*While Drums and Trumpets are sounding Alarms!*" (Dryden, *Works* 16: 28), but these shepherds prefer their pastoral (and phallic) flutes.

"Shepherd, Leave Decoying" turns the tables. Purcell wittily reclaims the phallic flutes for the shepherdesses, composing a duet for female voices accompanied by woodwinds (flutes and oboes). Singing in sweetly consonant harmony, the women remind listeners of the consequences of premarital sex, "women have the shot to pay" (56), before engaging in conventional sexual negotiation. If the men will marry them, they will happily "play." Purcell sets this word melismatically—more than one note per syllable of text—suggesting the pleasures in store for compliant shepherds.

In class, after reading the texts, teachers should play through both pieces and ask whether music can have gendered meanings. If so, what are they in this scene? They can then reveal further musical information and play the pieces again. Does the additional information affect the way we hear the work? How does music reshape our perceptions of the text and why?

Time permitting, teachers may wish to include the vigorous dance song "Come, Shepherds, Lead Up a Lively Measure," illustrating a seventeenth-century performance convention shared by masques, operas, and spoken comedies: the final reconciling dance. Who has prevailed, shepherds or shepherdesses?

Our second focus explores the juxtaposition of music, politics, and patriotism in *King Arthur*. Teachers should have students read act 5 and listen to the songs "Your Hay It Is Mow'd" and "Fairest Isle." Seventeenth-century song sheets for both are reproduced in the California Dryden (16: 507–08). The first song is sung by men in colloquial language, with pointedly anticlerical humor ("Why Shou'd a Blockhead Have One in Ten?"). Purcell's music vigorously supports the transgressive message of the text (i.e., Why tithe?) with its emphasis on the physical (work, food, drink) over the intellectual (book learning) or spiritual.

After discussing the text and reading and listening to the song, students should watch the Salzburg Festival performance, where the staging is like that of a pop concert: the tenor wields a microphone in the style of Mick Jagger as the backup chorus encourages the audience to sing along. Flimm clearly understood Purcell's setting: its high level of repetition and syllabic setting enables participation, like a college fight song. If students are willing to sing along too, they may gain insight into this once very popular tune. Teachers should discuss how the Salzburg performance might influence interpretation. Did modern audiences understand the political-religious references made in the song? If they did, would this knowledge affect the way they heard it?

The second song, an elegant minuet originally performed by a female singer depicting Venus, provides a striking contrast. It also includes regular meter, rhyme, and musical repetition but creates a very different effect. Rather than a simple syllabic setting, Purcell includes brief melismas (several notes per syllable of text) decorating important words such as "isle" and "pleasure." Compare this serene musical moment with Dryden's association of Venus with the Stuart monarchy in *Albion and Albanius* and, later, in *The Secular Masque*. What do these contrasting songs (and the other act 5 entertainments) suggest about his audiences and their ideal England?

A third option is to consider the relation between music and magic in *King Arthur*. Musical magic is used both to guide and to mislead Arthur and his soldiers in act 2 and to promote seduction in the act 3 frost scene.

Neoplatonic ideas about spirits help explain why Philidel's beneficent music in act 2 works better than the music of the evil Grimbald. Elemental spirits were ranked: spirits of air were higher up the spiritual ladder (in Dryden's

Christianized view, closer to heaven), while earthy spirits were corrupted by their proximity to hell.[2] In the original production, Philidel was probably played by the soprano Charlotte Butler (who also portrayed Cupid in act 3), and the baritone John Bowman played Grimbald (see Baldwin and Wilson); the pitch of the singers' voices served as an aural analogue for their relative spiritual merits.

Students should read this scene and then play "Hither This Way" and "Let Not a Moonborn Elf" back to back. Which song is more convincing? As Rodney Farnsworth has noted, Philidel proves an expert musical rhetorician in "Hither This Way," perfectly pitching his message to persuade Arthur and his men to follow. Grimbald's forces mimic Philidel's instructions musically and textually, but Philidel generates all the musical ideas. His airy soprano overmasters Grimbald's gruff tones, as becomes comically apparent when Grimbald himself tries to imitate Philidel's voice in "Let Not a Moonborn Elf."

A contrasting example of musical magic is the famous frost scene, wherein Osmond calls up a masque of Winter and Cupid to thaw the frigid Emmeline. We have screened the Salzburg video excerpt in class, and students find it charming, although one must emphasize that Dryden and Purcell had neither penguins nor babes in bikinis in mind. This scene is fruitful from a pedagogical standpoint because it opens up all sorts of questions about the connection among music, magic, and the erotic. Yet the seduction fails: Emmeline does not give in to Osmond's enticing show.

Given the critical reception of the frost scene—frequently cited as Purcell's masterpiece—the composer triumphed, even if Osmond did not. Dryden's hero and heroine, and by extension his audiences, must continually distinguish between music that guides and celebrates and music that seduces and betrays.

Afterword: Musical Dryden for Musical Students

In an upper-level undergraduate course or seminar, teachers may ask students to tackle, with appropriate preparation, a music-oriented topic. Here are a few suggestions:

Compare a musical scene from *King Arthur* with a similar one of magic, triumph, or love from the 1695 revival of the Dryden-Howard *Indian Queen*, also with music by Purcell.

In *King Arthur*, act 4, scene 2, Dryden is very specific about the music (a minuet, repeated) to be performed by the nymphs and sylvans attempting to seduce Arthur from his quest. Why would he want a minuet? What does Purcell do instead, and does it work, aesthetically and dramatically?

Compose or adapt music from other Purcell works for one of the *King Arthur* lyrics apparently not set in 1695 (e.g., act 3, scene 2) and discuss how it would work in the scene. This could be a group project, with in-class performances of scenes and their new music.

NOTES

[1] Dramatic operas are often referred to in secondary sources as semioperas, since they include both musical sections and spoken dialogue, unlike an all-sung French or Italian opera of the time. The term "dramatick opera" appears on the title page of *King Arthur*.

[2] Jack Armistead has written numerous articles about Dryden's occult knowledge ("Dryden and the Occult" and "Occultism"). Any of these may be used, along with Gary Tomlinson's *Music in Renaissance Magic*.

"Originally Shakespear's": Adaptation, Critique, and *All for Love* and *The Tempest*

J. Caitlin Finlayson

Rewriting the Bard

> As when a Tree's cut down the secret root
> Lives under ground, and thence new Branches shoot;
> So, from Shakespear's honour'd dust, this day
> Springs up and buds a new reviving Play.
>
> —Dryden, *The Tempest*

Every age reimagines the Shakespeare it wants. By pairing Dryden's *All for Love* (1677; *Works* 13: 1–111) with Shakespeare's *Antony and Cleopatra*, or Dryden and William Davenant's *The Tempest* (1667; 10: 1–103) with Shakespeare's *The Tempest*, students in an introductory drama course or in a survey of Shakespearean adaptation from the Renaissance to the twenty-first century can consider how Shakespeare is made to fit within the sociopolitical realities and theatrical contexts of a different period. A study of the critical evaluations of Shakespeare in the prefaces and prologues to Dryden's printed play texts and in his *An Essay of Dramatick Poesie* (1668; 17: 3–81) introduces students to the aesthetic sensibilities of drama after the reopening of the theaters by Charles II in 1660, at the end of the interregnum. It also establishes adaptation itself as a literary critique that is as valuable as new directorial interpretations of Shakespeare's works. Instructors can use Dryden's revisions of Shakespeare's plays to address changes to theatrical practice and to address the nature and interpretative consequences of genre modification. At a fundamental level, these theatrical rewritings invite students to evaluate adaptations in their own right. Students might also explore the effects of the modernization of language on interpretation and consider the question of linguistic impoverishment. Finally, Dryden's rewritings engage students in the question of whether adaptation is necessary to make Shakespeare accessible "for all times" (Jonson, line 43) or simply illustrates the modern critics' claim, in Ezra Pound's terms, that everything has to be made new (620). This essay proposes the use of Dryden's Shakespearean adaptations to discuss issues of performance theory, theater history, adaptation as critique, and genre modification as well as to explore Dryden's dramatic merit and his place in the development of English theater.

Adaptation, an act of appropriation, holds a mirror to both the adapter and the adaptee. Dryden's "new reviving Play[s]" begin the history of adaptation of Shakespeare as literary critique. Acknowledging the twenty-year gap in professional theater, Dryden points to his play's origins in a past form (the Renaissance stage) and writer (Shakespeare) but insists that from this "secret root" his new play—an offshoot, not a copy—has emerged, reviving both the theater and Shakespeare for a new, more sophisticated audience. Why adapt Shakespeare in the first place? Why not, my students ask, just stage *Antony and Cleopatra* as Shakespeare wrote it? Why give Miranda a sister? Consideration of Dryden's motivations introduces the exigencies of the Restoration stage, in particular the theater companies' need for a wide selection of material immediately available for production, and also highlights the division of Renaissance play texts between the two royal patent companies. Here it is useful to draw an analogy with current popular films of Shakespeare and show how audience familiarity, monetary incentive, and the lack of copyright contribute to continuing adaptation specifically in the film medium. The appropriation and adaptation of Shakespeare, students will come to understand, is ongoing, and the motivations that drive it (and the anxieties that plague it) are largely the same, then and now.

Students are generally surprised to discover that theatrical adaptation was in part a legal requirement, not simply a creative choice. Thomas Killigrew's King's Men, which included several professional actors from the Stuart period, were granted the right to perform most of Shakespeare's plays in their original format. This entitlement initially left Davenant's Duke's Men, the company for which Dryden wrote, with the rights to only two Renaissance plays, so they were in desperate need of material for performance. Davenant made a proposal to the Lord Chamberlain to reform "some of the most ancient Playes that were playd at Blackfriers . . . makeing them, fitt, for the Company of Actors," who were largely inexperienced (Clark, Introduction xlii). He was granted the legal right to perform ten of Shakespeare's plays in adapted form. Adaptation, then, was in part a matter of legal obligation. These plays, made fit for the Restoration stage, proved to be commercially profitable and generally more popular with audiences than Shakespeare's originals. This interesting fact raises a number of questions. What were Restoration notions of authorship and copyright? Why were these plays more popular than the originals? The circumstances that led to this adapting of Shakespeare's scripts mark the continuing divide between performance based on authentic, original practice and performance that modernizes and seeks novelty. Note the contrast today between the Original Practices Project of Shakespeare's Globe and the multitude of gangster films inspired by Shakespeare's plays.

Undergraduates new to theater studies often have little knowledge of how plays are staged and of how theatrical conditions, such as a male-only cast or the use of movable scenery, might in part dictate the type of work a playwright composes and stages. Adaptation helps show students that theatrical practice is more than a superficial, mechanical aspect of a play. When they read a Shakespeare-Dryden pairing, they are freed from basic elements of story and can focus on how changing theatrical practice affects the presentation of the action. One approach to Dryden's rewritings is through a comparative stagecraft assignment, in which students are introduced to the performance conditions of each period (stage design, actors, costumes, sets, etc.) and given the available production information on the plays. They are asked to examine one feature of a production, such as stage sets or female actresses, and consider how changing this feature changes the play and elements of the performance. *The Tempest* is an obvious candidate for this exercise, because its inclusion of magic, music, and masque is a bridge from Renaissance to Restoration theater. It lends itself to the use of scenery and the special dramatic effects that became such a key feature of the Restoration stage. Its embedded masque and music also point to opera and the semioperatic theatrical forms popular during the Restoration.

Critiquing the Bard

One method for broaching the subject of making Shakespeare "fitt" for the Restoration stage and highlighting the theatrical practices and aesthetics of the time is to begin with Dryden's often ambivalent commentary on Shakespeare in *An Essay of Dramatick Poesie* and in his adaptations' prefaces, prologues, and epilogues. Here, small-group work before discussion can be particularly useful. Through selected excerpts, students can assess his critique of Shakespeare as they would a critical article. They may consider how Dryden sets his own literary career in the context of Shakespeare's, what he values or rejects in Shakespeare's plays, and the difference in aesthetic sensibility he sees between his audience and Shakespeare's. The instructor should draw attention to the inconsistency in Dryden's viewpoint and ask students to consider why Dryden stages his critique by presenting it within the prologues and epilogues of his adapted plays. Discussion of his shifting principles of Shakespearean appropriation can act as a transition into a more focused examination of a particular play. It also reveals the writer's metatextual reflections on the act of writing, as Dryden self-consciously invokes his source and discusses his creative process.

From the outset, Dryden's contentious relationship to his predecessor is apparent. Shakespeare "had the largest and most comprehensive soul," Dryden tells us, yet "[he] is many times flat, insipid; his Comick wit degenerating into clenches, his serious swelling into Bombast. But he is always great, when some great occasion is presented to him." With one comment Dryden praises; with the next, he disparages. His criticism often links Shakespeare's lack of formal education to his unsuitability to a new, homogeneous, sophisticated Restoration audience influenced by French theater. Dryden articulates the Restoration view of Shakespeare as a natural genius: "Those who accuse him to have wanted learning give him the greater condemnation: he was naturally learn'd; he needed not the spectacles of Books to read Nature; he look'd inwards, and found her there." Typically, this view is immediately qualified by a comparison with Francis Beaumont and John Fletcher, whose natural gifts were "improv'd by study" (55) and whose plays, Dryden notes, outperformed Shakespeare's on the Restoration stage. This vacillating critique indicates Dryden's complex relationship to his source, Shakespeare: in part elitist posturing to differentiate himself from this great but natural poet and in equal part anxiety of influence, expressed most directly in his preface to *All for Love*: "[W]ithout Learning, [Shakespeare] should by the force of his own Genius perform so much, that in a manner he has left no praise for any who come after him" (13: 18). Both Shakespeare's and Dryden's *The Tempest* provide an opportunity for students to consider the portrayal of authority and creativity, a portrayal that leads into a discussion of Prospero, Shakespeare and Dryden as caught in anxieties of authorship. Dryden's collaboration with Davenant, who suggested characters and provided daily "amendments" to Dryden's play (10: 4), further complicates the authorship issue. In essence, Dryden's adaptations are an epilogue to Shakespeare—both retrospective and generative.

Language: Original versus Modernized

Dryden's criticism in *An Essay of Dramatick Poesie* that "*Shakespeares* language is likewise a little obsolete" (*Works* 17: 57) echoes the perennial undergraduate complaint that Shakespeare's words are antiquated and that students feel distanced from or intimidated by his mode of expression. Dryden in the preface to his *Troilus and Cressida* (1679; 13: 217–355) announces vitriolically that Shakespeare's version is a "*heap of Rubbish, under which many excellent thoughts lay wholly bury'd*" (226). "Words and Phrases," he states in his preface to *All for Love*, "must of necessity receive a change in succeeding ages" (18). Dryden, then, is part of the continual process of updating and modernizing Shakespeare's language on page, stage, and screen. His commentary can prompt students to consider in what form they are reading Shakespeare: original text, modernized text, or, as in comic books, paraphrased? Is modernization of punctuation and spelling a form of adaptation? Dryden's criticism raises these still-pertinent questions, and through it the instructor can lead into close reading of specific, important segments of the adaptation of language by Dryden.

The famous barge speech in *Antony and Cleopatra* provides a valuable illustration of Shakespeare's and Dryden's texts as palimpsests. By juxtaposing Thomas North's translation of this scene from Plutarch's *Lives of the Noble Grecians and Romans*; Shakespeare's ornate version in act 2, scene 2; and Dryden's more streamlined rendering in act 3, scene 1, of *All for Love*, students can consider how both playwrights approach the scene and use their sources. Students should consider in particular the effect of reassigning the poetic speech from Shakespeare's stoic, cynical Enobarbus to Dryden's Antony. The scene shifts from the paradoxical beauty and allure of Cleopatra's ability to make "defect perfection" in Shakespeare (238) to Antony's failure to control his personal desires in Dryden. This shift refocuses the play to domestic politics and "unlawful" (10), but sympathetically engaging, romantic love. Does Dryden's modernizing of the language impoverish or even misrepresent Shakespeare? Or should we view the reassigning and streamlining of this speech as a means of redirecting the play's focus from Cleopatra, whom Dryden renders more sympathetic and submissive, to Antony? Noting the importance of typecasting to the construction of plays in both Shakespeare's and Dryden's times, the instructor can introduce students to the original casting information for Dryden's version as a means of explaining the play's dramatic structure. In 1677 the casting of Elizabeth Boutell, who usually played virtuous heroines, as Cleopatra, in opposition to Katherine Corey as Octavio, "turn[ed] the adulterous mistress into an innocent heroine and place[d] her at the moral centre of the tragedy" (Mora 75).

The Restoration Actress and Sexual Voyeurism

Margaret Hughes's performance in *Othello* at the Vere Street Theatre in 1660 is generally thought to mark the beginning of women on the professional stage in England. Her story, as dramatized by Claire Danes in the film *Stage Beauty* (2004), provides at once a historical and pop culture entry point for a discussion of the artistic effects of including women onstage. Popular adaptations such as *The Tempest; or, The Enchanted Island*, written by Dryden in collaboration with Davenant and first performed by the Duke's Company in 1667, made deft use of this new performance practice. Students in a survey of drama course will have already learned that male actors played female roles on the Renaissance stage. The class will also have discussed Shakespeare's exploitation of transvestitism and cross-gendering as dramatic devices and the homoeroticism of young male actors' playing female romantic roles.

Dryden's additions of Miranda's younger sister, Dorinda, and Ariel's girlfriend, Milcha, attest to the novelty of female actresses and the expansion of female roles in the newly reopened theaters. Dryden continues the tradition of cross-dressing in Shakespeare's plays, however, by reimagining Sycorax as Caliban's sister, a part he assigns to a male actor. Inverting the tradition and responding to the new fad for roles featuring women in breeches, Davenant, as Dryden stipulates in his preface to *The Tempest*, created the character of a young male Hippolito performed by Mary Davis. Davis became Charles II's mistress shortly after the play's premiere. Breeches roles were popular for exposing the actresses' legs, and Davis's were considered particularly fine. The female actress, playing an inherently promiscuous male, destabilized notions of gender and sexual agency while pandering to the audience's (and the monarch's) appetite. These alterations supply four prominent roles for actresses to a Shakespeare play that has only one female character. Shakespeare's *The Tempest*, critics such as Stephen Orgel and Ann Thompson have noted, crafts women as an absence or memory: Claribel, Miranda's mother and nurses, and Sycorax. Dryden's version places women center stage. The average adult company in the Renaissance had only two to four young male actors, which necessarily limited the number of female roles, but Davenant hired roughly eight women to perform for his company, which necessitated the expansion of female roles.

One way of analyzing the spectacle of the female body on stage is by selecting scenes that primarily present these additional female roles. Dryden's *The Tempest* reframes Shakespeare's romance of loss and recovery, magic, authorship, authority, and male control of female sexuality into a domestic romantic comedy. Dryden interpolates a number of scenes involving Dorinda and Miranda, as well as their counterpoint, Davenant's breeches role character of Hippolito, a man who has never seen a woman. The interpolated scenes involving these three actresses come to dominate the action as the play progresses, making *The Tempest* a fruitful exemplum of the place of women on the Restoration stage. The prologue informs the audience that Hippolito is played by a woman, but, unlike Shakespeare's cross-dressing Rosalyn, this actress will not break the illusion by shedding her male attire in the final act. The prologue insists that she will believably perform the "perfect man" (36). Dryden exploits the liminality of the prologue to draw attention to the actress's cross-dressing, ensuring the audience's awareness of the woman beneath the man's apparel. He further suggests the eroticism of this concealment: "Or if your fancy will be farther led / To find her Woman, it must be abed" (37–38).

The first scene in which Dorinda appears (1.2) establishes her role as Miranda's sexual confidant. Miranda shares her discovery of a creature named Man, and the sisters muse about gender difference, exploring the concepts of brothers, fathers, and their origins in a manner that is overtly sexual and uncomfortably verges on incestuous. Having heard her father say that woman was made for man, Miranda reflects, "[M]y Father is a man," to which Dorinda, the more innately lascivious of the two sisters, responds, "Methinks indeed it would be finer, if we two / Had two young Fathers" (322, 323–24).

In act 2, scenes 4–5, gender, carnal desire, and the eroticism of female performance are further explored. Since the scenes are discrete additions to the text, students are more readily able to discuss how they not only present gender and sexuality but also reframe our conception of Shakespeare's Miranda. Act 2, scene 4, introduces Hippolito, an unsocialized, uncultured wild man. Dryden notes in the play's preface that Davenant suggested the character to act as a counterpoint to Shakespeare's naive Miranda. Though Miranda is unconsciously sexual in Dryden's adaptation, her transition from naive and controlled to sexually awakened and uncontained, possibilities only hinted at in Shakespeare's play, takes center stage as Dryden explores the budding sexuality of three characters removed from society. In contrast to Miranda's infatuation with the respectable Ferdinand in Shakespeare, this Restoration adaptation offers the audience an unsocialized, licentious rogue—played by a woman.

Hippolito's insatiable carnal appetite leads to the play's only act of violence: Ferdinand's nearly fatal stabbing (or sexual penetration) of Hippolito (or the female actress's body) (Rosenthal, "Reading" 208). While Shakespeare crafts

Prospero's paternal control of Miranda's virginity as both familial and political commodity, Dryden provides the audience with a more ambiguous spectacle of female agency and sensuality, the degradation of patriarchal control but also, ultimately, its quasi-recovery through sexual violence, a prevalent trope on the Restoration stage (207–08). Dryden's adaptations of Shakespeare allow students to historicize changing notions of gender and performance.

Genre: Changing the Politics of Romance

Moreover, these added scenes allow for a discussion of the reimagining of *The Tempest* as a romantic comedy rather than a tragicomedy and illustrate the aesthetic tastes of the Restoration audience. The added scene between Cleopatra and Octavia in *All for Love* also raises many of the gender issues mentioned above. In his preface, Dryden excuses its inclusion, arguing that it would be "both natural and probable, that Octavia, proud of her new-gain'd Conquest, would search out Cleopatra to triumph over her; and that Cleopatra, thus attacqu'd, was not of a spirit to shun the encounter . . . though the one were a Roman, and the other a Queen, they were both Women" (11). Like *The Tempest*, the scene foregrounds the romantic struggles of the characters and provides a more central role to Octavia in Dryden's version. Yet it also reduces the heroic tragedy of Shakespeare at times to a domestic narrative. This move away from heroic tragedy reflects the increasing popularity of romantic comedies that play out contemporary domestic life onstage, bringing the drama of the period into the present moment and into the family home. It also introduces students to how the moral landscape of Renaissance drama changed after the reopening of the theaters. Dryden in *All for Love* rewrites Cleopatra as a passive heroine in a play focused more on Antony and Cleopatra's domestic situation than on the political backdrop. His preface to his *Troilus and Cressida* can be useful here for a discussion of the changing conception of the hero and heroic drama. Once again engaging in an intratextual conversation with Shakespeare, Dryden argues for the neoclassical principles of unity and decorum, outlines the faulty features of Shakespearean drama that necessitate his revision, and redefines the tragic hero and heroic tragedy. Students in my Introduction to Drama course argued at length about the validity of Dryden's definition of the hero as "*a man who has so much more in him of virtue than of vice, that he may be left amiable to the audience, which otherwise cannot have any concernment for his sufferings*" (13: 236). They also debated the degree to which Dryden's Antony fulfills this definition. Close examination of how Antony is described by secondary characters in Shakespeare and Dryden can further clarify these playwrights' contrasting notions of the heroic. Dryden's adaptations provide a forum for students to explore theatrical and aesthetic developments in English drama and the consequences of these developments for the type of drama being written and produced in the Restoration.

Reading Dryden's theatrical style through Shakespearean adaptation provides a touchstone for students, enabling them to historicize both Shakespeare's and Dryden's plays in terms of production and stagecraft, genre, political allegory, gender, and performance. At the same time, approaching Dryden's plays as adaptations that reflect their contemporaneous world creates a more sophisticated framework from which students can read modern Shakespeare adaptations on stage, on film, and in comic books. Considering adaptation as critique opens up these plays to critical theory as practice and enables students to perceive writers' metatextual reflections on writing itself.

The State of Innocence and *Paradise Lost*: The Politics of Adaptation

Elizabeth Bobo

Although often dismissed as unworthy of its source, Dryden's opera *The State of Innocence and Fall of Man* (1677; *Works* 12: 320–82) has considerable value for students of English literary history. Students in my Seventeenth-Century Studies and Milton seminars report that reading Dryden's adaptation before reading Milton's *Paradise Lost* (1667) creates a framework in which to set the labyrinthine similes, epic descriptions, and myriad allusions soon to be encountered in the original. Looking backward opens provocative points of entry into the work of both authors and provides stimulating lessons in the politics of literary publication, genre, and adaptation. A comparative overview of early editions of both works develops student awareness of the roles played by publishers, editors, and various generations of readers in shaping canonical authors and their texts. Through this approach students learn to detect the various ways textual interpretation reflects the individual reader's interests, to include a work's dissemination and reception history in literary analysis, and to reconsider accepted accounts of literary periodization and influence. In starting with the first adaptation of—that is to say, one of the earliest responses to—a canonical text, this lesson exemplifies the shift in literary studies toward a history-of-reading approach. This approach, when practiced in the classroom, increases the possibilities for students to respond analytically to a text.

As do students today, Restoration readers liked *The State of Innocence*. During that time, it was Dryden's best-selling dramatic work. Provided access to early-edition facsimiles of both works in conjunction with *English Short-Title Catalog* descriptions, students discover that, in its first thirty years of publication, *The State of Innocence* appeared in ten affordable quarto editions. After the initial publication of *State*'s libretto, *Paradise Lost* had only one edition that was more affordable (the third, an unadorned octavo in 1678); its next three editions (1688, 1691, and 1695) were issued in prohibitively expensive, illustrated folio format. *Paradise Lost* did become a household book in the mid–eighteenth century, but in the decades after its 1678 octavo edition sold out, *The State of Innocence* quarto would have been the more affordable option for most readers. Consequently, Milton's imaginative expansion on the Genesis story gained prestige not only because of the beautiful folio editions available to an elite readership but also, and perhaps even more, because of Dryden's condensed and repoliticized quarto version made available to the popular readership.

Pairing Dryden and Milton in this print culture context illustrates the political nature of writing, reading, and adapting literature. Some of the most obvious marks of political affiliation can be found in paratextual materials. In *The State of Innocence*, these materials indicate that Dryden transforms the subject matter of the antimonarchic, radically Protestant Milton into a product that supports the royalist and perhaps even Roman Catholic cause. Indeed, the title page implies that the work supports not only the House of Stuart but also Catholic succession to the throne: the work is "Dedicated to her Royal Highness the DUCHESS" (*Works* 12: 80 [the 1677 title page of *State*]), Mary of Modena, the new Catholic bride of the future James II. The prominence of the word *duchess* on the title page mitigated the association that readers had between Milton's expanded treatment of Genesis and his revolutionary politics. Mentioning the book's dedication to the duchess suggested that the royal family endorsed the work. As the title page indicates, the adaptation seemed to support political affinities opposite to those Milton held, thereby enhancing the work's appeal to Restoration monarchists.

Following the dedication, the commendatory poem written by Dryden's friend Nathaniel Lee describes this adaptation as a corrective to the "rudely cast," "roughly [drawn]," "old fashion'd" work of the "dead Bard" (12: 537 [sig. A4r]). This claim that the new work aesthetically surpasses the older one suggests that the constitutional policy endorsed by the new work, absolutist monarchy, surpasses the republican ideals endorsed by the original author. When students read the next prefatory piece, "The Authors Apology," they find that Dryden deploys the conventional modesty topos to situate Milton as the master poet. Asserting, "The Original being undoubtedly, one of the greatest, most noble, and most sublime POEMS, which either this Age or Nation has produc'd," he dissuades the reader from comparing the two pieces (86; sig. br-v). This elevation of Milton's achievement may have actually discouraged readers from troubling themselves with the lengthy original. Among the first critics to use the epithet *sublime* to describe the poem, Dryden separates Milton from the mundane concerns of politics. In this way, he is able to identify his own work with the stylistic sublimity for which Milton was becoming known while glossing over any disagreeable political associations. Like the title page and the dedication, the prefatory poem and essay are integral parts of the adaptation, the general purpose being to appropriate Milton's literary achievement for Dryden's royalist patrons.

The decision to condense the blank verse epic into a rhyming drama also tamed Milton. That rhyming couplets were associated with royalist interests is suggested by Milton's reference to this style as "bondage" as opposed to the "ancient liberty" that he claims to have recovered for the heroic poem through his use of blank verse (*Paradise Lost* 210 ["The Verse"]). Furthermore, the dramatic genres, epitomized in the aristocratic masque form, had long been associated with the court. Dryden's generic choice was made "to recover the epic form for the Restoration—to lay the aesthetic groundwork for the great nationalist heroic poem" that Dryden hoped to write (Welch 223). In order to put the epic in the service of a royalist England, Dryden redirected the force of Milton's grand subject matter into the elitist opera. The transformation played an important role in advertising the work: "OPERA" is the only word on the title page larger than "DUCHESS." This detail and others like it become more significant once students are guided to consider the implications of generic choice. The libretto's masque-like stage directions, requiring elaborate scenery, special effects, impressive machines, instrumentation, and the casting of doubles for the singing parts, typified the wealth and privilege of royalist entertainments. Through these excesses Dryden not only dramatizes *Paradise Lost* but also creates the script for a hyperdramatic extravaganza, exemplary of the growing vogue for English operatic spectacles and the royalist politics they represented.

By transforming the epic to drama, Dryden also eliminates the narrator of *Paradise Lost*, an omission that undermines greatly the authority on which Milton's work was traditionally thought to depend. As Restoration politicians sought to exclude individual inspiration—or religious enthusiasm—from respectable political arguments, "*Paradise Lost* was taken up by two opposing sides that clashed in the political crisis over religious toleration" (Achinstein 2–3). The side defending individual choice was represented by Andrew Marvell's commendatory poem "On Paradise Lost" (1674); the side attacking toleration, by Dryden's *The State of Innocence*. By omitting the narrator, Dryden deprives the story of its divine inspiration transmitted through the pen of the prophetic poet, the classical *vates*, whom Milton Christianized. In keeping with his reduction of the roles of God and Christ, Dryden's erasure of the very concept of divine inspiration renders his work more palatable to a readership increasingly mistrustful of religious enthusiasm.

Dryden's elimination of the narrator detracts from the authority Milton had generated for his authorial persona by means of the epic's inspired narrator. Although English professors emphasize the distinction between the author and the narrator, readers of *Paradise Lost* traditionally do not. Critical assertions about Milton's connection to his sacred subject matter are usually grounded in the assumption that the narrative voice in the invocations is that of Milton himself. After having read Dryden, students, encountering the invocations, ask, "What would the work be like without them?" and "What does their inclusion add to the telling of story?" From this perspective, the mutually validating relationship between Milton's authorial persona and his narrator's claim to inspiration is no longer simply a requisite of the epic genre in the classical tradition. Students learn that the meanings and values of poetic devices change over time: invocation was demanded by the genre, but it also expressed a religiopolitical resistance that was increasingly unacceptable in public discourse.

The day before the play is assigned as homework, students participate in dramatic stage readings. To supplement facsimiles of original editions, Jack Lynch's online edition of the play is convenient and line-numbered; it can be used with in-class reference to Vinton Dearing's notes in the California Dryden. The first two of Lucifer's six soliloquies are read aloud for initial contrast to the corresponding passages in *Paradise Lost*. Lucifer's first soliloquy (1.1.1–16) corresponds to Satan's lines in book 1 of Milton (84–270), his second (2.2.1–21) to

Satan's lines in book 4 (32–133). This comparison sparks interest in the structural differences between the two texts and also invites discussion about what makes *Paradise Lost* political in the first place and what the function of Satan is in the epic. The in-class stage readings bring to life the differences between the complex characterization of Satan and the simplified one of Lucifer. Listening to Lucifer's couplets, students hear how his thoughts are bound up in the end-stopped lines, which themselves seem to limit any psychological development or investigation of motives.

For many current Milton scholars, the quality that renders *Paradise Lost* most threatening to absolutist thinking and thereby potentially subversive is its indeterminacy and incertitude. Students gain exposure to this critical trend through assigned readings of Joseph Wittreich (*Feminist Milton* and "Milton's Transgressive Maneuvers") and Peter Herman (*Destabilizing Milton*). According to both Wittreich and Herman, the political threat posed by Milton's work is not so much that its characters or episodes have direct correspondences to real events during the Interregnum or Restoration as that Milton wrote the poem in a way that lends itself to multivalent, even contradictory interpretations. This multivalence is illustrated in the tradition of responses to Satan, including the debate over whether or not he is the hero. If one agrees with the current assessment of Milton's text as unstable, then Dryden changed the politics of the original by reducing the complexities, thereby foreclosing on the possibility of ambiguous interpretation. This reduction is found in his characterization of Lucifer. In cutting up and dividing among the fallen angels Satan's initial speeches, Dryden denies Lucifer the elevated and noble lines that helped create Satan's heroic stature and problematized the valuation of rebellion in *Paradise Lost*. Instead Dryden's version confers on the act of rebellion a single meaning, that of a council of traitors (by that time associated with the regecides) conspiring to overthrow a divine king, a stable, negative meaning for monarchist Restoration readers.

Second only to Satan, the figure of Eve compels student discussion. After students are introduced to the 1980s debates over the relation between Milton studies and feminist criticism, they compare the two authors' representations of the first woman. Isolated quotations might suggest that Dryden offers a pro-woman corrective to what has been interpreted by many as a misogynistic subtext in Milton's treatment: Dryden's Raphael states that Eve is "[a]n equal" (107 [2.2.64]) while in Milton's version Adam and Eve are "[n]ot equal" (4.296). But Dryden's Raphael immediately qualifies his assertion, "An equal, yet thy subject. . . ." As Hugh MacCallum clarifies, "Far from taking a less patriarchal view of marriage than Milton, . . . [Dryden] throws more stress than does his source on the vulnerability of Eve. . . . Milton's Eve, in contrast, is expected to use her reason . . ." (122). Most critics agree that Dryden's prelapsarian Eve resembles a coquettish ingenue of the Restoration stage, but those who do not agree give students diverse claims to defend or refute. For example, Jean Gagen claims that Dryden's Eve is "more dignified and less reprehensible," more "purified in motives and behavior" than Milton's Eve (144–45). In contrast, Louis Martz calls her "willful, vain, argumentative, sexy, quick in repartee, indulgent in ironic self-pity" (195). Wittreich adds that Dryden restores "the Eve/Satan typology" to prevent what might be seen as ambiguous treatment of her by Milton ("Milton's Transgressive Maneuvers" 249). Reading both versions of Eve puts students in a stronger position to formulate their own opinions about the function of this figure.

As students decide for themselves what Dryden and Milton might have been doing with Eve, they are introduced to the extensive use of her in early modern controversial writing about women and government. As Shannon Miller shows, "Cultural invocations of rewritings of *Paradise Lost* in the late seventeenth century highlight how issues of gendered hierarchy could be negotiated through *Paradise Lost*" (208). The various uses of the first marriage in debates about political theory provide a historicist context in which to frame the comparison. Interest in further research turns some students to Miller's *Engendering the Fall* to see how seventeenth-century women writers, Robert Filmer, John Locke, and others employed the Genesis narrative of origins to justify opposing arguments. Considering Dryden's revision of Milton's Eve as one of many among his contemporaries reframes an exercise in contrast into an exercise of comparison. Read against the way seventeenth-century women writers interpreted the first marriage, Milton's and Dryden's representations of Eve prove to have more similarities than differences. Students discover, here as elsewhere, the benefits of looking beyond first impressions.

For the purpose of illustrating how philosophical and theological discourses reflect political interests, juxtaposing the two works is more effective than studying either text by itself. Despite his diminution of Milton's complexities, Dryden maintains the theme of free will, rewriting it into an incongruously static and lengthy scene among Adam, Raphael, and Gabriel. Studying this dialogue provides for students a relatively simple window into complex history-of-thought concepts such as libertine and Hobbesian determinism, the Anglican distinction between God's foreknowledge and God's decree, and Milton's endorsement of choice in his prose as well as in his poetry. It helps to show that critics disagree about what Dryden accomplishes in the free will scene. Elucidating both the theological issues and their political ramifications, Bruce King offers the conventional interpretation that the defense of free will (voiced by the angels) wins out over the Hobbesian, determinist position (voiced by Adam), thereby reflecting Dryden's opinion in the matter (375). K. W. Gransden disagrees, claiming that Adam wins the argument "hands down" (130). Nicholas Von Maltzahn complicates the discussion by asserting that in the 1670s Dryden's sympathies were more determinist than pro–free will; he sees the angels' proposal as a defense not of human freedom but of "a more dubious compatibilism—maintaining that 'free will does not preclude determinism and vice versa'" (48). In comprehending the terms of the philosophical-theological debate and in attempting to decide for themselves how contemporary readers might have understood this scene, students learn about ideas crucial to seventeenth-century intellectual history and the practice of analyzing literature in this context.

Beyond serving as a memorable summary of its predecessor, *The State of Innocence*, read in advance of studying *Paradise Lost*, introduces students to current theories and methods of historical literary analysis. They see that interpretations—found in the forms of paratext, adaptation, and reception—force onto an original text the concerns of readers of a particular generation and cultural context. Dryden's *The State of Innocence* was not only a popularizing, musical adaptation of Milton's work but also a royalist retort to and counterattack against Milton's lifelong argument for conscientious resistance to earthly oppression in religion and government. In looking backward from the then-best-selling but now-neglected work to its predecessor, students gain experience in primary textual analysis in a print culture context. Attending to the variety of ways in which literary works can be ideologically loaded, they can use the methodologies of this lesson to further develop their own criticism of other texts, both lesser known and canonical.

PROSE AND TRANSLATION

Dryden and Rochester: Tracing Literary Rivalries in Dryden's Prefatory Texts

Jennifer Brady

Students at Rhodes, the liberal arts college where I teach, bring few preconceptions to John Dryden's plays. *Marriage à-la-Mode* (1673; *Works* 11: 219–316), *Aureng-Zebe* (1675; 12: 147–250), and *All for Love* (1677; 13: 1–111) are all terra incognita to undergraduates who, if they encounter Dryden at all before taking a course on Restoration drama, will have done so in a historical survey of British literature typically offering a smattering of his poetry and token excerpts from his critical essays. It is difficult for students to grasp a career spanning more than forty years of intensive productivity and encompassing so many genres. Most of Dryden's texts are frankly occasional and enmeshed in the partisan political and literary controversies of his age. Dryden can seem a remote figure, *dry* (a pun that every generation of students surely rediscovers for itself) and formidable, a challenge for readers struggling to make sense of the unfamiliar terrain of Restoration literature.

In my upper-division course on Restoration drama, a survey of ten plays produced from the 1670s through the 1690s, I teach two plays by Dryden at the midpoint of the semester, directly following a unit of the course titled "Court and Theater Milieu." Dryden's *Marriage à-la-Mode* (or, less often, his heroic drama *Aureng-Zebe*) and *All for Love* become centerpieces of the course. Because the other playwrights are represented by only one play, two plays give Dryden pride of place. The course is designed not only to show his centrality to the period but also to situate him in the volatile culture of patronage relations in the 1670s. Students who read *Marriage à-la-Mode*, which Dryden dedicated to John Wilmot, the second earl of Rochester, and which was advertised on the title page as a comedy "Written by JOHN DRYDEN, Servant / to His Majesty" (220), will have just finished a week on Rochester's verse satires and have read "A Character of King Charles II" (1750), by George Savile, marquis of Halifax, both materials provided as handouts, in addition to reserve readings (see Hammond, "King's Two Bodies"). The packet of Rochester poems includes not only "A Satyr on Charles II" (1673–74) and "An Allusion to Horace, the Tenth Satyr of the First Book" (1675–76) but also several of the poems that establish Rochester's libertine persona and credentials, such as "Against Constancy" (1676), "The Disabled Debauchee" (1675), and "To the Postboy" (1676) (Wilmot, *Complete Poems*). The "Court and Theater Milieu" unit prepares students for Dryden's complex dedications and prefaces in which the playwright, dependent for his livelihood on court patronage, which was always sporadic and uncertain, aired his deepening mistrust of Charles II's court.

When teaching *Marriage à-la-Mode* and *All for Love*, I begin by discussing the rhetorical strategies of the prefatory texts. I devote as much as forty-five minutes of the first class to the dedication of each play; for *Aureng-Zebe*, I allot less time to prefatory material. Many modern anthologies of seventeenth-century drama still omit the paratexts, despite the growing scholarly consensus that they are central to studies of textual patronage and the history of authorship (see Bergeron; Cotterill; Loewenstein). For many years I relied on New Mermaids or Regents Restoration Drama editions of individual plays, since they include prefatory materials, but recently I was delighted to find David Womersley's *Restoration Drama: An Anthology*, which publishes a generous breadth of work from the period, including Dryden's *The Conquest of Granada* (1670) and *All for Love*, with all their critical apparatus intact. I now supplement Womersley's edition with one or two single plays and count myself lucky, as a believer in the value of teaching the critical preface, to have this excellent anthology available as a resource for undergraduates.

The prefatory texts may at first seem an unpromising entryway into an appreciation of Dryden's plays. Although Dryden does treat aspects of his plays' early reception in the critical prefaces and famously compares his version of *Antony and Cleopatra* with Shakespeare's in the preface to *All for Love*, the prefaces are largely taken up with extraliterary concerns. Dryden's dedications to aristocratic patrons disgusted Samuel Johnson, who complained that "in the meanness and servility of hyperbolical adulation, I know not whether, since the days in which the Roman emperors were deified, he has been ever equalled" in denouncing Dryden's prostitution of his talent. "When once he has undertaken the task of praise, he no longer retains shame in himself, nor supposes it in his patron," Johnson adds ("Dryden" 113). The hyperbolic praise served up in the dedication of *Marriage à-la-Mode* to Rochester exemplifies the style of flattery Dryden practiced on such occasions. He makes the earl of Rochester a virtual god: "In this Dedication therefore, I may seem to imitate a Custom of the Ancients, who offer'd to their Gods the Firstlings of the Flock, which I think they call'd Ver Sacrum, because they help'd'em to increase" (11: 221). Students can find Dryden's praise of Rochester estranging, foreign to their sense of propriety and occasion, though the issues of patronage and dependency raised in and by the prefaces will naturally be less freighted for them than they were for Johnson.

Why focus on Dryden's prefaces, then, when reading them can prompt us to blush, to feel on his behalf a shame he seems not to have internalized as their writer? The dedicatory texts are not merely exercises in flattery, though flattery is a crucial component of their rhetoric. He is a shrewd observer of the vanities of court life. These texts prefigure the criticism of court-centered ambitions offered in the plays, suggesting his deep-seated unease about court life. The chronic disloyalty of courtiers, their fickleness, their penchant for malice, their abject fawning before those above them, and their ruthless determination to crush those beneath them are all staples of Dryden's plays of the period as well as recurrent topics in his prefaces. There is Melantha, the ubiquitous town lady in *Marriage à-la Mode* who haunts the court and changes her loyalties as often as she replaces her fashionable French idioms; there are the servile crowd of courtiers at Agra in the restoration year of 1660 who "chang'd affections bring" to each new regime (1.1.52); and there is the corrupt and treacherous Egyptian court in *All for Love*, awaiting Octavius's inevitable takeover of their country while plotting their survival. The depictions of court life in these three plays are consistent both with one another and with the negative depiction of courtiers in the prefatory texts. In the preface to *Aureng-Zebe*, Dryden includes a scathing portrait of the "Character of a Courtier without Wit" that underscores the malice, backbiting, and undisguised careerism he associates with the court (12: 150). He repeatedly announces his preference for privacy over a life lived in the public eye. In the 1678 dedication of *All for Love* to Thomas, earl of Danby, the "*Croud of Suitors*" importuning Danby at court are "*so clamorous a Train*" (13: 8–9) of petitioners that Dryden pities the Lord High Treasurer. While these prefaces flatter their aristocratic dedicatees, Dryden maintains a stance of detachment, of being above the fray; he is a suitor but not one of the clamorous mob sordidly vying for favors.

Dryden's tense relations with the mercurial earl of Rochester are reflected in the nuanced ambivalence of the 1673 preface to *Marriage à-la-Mode*. During the 1670s, Dryden's anxiety about his reception at Charles II's court came to center on the dissolute and charismatic godson of the monarch. That Rochester's inconstancy in his love affairs was replicated in his literary relations made him a poor candidate for any long-term support. Even in the dedication of *Marriage à-la-Mode* to Rochester, Dryden airs his mistrust of the alliances formed by courtiers:

> That which with more reason I admire, is, that being so absolute a Courtier, you have not forgot, either the ties of Friendship, or the practise of Generosity. In my little Experience of a Court (which I confess I desire

> not to improve) I have found in it much of Interest, and more of Detraction: Few men there have that assurance of a Friend, as not to be made ridiculous by him, when they are absent. (11: 221–22)

In teaching this passage, I ask students to attend to the implications of its parenthetical phrase. Dryden uses the aside to dissociate his values from those of the court, underscoring his distaste for its intrigues. He positions himself (like his pastoral lovers, Leonidas and Palmyra, in the play) on the periphery of court life. Rochester, by contrast, is the consummate courtier, accustomed to the malice that sabotages friendship at court. Even if the passage professes to celebrate Rochester's exceptionalism—his rare loyalty to his friends and his determination to shield them from the malice of others—it conveys Dryden's acute awareness of his own vulnerability to ridicule.

A close scrutiny of the preface to *Marriage à-la-Mode* helps students grasp how Dryden negotiates his own and Rochester's different temperaments, class identities, and practices as writers. In his concluding remarks, Dryden stresses Rochester's nobility and dilettantism. Ostensibly deferring to Rochester's superior wit and genius, he claims that he has "so much of self-interest, as to be content with reading some Papers of your Verses, without desiring you should proceed to a Scene or Play," a double-edged compliment that underscores Rochester's aristocratic preference for the manuscript tradition over print and the low expectation of sustained productivity associated with a courtier-poet who can cavalierly criticize others' plays without ever writing so much as a scene. "People of my mean condition, are onely Writers, because some of the Nobility, and your Lordship in the first place, are above the narrow praises which Poesie could give you," Dryden writes, distinguishing his own professional ambitions from Rochester's dilettantism (223). In this passage, Dryden bows and scrapes to the aristocrat who is his patron and intercessor at court, while coolly announcing his own, more serious investment in the accolades awarded writers who combine genius with a strong work ethic.

As the coded reservations in this preface make clear, the rupture in Dryden and Rochester's alliance was inevitable. Their rapprochement was of brief duration. Rochester's "Allusion to Horace" soon targeted Dryden's overproductivity ("Five hundred verses every morning writ / Proves you no more a poet than a wit" [Wilmot, *Allusion*, lines 93–94]) as the source of his work's uneven quality. Dryden responded in his preface to *All for Love*, excoriating Rochester for his arrogance and exhibitionism. Here Dryden's panegyric on Shakespeare is interrupted, even derailed, by his angry preoccupation with his contemporary rival. Over several pages, Dryden turns from extolling Shakespeare to attacking Rochester: Rochester is not, he puns, "qualified to decide Sovereignly, concerning poetry" (13: 13); he is a witty man but fatally self-indulgent and high-handed. In his preface to *Marriage à-la-Mode*, Dryden had obsequiously petitioned Rochester not to enter into a competition with other writers: "Your Lordship has but another step to make, and from the Patron of Wit, you may become its Tyrant: and Oppress our little Reputations with more ease then you now protect them" (11: 223–24). Five years later, his foreboding has been realized; he now likens Rochester to Dionysius and Nero, tyrants with laureate pretensions who used their power to suppress more talented writers. Surrounded by drunken flatterers who encourage his vanity and his malicious urge "to destroy the fame of others" (13: 15), Rochester has become a destructive literary despot. In a final gesture of contempt for his powerful aristocratic rival, Dryden refuses to name him.

The anger fueling Dryden's preface to *All for Love* stems from his awareness of his social vulnerability in any contest with the earl. As the godson of a notoriously indulgent, permissive monarch, Rochester was insulated from repercussion and given free rein to bully, ridicule, and attack those beneath him. Dryden prided himself on his restraint in responding to the many satires written against him over his career, but Rochester's satire stung, provoking Dryden's response, because it circulated at court, exposing Dryden to ridicule in the milieu where his reception mattered most. At stake for him, bluntly, was his livelihood.

Rochester's forte as a satirist lies in his willingness to shame his targets. In his "A Satyr on Charles II," Rochester draws on his private communications with Nell Gwyn, Charles's mistress, to mock in graphic detail the aging king's flagging sexual stamina ([*Complete Poems*] lines 28–31). Such ad hominem ridicule is also prominent in "An Allusion to Horace," where Rochester targets Dryden's blundering efforts to pass as a rake in the company of his social superiors and his failure to impress the ladies with his bawdy talk:

> Dryden in vain tried this nice way of wit,
> For he to be a tearing blade thought fit.
> But when he would be sharp, he still was blunt:
> To frisk his frolic fancy, he'd cry, "Cunt!"
> Would give the ladies a dry bawdy bob,
> And thus he got the name of Poet Squab.
> (*Allusion*, lines 71–76)

Both "A Satyr on Charles II" and "An Allusion to Horace" circulated at court, lampooning their targets; neither the king nor Dryden could undo or efface the impact of these scurrilous verses on the coterie audience for whom they were written. Manuscript circulation fed Rochester's need for notoriety at the same time as its anonymity gave Rochester the benefit of deniability. The famous pun on Dryden's name in "An Allusion to Horace" connects him to a "*dry* bob," meaning that the poet lacks the ability to ejaculate; Dryden is exposed as a dull provincial who has been masquerading as a rake. "An Allusion to Horace" achieves its primary aim when Poet Squab is summarily expelled from the charmed circle of libertine wits over whom Rochester presides.

In pairing these two writers in my course, I emphasize the inevitable dissolution of their alliance as each evolved in the 1670s into his rival's antithesis.

Rochester represents the aristocratic dilettante working in the still-viable tradition of manuscript publication, Dryden the industrious and disciplined professional writer whose renown is dependent on his resourceful use of print publication. Rochester is the debauched courtier memorialized in his own verses and idealized in Sir George Etherege's portrait of the libertine hero Dorimant in *The Man of Mode* (1676). Dryden is, by contrast, Charles II's poet laureate, an ambitious writer with complicated ties to the court and a strong preference for the private life. Students who read his critical prefaces in chronological order—from the dedication of *Marriage à-la-Mode*, with its hyperbolic praise of Rochester and its nuanced subtext of disaffiliation and reserve, through Dryden's expressed anxieties about malicious courtiers in *Aureng-Zebe*, to his final angry rupture with Rochester in *All for Love*—come to see Dryden differently. They are engaged by his struggle to establish himself as a professional writer in a courtly milieu where he was never particularly comfortable. They see his personal and social vulnerability to ridicule. They probably—and this response reflects my own bias as well as the nearly unavoidable pedagogical consequence of juxtaposing in a course two writers who exemplify rival literary traditions—end up preferring Dryden to Rochester.

Dryden is not shamed by the praise he lavishes on his aristocratic patrons precisely because he maintains a distance from them, a self-protective space. He reveals in the preface to *Aureng-Zebe* his disgust "when he sees, he can hardly approach Greatness, but as a Moated Castle; he must first pass through the Mud and Filth with which it is encompass'd" (12: 150). The caustic depiction of court life in his plays is thus anticipated in his sober reflections as he surveys from a discreet distance the backstabbing court of Charles II.

Dryden had an unexpected ally in his growing distaste for courtiers, the king himself, who shrewdly appointed him his poet laureate in 1668. In my Restoration class, students are assigned Halifax's sardonic portrait of Charles II, which includes penetrating insights into court life under a king notorious for his "Love of Ease." There is a marvelous passage in Halifax's "A Character of King Charles II" depicting the attempts of Charles to flee from courtiers importuning him for favors to the sanctuary of his mistresses' private chambers, where he could slumber after dinner in comparative peace and quiet. Halifax evokes the scene memorably:

> The being galled with Importunities, pursued from one Room to another with asking Faces; the dismal Sound of unreasonable Complaints, and ill-grounded Pretences; the Deformity of Fraud ill-disguised; all these would make any Man run away from them; and I used to think it was the Motive for making him walk so fast. (Savile 492–93)

Marriage à-la-Mode, which Charles II first read at Windsor in 1671 on Rochester's recommendation, was a particular favorite of the king's. He must have loved Dryden's representation of Melantha, the ditzy gate-crasher whose transparent ambitions to ingratiate herself at court prove her undoing. But this comedy would have appealed to Charles for another reason. Leonidas and Palmyra, the romantic protagonists, repeatedly voice their nostalgia for their pastoral bliss before the unwanted discovery of their royal bloodlines and before Leonidas's restoration to the throne robbed them of their privacy. "So many of his hours in publick move / That few are left for privacy, and Love," the prince laments (2.1.413–14). Dryden surely invites Charles to see an idealized version of himself in this scene, where Leonidas bemoans the burdens of monarchy, especially its precipitous loss of privacy. From their different vantage points, at the center or on the periphery of power, both the king and his poet laureate had reason to share a mistrust of the "asking Faces" at court. Dryden's critique of courtly careerism is developed in plays such as *Marriage à-la-Mode*, but it is first announced, sotto voce, in the prefatory texts, where he proves himself to be an astute, unillusioned observer of the very public lives lived in Charles II's court.

Students in my Restoration drama class write essays on various topics that spring directly from our discussions. They may focus on the prefatory texts as commentary on Dryden's relations to the court and to Rochester, or they may choose to write on the representation of court life in the plays themselves. Many explore the pronounced nostalgia in Dryden's plays for irrecoverable idealized worlds, often focusing on his depiction of Palmyra and Leonidas. In my experience, students respond most vividly to *Marriage à-la-Mode*, a play they find unexpectedly bawdy and unexpectedly moving. It is often their favorite play in the course.

NOTE

I want to thank Dan Gates, Jayne Lewis, Brian Shaffer, and Sara van den Berg for their very helpful suggestions on draft versions of this essay.

Forgetfulness and Authorial Presence in Dryden's Prose

Aaron Santesso

My first encounter with student responses to Dryden's critical prose was inauspicious: beside a typical sentence in a library copy of the "Discourse concerning the Original and Progress of Satire" (*Works* 4: 3–90; "By this time, my Lord, I doubt not but that you wonder why I have run off from my Biass so long together, and made so tedious a Digression from Satire to Heroique Poetry" [15–16]), a weary undergraduate hand had scrawled, "So do I." This did not bode well. Endless digressions, a dusty debate, strange syntax: on the face of it, Dryden's "Discourse" seems like a tough sell to undergraduates. Yet the piece, strategically excerpted, can be a revelation: not only strikingly ambitious—Dryden means it when he warns the reader that he is attempting a "new method" of writing (68)—but also littered with charming, surprising, and memorable moments.

When I teach the "Discourse," I focus on a seemingly offhand remark that to my mind is one of the most pregnant lines in seventeenth-century criticism: "I ought to have mention'd [*Hudibras*] before, when I spoke of Donn; but by a slip of an Old Man's Memory he was forgotten" (81). The line always jumps out, and for good reason. My students know from hard experience that such an admission would not go over well in their own critical prose; why, then, would Dryden include it?

I use this single line as a way of opening up not just Dryden's criticism on satire, or even his criticism as a whole, but also seventeenth- and eighteenth-century prose in general. In a satire class, the line—characteristic of the innumerable apologies, backtracks, and diversions of the "Discourse"—can be taken as a kind of condensation of the main argument: satire must be unified by an overall theme, but it can and indeed should digress, being by its nature a "hotch-potch" (37).[1] Yet there is much more going on here. On the broader critical front, it shows the emergence of the idea of authorial personality, especially as it relates to the practice of criticism. Elsewhere in the "Discourse," Dryden suggests that "[a]ny thing, tho' never so little, which a Man speaks of himself, in my Opinion, is still too much" (60). This statement of course is shamelessly disingenuous, coming as it does in the midst of a work of criticism that serves as an autobiography of sorts. Dryden describes (albeit nonsequentially) his development from schoolboy to young writer "without Name or Reputation" to "public Mark" to elder statesman (4, 8). Students often understand ideal criticism as neutral, or formal to the point of mechanical; Dryden's essay can therefore be unsettling in the way it confronts readers with the undeniable presence of an individualized author, a person with foibles and weaknesses. All of this provides a wonderful opportunity to describe the invention of the "author" (a conversation that in my classes moves from Jonson's 1616 Folio to the 1710 Copyright Act to the modern debate between Roland Barthes and Michel Foucault. One might not automatically associate Dryden and Oscar Wilde, but Wilde's suggestion that criticism "is the only civilised form of autobiography" is both provocative and pertinent here (1125).

To pursue the idea of a work of criticism as autobiography, I ask my students whether the author of a critical work is really an "author," in the same sense that Daniel Defoe or Jonathan Swift or J. K. Rowling is an author. It is a question prompted by personal experience: most of us have encountered (alas) the traditional idea that writers of fiction open up their souls, while critical authors close them up. Dryden himself is well aware of this idea, yet when we get to the comparative section of the "Discourse," the person of the author begins to seep through cracks in the prose. Dryden assures us that he is "labouring . . . to divest my self of partiality, or prejudice," then plunges cheerfully into a deeply subjective and openly prejudiced comparison of classical satirists: "I must confess, that the Delight which *Horace* gives me, is but languishing. Be pleas'd still to understand, that I speak of my own Taste only: He may Ravish other Men; but I am too stupid and insensible, to be tickl'd" (50, 63). The mention of "Taste" provides another teaching opportunity: I ask my students whether all our aesthetic judgments aren't based on taste and whether taste isn't simply a synonym for personal response. Especially for junior undergraduates, the idea that taste is trainable can be controversial (Bourdieu is particularly useful here).

Gradually, the trickle of personality in the "Discourse" becomes a flood, more or less overwhelming the argument—and it is here we really feel Dryden's "new method" of writing. After attacking modern "lampooners," he suggests that his emotions are getting the better of him: "This is almost a digression, I confess to your Lordship; but a just indignation forc'd it from me. Now I have remov'd this Rubbish, I will return to the Comparison of *Juvenal* and *Horace*" (61).[2] And a paragraph that begins by comparing Horace and Juvenal ends, somehow, with Dryden's admitting that attacks on his "Reputation" hurt him and praising his refusal to respond to "scurrilous lampoons" (60). But while such lines conjure up an image of a distracted, angry victim of critical injustices, Dryden carefully balances them with repeated, disarming apologies for "rambling" (73). Over and over he begs pardon for digressing, but his apologies are almost gleeful, and he seems somewhat proud of his ostensible lack of focus. Taken together, these moments create a picture of a rambling, harmless old man, not entirely in control of his own prose—and what better way to cause us to lower our guard? After all, Dryden is not the first critic to have employed a forgetful persona: Sir Thomas Elyot, for example, writes very similar lines in his "Value of Poetry in Education" ("But in defending of orators and poets, I had almost forgotten where I was" [68]). In this sense, then, Dryden is using less of a new method than an old trick.

So perhaps we might see Dryden as luring us into a trap: charmed by the forgetful narrator, we hesitate to reject entirely his theory of satire. But there is another possibility: what if Dryden really did forget about *Hudibras*? In this reading, the line is, to borrow a phrase from earlier in the "Discourse," "Nature without Art" (29). Many students feel that genuine forgetfulness is more plausible: if Dryden wants us to lower our guard, presenting an absentminded narrator is a risky way to go about it. After all, he is trying to bring order to chaos, to offer a systematic evaluation and final judgment, so adopting the persona of someone who misplaces key pieces of information seems counterintuitive. Perhaps he simply forgot. But even if we imagine that he is writing in an unmediated, pseudo-stream-of-consciousness way, why would he not omit his admission when preparing the piece for publication?

The answer I give in the classroom is simple: all writing, critical writing included, is a balance between manipulation and artlessness. However rhetorically adept Dryden is—and he is adept—he is shrewd enough to know that revealing something of himself makes the rhetoric easier to accept. This little sentence can gently remind students that the critical author is a human being, and that criticism, as much as the work it criticizes, can be autobiographical and emotional.

Why, then, does Dryden mention his forgetfulness? Perhaps because it worries him. He was sixty-three when he wrote "Discourse"; he would die six years after the piece appeared. A few years earlier, he had written the preface to *Sylvae* and recognized in Lucretius "the inconveniencies of old age, which make him incapable of corporeal pleasures; the decay of understanding and memory, which render him contemptible, and useless to others" (*Works* 3: 12). Many writers, from Hesiod to Friedrich Nietzsche, have celebrated the power of forgetfulness as a way of overcoming pain or the chains of the past. Plato, on the other hand, is pessimistic: for him, forgetfulness is quite simply a bad thing, something that distances us from the truth and alienates us from ourselves. Dryden, I think, is rather on the Platonic side of things here, and his words on his forgetfulness form a jarringly honest moment in his criticism; they may indeed be the most human moment in all his writing.

It is also possible, however, to use the line to move a class in an entirely different direction, to read "a slip of an Old Man's Memory" as less about humanity or authorial personality and more about genre. The line may signal a prose writer's willingness to experiment. Dryden joins several prose authors of his period in laying claim to a faulty memory. William Congreve (in *Incognita*), Delariviere Manley, and especially Aphra Behn all employ narrators that realize they have "forgotten" to divulge key points to the reader (Congreve 1: 125; Manley 62). Students quickly recognize this admission as a strategic move. It serves Behn well in *Oroonoko* to delay the revelation that her Westernized hero and heroine are covered with tribal tattoos (40). Forgetfulness can also function as a rhetorical trope: Behn and others use the claim of forgetfulness as a marker of authenticity: the narrator who introduces herself as an eyewitness is, ironically, more credible if she occasionally slips. One might therefore read Dryden's essay as a hybrid work, one that experiments with literary tropes as a way of establishing critical authority.

In a class that considers the development of literature more broadly, this device provides a chance to begin a conversation about the general possibilities of prose itself. When Dryden was writing the "Discourse," prose was in a sense still a new, exciting thing. Literary criticism in English was barely a century old; long prose narratives had been popular for about the same amount of time, and seen as respectable for less than that; the success of Bacon's *Essays* surprised no one more than Bacon himself. For Dryden, after a career built on efficient, carefully controlled verse, prose remained an astonishing, exciting space.[3] Part of the charm of his prose comes from the feeling it conveys of being slightly overwhelmed with its potential, as if someone had spent his or her life in a small apartment and were now kicking around a big house and not knowing quite what to do. What exactly is one going to put in all this room?

Dryden's answers to this question, like the answers of other authors over the ensuing decades, can be conventional—but they can also be progressive and even revolutionary. Despite the reputation of the "Discourse," and of Dryden's criticism generally, as relatively conservative and indeed normative, in its embrace of forgetfulness it anticipates later, avant-garde works. Instead of simply using the work as an introduction to satire of the period, in other words, one could also use it as an introduction to experimental prose. *Tristram Shandy*, for example, is a veritable compendium of forgotten ideas (from "But I forgot my uncle Toby, whom all this while we have left knocking the ashes out of his tobacco pipe" to "I am a Turk if had not as much forgot my mother" [Sterne 72, 438]). Sentence after sentence begins, "I forget which" or "I forget what" or "I forget who." Lesser-known works too offer parallels: Richard Griffith's *Something New* (1772) offers the same forgetful narrator, playful exercises, thought experiments, surreal digressions, use of aposiopesis, and so on. Dryden's "Discourse" can even be seen as an ancestor of future forgetful narrators, in works from *The Turn of the Screw* to *Catcher in the Rye*. A few short excerpts from Samuel Beckett or Thomas Pynchon will go a long way toward countering concerns that eighteenth-century literature is dusty and distant. Dryden's "Discourse" is an opportunity to introduce to early undergraduates, particularly those majoring outside the humanities, basic ideas that often come as a revelation: that narrative need not necessarily be chronological and straightforward to be effective, that the presiding third-person narrator may be untrustworthy, that instability is part of the novelistic and indeed literary tradition.

So, this one line about the slip of an old man's memory offers widely different interpretative possibilities and opens up different classroom conversations: it can be read as the strategic deployment of a charming persona, or as a searingly honest moment, or as an experiment in a new way of writing prose. It can be connected with early criticism, with seventeenth-century prose, or with modern novels. The one thing it is not is dry and irrelevant.

NOTES

[1]Dryden's "Discourse" is as much of a "Mixture" as the genre it describes, and the numerous apologies are a tongue-in-cheek way of drawing attention to the nature of a "Satura" (37).

[2]This is an opportunity to explain in a different way (as opposed to that described in note 1) why Dryden's interruptions, digressions, and apologies are legion: "And give me leave, my Lord, since I have here an apt occasion, to say . . ."; "But I am enter'd already upon another Topique . . ."; "But I have said enough, and it may be, too much on this Subject. Will your Lordship be pleas'd to prolong my Audience, only so far, till I tell you my own trivial Thoughts" (61).

[3]He describes, in the "Discourse," his writing of the *Essay of Dramatick Poesie* as setting sail into a "vast Ocean" (4–5).

Teaching Dryden's Latin Translations: Lucretius, Vergil, and the Honeybee

Adam Potkay

Erotic obsession and how to cope with it, the fact of death and the thirst for life, the delicate balance between human beings and their environment and all that threatens that balance—what student wouldn't be captivated by such concerns? Yet how many of us associate them with Dryden's poetry? Dryden, we all know, is a politically and socially engaged poet, and it's a challenge for us to teach his topical poetry to undergraduates far removed from the public issues and persons he addressed. The Great Fire and the Dutch Wars, the Exclusion Crisis and Popish Plot, Church of England ecclesiology in relation to Roman Catholicism and Protestant Dissent, royal bastards who are rebellious and promising satirists who die young—I admit that I've found all these concerns a hard sell, even at a liberal arts college named for King William and Queen Mary. But these are the concerns of *Annus Mirabilis*, *Absalom and Achitophel*, and "To the Memory of Mr. Oldham." Perhaps a more welcoming way to initiate students into Dryden's poetry is through his translations, which are perennially accessible and compelling.

Dryden's translations from Lucretius's *De rerum natura* (*Works* 3: 44–66; "On the Nature of Things")—which Dryden's California editors deem a "neglected masterpiece" (281)—offer therapeutic advice on how to deal not only with the fear of death but also with a maddening erotic attachment. This sexual perturbation is apt to be familiar to students of college age, but just in case it isn't, I typically introduce the story of Dido and Aeneas, which ends with Dido's suicidal rage against Aeneas for abandoning her, through book 4 of Dryden's translation of Vergil's *Aeneid* (5: 450–84) or through his "Dido to Aeneas," adapted from Ovid's "Epistles," or *Heroides* (1: 132–38). Another poem Dryden translated from the Latin is Vergil's *Georgics* (5: 137–266), a didactic poem on agriculture and the worth of poetic as well as manual labor but also on the sexual force that works through all things and on death, along with Eros, as a limitation of our purposeful activity. I focus my teaching of the *Georgics* on book 4, in which the myth of Orpheus and Eurydice, the poet's failed attempt to bring his dead beloved back from the underworld, is framed by a story about bees: the hive, its collective death, and its ritual restoration in an act that rights the balance between man and the gods, man and the earth. Dryden found the *Georgics* to be "the best Poem of the best Poet," the masterpiece of Vergil's maturity (5: 137–38 [dedication to *Georgics*]); the same tribute might be paid to Dryden's English version of the poem.

As the table of contents of Keith Walker's Oxford World's Classics edition of Dryden (*Major Works*) makes clear, much of Dryden's poetic work lies in the translation or imitation of earlier poetry, Latin poetry in particular (Lucretius,

Ovid, Horace, Juvenal, Persius, Vergil). Dryden first theorized poetic translation in his preface to a translation of Ovid's *Epistles* (1680), in which he advocated paraphrase (or "translation with latitude") over metaphrase (strict translation) and imitation (taking undue license with the original) (*Works* 1: 114–19). In the last twenty years of his poetic career, Dryden would increasingly find his own poetic voices in the paraphrasing of other authors.

If we are inclined to think of literary translation as beneath the dignity of original composition, we entertain a view quite alien to Dryden's and to that of readers and critics, from the fourth earl of Roscommon (*An Essay on Translated Verse* [1685]) to Samuel Johnson (*Lives of the Most Eminent English Poets* [1781]), who ranked verse translation highly. The translations of Dryden, as later of Alexander Pope, were considered to be among these authors' greatest achievements. I teach Dryden in an upper-level period course on British literature from 1660 to 1744, once "the age of Dryden and Pope," an era that comprises the great age of literary translation in English—if not its golden age (that title should go to the Tudor-Stuart Renaissance, which gave us Golding's Ovid and Chapman's Homer), then its incandescent silver age. Translation was taken seriously, as a way of engaging and Englishing a Greco-Roman literary corpus that was still held to be, in most regards, unequaled by the vernacular literatures of Europe. The translator's art, less expressive than interactive, forges connection and renewal, salvaging voices that would otherwise be lost, collaborating with the past in the interest of the future. The ethics of translation are well expressed by Catherine Talbot in a letter from the 1740s:

> [A] faithful and elegant translator is a character of the highest virtue in the literary republic. It [translation] implies public spirit the most void of ostentation; a kind regard for the illiterate [i.e., those without Greek or Latin]; a love of our own native country, shown by enriching its language with valuable books; a just regard for merit of whatever country, by placing the merit of some valuable foreigners in the truest and fairest light. . . .[1]

In various incarnations of this course I've taught most all of Dryden's Latin and Greek translations. All have their inherent charms, and each has the additional benefit of establishing the various genres so important to Restoration and eighteenth-century literature. Thus students who steep themselves in a sampling of epic through either Dryden's *First Book of Homer's* Iliad (7: 260–85; from *The Fables*) or selected books of his *Aeneis* (I sometimes do books 2 [Aeneas in Carthage recounts the Fall of Troy], 4 [Dido and Aeneas], and 6 [epic descent into the underworld]) are apt to have a much greater appreciation for the mock-epic elements found in "Mac Flecknoe" and Pope's *Dunciad*. Reading Dryden's imitations of Horace and Juvenal is a wonderful introduction to satire. From Juvenal I've used the misogynist sixth satire to start a conversation about gender politics that extends to Pope's "To a Lady" and the responses that it, and

Pope more generally, elicit from women authors (Mary Leapor, Lady Mary Wortley Montagu, and Anne Ingram, Viscountess Irwin). Dryden's rollicking paraphrase of Juvenal's tenth satire (4: 144–203) may be profitably contrasted with Johnson's Christianized—and bowdlerized—version of the same, *The Vanity of Human Wishes*, in a conversation about changing literary and sexual mores between the Restoration and the mid–eighteenth century. A section on the verse epistle can commence with Dryden's paraphrase of Ovid's "Dido to Aeneas," a work that leads naturally to Rochester's "A Letter from Artemizia in the Town to Chloe in the Country" and to Pope's "Sappho to Phaon," "Eloisa to Abelard," or Horatian epistles. Pope's *Essay on Man* is illuminated by beginning one's teaching of philosophical verse, or the didactic poem, with Dryden's paraphrase of Lucretius's *De rerum natura*.

Students are susceptible to the charms of Dryden's Lucretius, not least because of the Latin poet's existential and erotic concerns: the meaning of life, atoms and the void, why death ought not to be feared, and finally—Dryden's favorite part of Lucretius, book 4—"the truest account of the disease [of erotic obsession] and its remedy" (3: 12 [preface to *Sylvae*]). Some students also like, as Dryden puts it, Lucretius's "noble pride, and positive assertion of his opinions" (10)—an antidote, perhaps, to modernist poetry, which asserts little or nothing. Lucretius offers a systematic poetic exposition of Epicurus's philosophy, though students may be surprised to learn that Epicurus was no epicure. Although he considered pleasure (*hēdonē*) the greatest good, his notion of it is best understood as the absence of pain: pleasure is unruffled tranquillity, composure, peace. Epicurus taught that three main things trouble the mind: fear of eternal punishment after death; in life, undue public ambition; and, finally, erotic attachment. Cupid's arrows were to be avoided at all costs. (Although counseling a male readership to avoid what we'd call falling in love, with either women or young men, Lucretius is all for marital, reproductive sex, and even offers advice—now valuable for entertainment purposes only—on the best sexual positions for conception.)

But if Lucretius advised against erotic desire, he also depicted it, as Dryden notes, in a "lively" and "alluring" manner (12). To follow Lucretius faithfully, Dryden avows he was bound "to turn him into . . . luscious *English*"; thus he reproduces the tension in Lucretius between condemning and sumptuously describing the coupling of lovers. Dryden claims but does not show that there is no satisfaction

> when the Youthful pair more clossely joyn,
> When hand in hands they lock, and thighs in thighs they twine
> Just in the raging foam of full desire,
> When both press on, both murmur, both expire,
> They gripe, they squeeze, their humid tongues they dart,
> As each wou'd force their way to t'others heart. . . . (4.71–76)

If Lucretius and Dryden after him truly wanted, on Epicurean principles, to wean us away from carnal thoughts, they could've done a better job than this. Yet the literary point to be made here is that, as in Pope's *Essay on Man*, the best didacticism is the most vexed didacticism.

Expiring in the above passage means "breathing out" (Johnson's *Dictionary*, def. 1) and also "dying," and *dying* is a traditional euphemism for "reaching orgasm"—but when it comes to accepting one's final expiration, Dryden gives personified Nature finely crafted lines on why not to fear annihilation. One reason is that Nature has nothing new left to give:

> To please thee I have empti'd all my store,
> I can invent, and can supply no more;
> But run the round again, the round I ran before.
> (3.138–40)

In my experience, students love that last triplet, and here, as throughout, Dryden's Lucretius abounds with good examples of sound imitating sense. In the triplet's final alexandrine we have both a circular line about circularity, built on the figures of polyptoton (the verb *to run* cast in different tenses) and anadiplosis (ending one phrase with the "round" that starts the next), and a plodding line about plodding on, its regular iambs extended across a greater length. Perhaps not all students enjoy mastering this technical appreciation of poetry, but a good many do, and Dryden (as later Pope) affords numerous such passages for them to linger over.

The last genre to which Dryden can introduce students is georgic, a crucial genre in eighteenth-century poetry, from Pope's *Windsor Forest* through William Wordsworth's *Michael*, but one that students are not apt to find immediately attractive. I draw them in by having them read and write on selections from Dryden's paraphrase of Vergil's *Georgics*. Vergil's poem follows naturally from Lucretius in that it is Epicurean and didactic. According to Vergil's learned speaker, the poet as gentleman farmer, understanding the nature of things is best, but a close second best is "[t]o lead a soft, secure, inglorious life" near "a winding Vally, and a lofty Wood" (2.689–91). But as with Lucretius, Vergil's didacticism is vexed: in tension with his ideal of tranquillity, book 3 of the *Georgics* introduces, along with advice on how to breed animals, a frank acknowledgment of the uncontrollable force of sexual desire. Eros stirs up competitive violence between animals as between human beings, and even between kings. Politically inclined teachers can note in Dryden's depiction of sexually competitive bulls (3.325–80) a sustained allusion to the conflict between King William III and the deposed King James II, who here "surveys the pleasing Kingdoms, once his own" (354).

My teaching of the *Georgics* focuses on book 4, which contrasts the erotic madness of men with the asexual calmness of bees ("No lust enervates their

Heroic Mind" [290]). Orpheus mourns for a dead love that cannot be brought back to life, and yet, in a strange turn, we are taught a mythic way to restore a lost hive. *Georgics* 4 begins with advice about raising bees but also with political observations about the hive, a commune under a king ("All is the States, the State provides for all" [229]). The second part of the book (lines 401–806) concerns the legendary beekeeper Aristaeus, whose hive suddenly dies in a seemingly inexplicable manner. Aristaeus eventually discovers the reason for his hive's demise: it is his punishment for the attempted rape of Eurydice, a chase that ended with her accidental death. He receives instruction in making a proper sin offering of eight cattle to the wood nymphs, and after nine days a new swarm of bees magically arises from the sacrificed animals (Vergil here offers a mythical account of the origin of the ancient practice of bugonia, aimed at generating bees from the corpses of oxen).

Why all this fuss about bees? It's a question urban and suburban students are apt to ask, and fortunately there's a good answer to it. In addition to producing honey, which was a foodstuff more consequential to Vergil's world and Dryden's than to our own (sugar and sucrose-surfeited) world, the European honeybee, introduced to North America four hundred years ago, serves a crucial role in our agriculture. Tomatoes, peppers, apples, pears, squash, and almonds are all bee-pollinated foods. Yet, as recent articles in the *New York Times* and *On Earth* attest, managed honeybees are approaching a state of crisis. Increasing cases of colony collapse disorder, or the sudden death of hives, has beekeepers, farmers, and environmentalists as alarmed as Aristaeus was about his loss (see Levy; Klinkenborg). For although our loss today is partly explainable and thus potentially reversible—it involves the diminishing of wild flowering plants through human overpopulation and overdevelopment— it is also partly unexplainable.

What, finally, does it mean that in Vergil bees can be regenerated while individual people cannot? In most recently teaching the *Georgics*, the essay questions I posed concerned poetry and its limited power to restore life—for human beings, for bees. I asked my students to consider the following quotation from Susan Stewart: "The cultural, or form-giving, work of poetry is to counter the oblivion of darkness . . . it is precisely in material ways that poetry is a force against effacement—not merely for individuals but for communities through time as well" (1–2). How does Stewart's reflection on the task of poetry relate to the tale of Orpheus and Eurydice? To what degree is Eurydice drawn out of the darkness—or not? This last question extends to the frames of poetic making and translational remaking: to what degree is Orpheus's task the same as Vergil's, and Vergil's the same as Dryden's? My students found these broad questions provocative, and the recent crop of essays I received in response to them was particularly good. Some students reflected on the ritual backgrounds of poetry. As one put it, "Vergil conceives that poetry is very much the ritualized act that Aristaeus's sacrifice of cattle is, a restoration of the natural order of things—an offering to quell desires, to assuage grief, to right wrongs" (Matthew Van Cura). Other students reflected on the collective life of bees. "It is the task that defines the bee, not the bee the task," wrote Emily Fuhrman. Human beings have not only individual projects but sometimes fatal desires, such as Aristaeus's attempted rape of Eurydice and Orpheus's rash backward glance at her. "Human beings can easily ruin things forever because they are controlled by their whims, while bees think as a unit and are not slaves to their impulses" (Krystyna Lopez). My students generally don't stray far from liberal individualism; perhaps the most surprising thing about teaching Dryden's Vergil was to see this strain of selfless thinking inspired by Vergil's bees as well as the crisis of bees today—and perhaps, in part, by Dryden's pollinating art of translation.

NOTE

[1]This letter, in which Talbot encourages Elizabeth Carter to translate Epictetus from the Greek, is quoted in Staves, *Literary History* 310–11.

Questioning Nature: Dryden's *Fables, Ancient and Modern*

Philip Smallwood

The most promising way for inexperienced readers of poetry to take pleasure in Dryden is to begin not at the beginning, with the widely anthologized political poems and occasional verses, but with the poems in *Fables, Ancient and Modern*, written in 1700 as the sun went down on Dryden's career (*Works* 7: 16–532). This final work of Dryden's lifetime consists of verse translations from Homer, Chaucer, Boccaccio, and Ovid and is preceded by his famous preface, which is the most lively and graceful of his essays in critical prose.

After a long period of neglect, scholarly work on *Fables* has done a great deal to reinvigorate these verse tales for the advanced student and scholarly reader.[1] But *Fables* is an ideal introduction both to Dryden and to the wider values of Augustan poetry. Despite the privileged attention traditionally given to the methods of practical criticism, many modern students reach the university poorly equipped by their schools and colleges in close reading techniques, though they are often adequately prepared with regard to literature's contribution to feminist lore, the virtues of domination subversion, and the major moral crises of our times relating to identity politics or human rights.

A compelling set of ethical, political, social, and philosophical issues is raised by *Fables*. There are, for example, in Ovid's "Cinyras and Myrrha," the moral agonies of incestuous desire and the law against it, while in "Baucis and Philemon," again from Ovid, we find marital affection, hospitality to strangers, and the unbearable pain of bereavement. The self-destructive power of desire, with its two shrines to pleasure and despair, forms the centerpiece of Dryden's longest poem in *Fables*, a miniature epic in three books from Chaucer's The Knight's Tale. The comedy of husbands and wives is explored in Dryden's translation of book 1 of Homer's *Iliad*, where wild parties on Olympus produce for Jupiter the domestic aftermath of slackened sexual performance and for the human race a ten-year-long war.

A related portrait of the pains and pleasures of marriage is supplied by the farmyard crowings of Chanticleer and Dame Pertelote in "The Cock and the Fox," a poem that has much to say, if indirectly, about gender and power relations in Charles II's court. Reference to earlier poems is often found by readers of *Fables*, and Dryden may indeed have been thinking of a future creative engagement with Chaucer in the famous opening portrait of Charles in *Absalom and Achitophel*. In *Absalom* he brings a king to the farmyard, in the fable a cock to the court. The Chaucer translations have the additional value, pedagogically, that access to the translated and to the original poetry can be firsthand. Students and tutors can compare Dryden's Middle English source with his modernized version and thus acquire an immediate idea of what it means to make new poetry from old—to produce a "Transfusion," to use Dryden's terminology, of the past into the present (41). Dryden exhibits close attention to transfusion as a principle of nature in his translation of the fifteenth book of Ovid's *Metamorphoses*, "Of the Pythagorean Philosophy," which argues on moral grounds for the vegetarian life.

Two poetical samples from *Fables* that I commend for their teachability involve women arguing in verse. They put debates about reason and truth into female formulation; and both contain judicial dilemma, sexual desire, class, love, and the politics of domestic and social repression.

Dryden's "The Wife of Bath Her Tale" begins with an evocation of a fairy world of long ago and far away, and nothing of the real-world grit that one might think attractive to student tastes is evident at the opening. Yet almost immediately we have an account of a rape.

> It so befell in this King *Arthur*'s reign
> A lusty Knight was pricking o'er the Plain;
> A Bachelor he was, and of the courtly Train.
> It happen'd as he rode, a Damsel gay
> In Russet-Robes to market took her way;
> Soon on the Girl he cast an amorous Eye,
> So straight she walk'd, and on her Pasterns high:
> If seeing her behind he lik'd her Pace,
> Now turning short he better lik'd her Face:
> He lights in hast, and full of Youthful Fire
> By Force accomplish'd his obscene Desire.
> (453 [lines 46–56])

The village community is outraged, and the knight is duly collared by the law and brought to book at King Arthur's court. But the women of the court, led by Queen *Geneura* (Guinevere), won't allow his execution, the rapist's punishment. Instead, with the suggestion of a more nuanced female judgment that is at once more accommodating of sexual criminality and more punitively complex than a male-dominated judiciary, they command him on pain of death to find the answer to the question, "*What the sex of women most desire?*" (line 97).

Here one might pause to examine the question and to probe the moral intent of the task. Do the women of the court already know what the correct response should be, and is the task therefore merely an elaborate tease, a kind of ultimate psychological revenge on one sex offender by collective womankind? But perhaps there is no right answer to the question. Is the court of ladies commissioning a public opinion survey, a piece of rather badly designed market research? Do they want a consensus view? Or are they seeking a spread of opinion? We are not told. Nor is the knight.

Off he goes, the deadline set for his return in a year and a day. The answers he receives are what we might expect according to the logic of this mission impossible: *quot feminae tot sententiae*. Some female respondents are keen on a world where free love reigns; others primly insist on the strict observance of the marriage vows. None of this will help the knight save his skin. There then follows a little digression satirizing women's inability to keep secrets, and on the final day of his quest the knight meets a "Quire of Ladies in a round" (215), and the oldest and the ugliest of the gathering tells him what he needs to hear. Without further ado, they return to King Arthur's court, and the solution to the puzzle is disclosed. The answer, of course, pertinent from the moment the ladies of the court take over the judicial function from Arthur ("to Nuptial Ties a Slave" [65]), is sovereignty: the settlement in the governance of domestic life as to who in the house wears the trousers.

Despite his crime against women, the knight thus finds salvation at the hands of one, but there is a catch: he must marry the crone. You promised, she insists; that was the deal you struck with me! With the gift of life comes the prospect of a living death for this "Bachelor . . . of the courtly Train." But marry they do and to bed they go, he struggling under the sheets to escape his consort's clasping arms. She then upbraids him in true wifely fashion, and there follows a long passage (lines 348–508) that is the heart of the poem. Students will see that this passage—all on the nature of true nobility—is greatly elaborated on by Dryden in comparison with the Chaucerian original.

The speech, in which the crone's voice transforms into the voice of Nature and the poem moves from comedy to the heroic, is an eloquent condemnation of the empty pride of ancestry and titles. The crone appeals to the virtues of Christian poverty and decries the arrogance of the droit du seigneur. The knight has no answer except to wish once again that he was not wedded to such an old and grotesque woman. Take your choice, is the crone's reply: it's me or the ax's edge. Morally exhausted, the knight resigns sovereignty to his wife. But, of course, as this is a fairy story from "Days of Old" (1), he pulls back the curtain to find what was once a decrepit old woman magically rematerialized as the most attractive maiden. Dryden supplies the moral—from the Wife of Bath's Prologue.

What, then, are we to conclude from this improbable tale about the proper punishment for rape? Loss of life? Loss of liberty? Compulsory self-assessment? Can the sin be cleansed by the good conduct of the culprit, or is its stain permanent? Do Dryden and Chaucer make too light of the crime by writing it into a fairy story? The punishment turns out to be a humiliating politico-cosmological lecture designed to discredit completely the established framework of social and economic privilege. Has the knight suffered enough by this punishment? Can one be punished enough for such a crime? One might let the students decide.

Another provocative poem from *Fables* in which politics and sexual politics coincide is "Sigismunda and Guiscardo," translated from Boccaccio. We have what seems a seventeenth-century justification of a woman's right to choose, coupled with an analysis of the perverted morality of honor killing. The poem makes in addition some powerful observations on parental affection: its obsessiveness, its capacity for cruel distortion, its element of sexual jealousy—particularly in the relationship between a father and a daughter (a theme taken up again in Dryden's translation from Ovid's "Cinyras and Myrrha").

Sigismunda, daughter of the tyrant Tancred, prince of Salerno, and a young widow, having observed a decent period of mourning, falls in love with Guiscardo, a servant and, though genteelly born, in effect a slave. The couple has fancied each other from a distance. She contrives to meet him in a secret place, and the rendezvous accommodates their first sexual encounter and also sanctifies it with the ceremony of legal marriage. They go on meeting covertly but are caught in the act by Tancred, who has Guiscardo arrested. In no hope of securing his reprieve, Sigismunda defends her right to love and to wed according to Reason's law, and with passionate logic she proceeds—at great length and with much power—to state her dignified claim to choose the best and the most virtuous of men without regard to social class. Her case, which has an obvious relation to the diatribe of Chaucer's crone, is constructed on fundamental and universal principles:

> Search we the secret Springs,
> And backward trace the Principles of Things,
> There shall we find, that when the World began,
> One common Mass compos'd the Mould of Man;
> One Paste of Flesh on all Degrees bestow'd,
> And kneaded up alike with moistning Blood.
> The same Almighty Pow'r inspir'd the Frame
> With kindl'd Life, and formed the Souls the same:
> The Faculties of Intellect, and Will,
> Dispens'd with equal Hand, dispos'd with equal Skill,
> Like Liberty indulg'd with Choice of Good or Ill.
> Thus born alike, from Vertue first began
> The Diff'rence that distinguish'd Man from Man.
> (lines 499–511)

Deaf to such lofty eloquence and weeping with sorrow and jealous rage, Tancred has Guiscardo put to death and delivers his ripped-out heart to Sigismunda. She has planned her suicide in anticipation of this disaster and performs the fatal act. With her dying words she asks that she and Guiscardo, as a public declaration of their mutual commitment in marriage, be buried as one flesh indivisible.

Almost every student of Dryden I have taught has been moved by Sigismunda's speech, and her brave self-possession and force of intellect are appreciated even by those who find it hard to accept metrical ratiocination as a legitimate conduit for poetry. You do not have to be an official feminist to applaud Sigismunda, and the analysis of the relations between fathers and daughters strikes a chord in the minds of sons who have mothers.

In *Fables*, Dryden's end-of-career questioning of Nature, in its complex relation with law and custom, social habit and natural taboo, subsumes the politics of party and faction in comedy, argument, and myth. The collection is his most accomplished poetical production and was widely admired by his contemporaries and immediate successors, beyond even his great 1697 translation of Vergil's *Aeneid*. Numerous poetical lamentations, or *luctus britannici* on the death of Dryden, memorialize the collection, and it was one of the reasons why his reputation reached the height it did in the early years of the nineteenth century, when taste had turned against satire and the old politics was dead.

Poems that depend on the virtues of narration, on the resonance of English poetical diction, and on the role of argument in verse can do much to overcome the resistance of modern students untutored in the linguistic niceties of English poetry. Dryden's "Alexander's Feast; or, The Power of Music" (1697), reprinted in *Fables*, also offers a matchless occasion to introduce the poetical resonance of Dryden by way of music and a recording of the eighteenth-century setting of Dryden by Handel.

"Mac Flecknoe" and *Absalom and Achitophel* have long monopolized entry to the university experience of Dryden—thanks, perhaps, to T. S. Eliot's famous essay. But this focus seems too narrow for the enjoyment of such a vast and comprehensive mind as Dryden's, and a return to the study of his plays has the disadvantage that it does not always allow the beginning reader to engage with Dryden's best or most competent work. The great poetry of the last works in translation has none of these limitations, and a return to *Fables* subordinates the teacher of literature to the literature taught. It places the discovery of the poems, and what is found in translation, directly in the hands of students who have knowledge of their own to bring to them. Such an approach avoids the intricacies of the Popish Plot and the Exclusion Crisis (barriers to the poetry for nonhistorians), but it also invites a historical reading of Dryden's creative biography and poetical genealogy, recognizing the move from politics to Nature as a purpose of his translated work. To teach Dryden today, we need first to recapture some portion of the enthusiasm of those early readers, including William Congreve, Joseph Warton, and Walter Scott, who were transported by *Fables, Ancient and Modern*.

NOTE

[1]See D. Hopkins; Hammond, *Dryden*; Reverand. The advent of the complete Longman edition of Dryden's poems (Dryden, *Poems of John Dryden*), with its single-volume distillation (Dryden, *Selected Poems* [Hammond and Hopkins]), has made *Fables* available in amenably annotated form. Extracts from several of the fables are included in Hopkins's Everyman selection of Dryden, *Selected Poems*.

NOTES ON CONTRIBUTORS

Anna Battigelli, professor of English at the State University of New York, Plattsburgh, is the author of *Margaret Cavendish and the Exiles of the Mind*. She is a coeditor, with Laura Stevens, of *Eighteenth-Century British Women and Catholicism*, a special topics issue of *Tulsa Studies in Women's Literature*.

Elizabeth Bobo, assistant professor at the University of Louisiana, Lafayette, is writing "Marketing Milton: Publishers, Politics, and the English Literary Canon: 1667–1736," a book that examines how Milton's earliest promoters popularized the author.

Thomas F. Bonnell is the author of *The Most Disreputable Trade: Publishing the Classics of English Poetry, 1765–1810*. He recently finished editing volume 3 of *James Boswell's* Life of Johnson*: An Edition of the Original Manuscript*.

Jennifer Brady, professor of English at Rhodes College, coedited *Literary Transmission and Authority: Dryden and Other Writers* with Earl Miner. She contributed to *Enchanted Ground: Reimagining John Dryden* and to *John Dryden: Tercentenary Essays*.

Margaret Anne Doody is John and Barbara Glynn Family Professor of Literature at the University of Notre Dame. She has written on Augustan poetry, eighteenth-century novelists, and the novel as a genre. She is working on a book on Jane Austen.

Dianne Dugaw is professor of English at the University of Oregon. Her books include *Memoirs of Scandalous Women*, *"Deep Play": John Gay and the Invention of Modernity*, and *Warrior Women and Popular Balladry*. Her recording *Dangerous Examples* presents a sample of early modern female warrior ballads. She writes on literature, folklore, and gender and sexuality.

J. Caitlin Finlayson, assistant professor at the University of Michigan, Dearborn, has published on graphic novels and adaptations of stage productions of Shakespeare as well as on the relation between the verbal and visual in Renaissance pageantry.

Daniel Gustafson is assistant professor of English at the City College of New York, where he teaches Restoration and eighteenth-century literature and drama. He is working on a book-length study of the afterlife of later Stuart drama in the eighteenth century.

Blair Hoxby is associate professor of English at Stanford University. He is the author of *Mammon's Music: Literature and Economics in the Age of Milton*. He is completing monographs entitled "What Was Tragedy? Theory and the Early Modern Canon" and "Reading for the Passions."

Ann A. Huse is assistant professor of English at John Jay College of Criminal Justice. She is the author of an essay on Dryden's French mistress and an essay on Rochester's poetry on the French pox and is currently working on a book about place and patronage in the seventeenth century.

Christopher D. Johnson is professor of English and department chair at Francis Marion University. He is the editor of *New Contexts in Eighteenth-Century British*

Fiction and is preparing an edition of Sarah Fielding's *The History of the Countess of Dellwyn*.

Deborah Kennedy is professor of English at Saint Mary's University, Halifax. She is the author of *Helen Maria Williams and the Age of Revolution* and *Poetic Sisters: Early Eighteenth-Century Women Poets*.

Jayne Lewis is professor of English at the University of California, Irvine. She is the author of books and articles on eighteenth-century literature and culture, most recently *Air's Appearance: Literary Atmosphere in British Fiction, 1660–1794*.

Kathryn Lowerre is the author of *Music and Musicians on the London Stage, 1695–1705*, and articles on musical-theatrical topics. She is an editor of the collected works of composer John Eccles and of *The Lively Arts of the London Stage, 1675–1725* (forthcoming).

Scott R. MacKenzie is assistant professor of English at the University of British Columbia. His book *Be It Ever So Humble: Poverty, Fiction, and the Invention of the Middle-Class Home* won the 2010 Walker Cowen Memorial Prize.

Adam Potkay is William R. Kenan Professor of Humanities and of English at the College of William and Mary. His most recent books are *The Story of Joy from the Bible to Late Romanticism* and *Wordsworth's Ethics*.

Will Pritchard is associate professor of English at Lewis and Clark College. He is the author of *Outward Appearances: The Female Exterior in Restoration London*.

Cedric D. Reverand II, the George Duke Humphrey Distinguished Professor of Literature at the University of Wyoming, has written extensively on Dryden and Pope. He is the general editor of *Eighteenth-Century Life*.

John Richetti is A. M. Rosenthal Professor Emeritus of English at the University of Pennsylvania. He is the author of *The Life of Daniel Defoe: A Critical Biography* and the editor of *The Cambridge History of English Literature, 1660–1780*.

Aaron Santesso is associate professor of literature at Georgia Tech. He is the author of *A Careful Longing: The Poetics and Problems of Nostalgia* and a coeditor, with Claude Rawson, of a collection of essays on Dryden. With David Rosen he is the author of *The Watchman in Pieces: Surveillance, Literature, and Liberal Personhood*.

Philip Smallwood is professor emeritus of English at Birmingham City University and visiting fellow in the School of Humanities at Bristol University. He has written widely on Augustan poetry and criticism. He is the author of *Critical Occasions: Dryden, Pope, Johnson, and the History of Criticism*.

Katie Sullivan is associate professor of theater at Saint Mary's College in Notre Dame. She teaches acting, voice, and movement classes and directs one production a year.

Elliott Visconsi is associate professor of English at the University of Notre Dame. He is the author of *Lines of Equity: Literature and the Origins of Law in Later Stuart England* and is at work on a study of the separation of church and state in the early modern period.

Kirstin R. Wilcox is senior lecturer at the University of Illinois, Urbana, where she teaches courses in fiction, Restoration and eighteenth-century literature, and women's writing. Her research centers on transatlantic women's writing in the eighteenth century, particularly poetry.

Amanda Eubanks Winkler is associate professor in the Department of Art and Music Histories at Syracuse University. She specializes in English theater music of the seventeenth and eighteenth centuries. She is the author of *Music for Macbeth* and *O Let Us Howle Some Heavy Note*.

Lisa Zunshine is Bush-Holbrook Professor of English at the University of Kentucky, Lexington. She is the author of *Why We Read Fiction* and *Strange Concepts and the Stories They Make Possible* and the editor of *Acting Theory and the English Stage*.

SURVEY PARTICIPANTS

Anna Battigelli, *University at Plattsburgh, State University of New York*
Elizabeth Bobo, *University of Louisiana, Lafayette*
Thomas F. Bonnell, *Saint Mary's College*
Jennifer Brady, *Rhodes College*
Margaret Anne Doody, *University of Notre Dame*
Dianne Dugaw, *University of Oregon*
J. Caitlin Finlayson, *University of Michigan, Dearborn*
Mark K. Fulk, *State University College of New York, Buffalo*
Christopher D. Johnson, *Francis Marion University*
Blair Hoxby, *Stanford University*
Deborah Kennedy, *Saint Mary's University, Halifax*
Kathryn Lowerre, *Michigan State University*
Scott R. MacKenzie, *University of British Columbia, Vancouver*
Adam Potkay, *College of William and Mary*
Cedric D. Reverand II, *University of Wyoming*
John Richetti, *University of Pennsylvania*
Gail Shivel, *Florida International University*
Philip Smallwood, *Birmingham City University*
Katie Sullivan, *Saint Mary's College*
Kirstin R. Wilcox, *University of Illinois, Urbana*
Amanda Eubanks Winkler, *Syracuse University*
Lisa Zunshine, *University of Kentucky*

WORKS CITED

Abrams, M. H., and Geoffrey Galt Harpham. *A Glossary of Literary Terms*. 9th ed. Boston: Wadsworth Cengage Learning, 2009. Print.

An Account of Marriage; or, The Interests of Marriage Considered and Defended against the Unjust Attacques of This Age. London, 1672. Print.

Achinstein, Sharon. "Milton's Spectre in the Restoration: Marvell, Dryden, and Literary Enthusiasm." *Huntington Library Quarterly* 59.1 (1997): 1–29. *JSTOR*. Web. 1 Aug. 2009.

Addison, Joseph, and Richard Steele. *The Spectator*. Ed. Donald F. Bond. 5 vols. Oxford: Clarendon, 1965. Print.

Aden, John M. *Critical Opinions of John Dryden: A Dictionary*. Nashville: Vanderbilt UP, 1963. Print.

Amarisinghe, Upali. *Dryden and Pope in the Early Nineteenth Century*. Cambridge: Cambridge UP, 1962. Print.

Armistead, Jack M. "Dryden and the Occult as Dramatic Code: *Tyrannick Love*." *Papers on Language and Literature* 24 (1988): 367–83. Print.

———. "The Occultism of Dryden's 'American' Plays in Context." *Seventeenth Century* 1 (1986): 127–52. Print.

Avatar. Dir. James Cameron. Twentieth-Century Fox, 2010. DVD.

Ayres, Philip J. *Classical Culture and the Idea of Rome in Eighteenth-Century England*. Cambridge: Cambridge UP, 1997. Print.

Baldwin, Olive, and Thelma Wilson. "Purcell's Stage Singers." *Performing the Music of Henry Purcell*. Ed. Michael Burden. Oxford: Clarendon, 1996. 105–29. Print.

Barnett, Dene. *The Art of Gesture: The Practices and Principles of Eighteenth-Century Acting*. Heidelberg: Writer, 1987. Print.

The Batchellors Answer to the Maids Complaint. . . . London, 1675. Print.

Behn, Aphra. *Oroonoko*. Ed. Joanna Lipking. New York: Norton, 1997. Print.

Berg, Alec, and Jeff Schaffer, writers. "The Gymnast." *Seinfeld: Season 6*. Dir. Andy Ackerman. NBC. 3 Nov. 1994. DVD. Castlerock; Sony Pictures Home Entertainment, 2005.

Bergeron, David M. *Textual Patronage in English Drama, 1570–1640*. Aldershot: Ashgate, 2006. Print.

Bevis, Richard W. *English Drama: Restoration and Eighteenth Century, 1660–1789*. New York: Longman, 1988. Print.

Black, Joseph, et al., eds. *The Broadview Anthology of British Literature: The Restoration and the Eighteenth Century*. Vol 3. Peterborough: Broadview, 2012. Print.

Blow, John. *Countertenor Duets by Purcell and Blow*. Dir. Robert King. Hyperion, 1992. CD.

———. *An Ode on the Death of Mr. Henry Purcell.* Perf. La Canzona. EMI Classics, 2000. CD.

———. *Ode on the Death of Mr. Henry Purcell.* Perf. Deller Consort. Harmonia Mundi France, 2008. CD.

Braverman, Richard L. *Plots and Counterplots: Sexual Politics and the Body Politic in English Literature, 1660–1730.* Cambridge: Cambridge UP, 1993. Print.

Bredvold, Louis. *The Intellectual Milieu of John Dryden*. Ann Arbor: Michigan UP, 1934. Print.

Brewer, John. *The Pleasures of the Imagination: English Culture in the Eighteenth Century.* New York: Farrar, 1997. Print.

A Broad-side against Marriage Directed to That Inconsiderable Annimal, Called, a Husband. London, 1675. Print.

Brower, Reuben. "Dryden's Epic Manner and Virgil." *PMLA* 12 (1940): 119–38. Print.

Brown, Laura S. "The Divided Plot: Tragicomic Form in the Restoration." *ELH* 47 (1980): 67–79. Print.

———. "Dryden and the Imperial Imagination." Zwicker, *Cambridge Companion* 59–74.

Burden, Michael. "Aspects of Purcell's Operas." Burden, *Henry Purcell's Operas* 3–27.

———, ed. *Henry Purcell's Operas: The Complete Texts*. Oxford: Oxford UP, 2000. Print.

Burgh, James. *The Art of Speaking*. London: T. Longman et al., 1761. Print.

Burns, Edward. *Restoration Comedy: Crises of Desire and Identity*. Houndmills: Macmillan, 2000. Print.

Butt, John. *The Augustan Age*. London: Hutchinson, 1962. Print.

Byron, George Gordon. *Don Juan*. Ed. T. G. Steffan, E. Steffan, and W. Pratt. London: Penguin, 2004. Print. Penguin Classics.

Caldwell, Tanya. *Time to Begin Anew: Dryden's* Georgics *and* Aeneis. Lewisburg: Bucknell UP, 2000. Print.

———. *Virgil Made English: The Decline of Classical Antiquity*. New York: Palgrave, 2008. Print.

Canes, Vincent. *An Account of Dr. Still's Late Book against the Church of Rome.* N.p., 1672. Print.

———. *Fiat Lux*. N.p., 1661. Print.

Canfield, J. Douglas. "The Ideology of Restoration Tragicomedy." *ELH* 51.3 (1984): 447–64. Print.

———. "The Jewel of Great Price: Mutability and Constancy in Dryden's *All for Love*." *ELH* 42 (1975): 38–61. Print.

———. "John Dryden." *Seventeenth-Century British Nondramatic Poets*. Ed. M. Thomas Hester. Detroit: Gale Research, 1993. 81–111. Print. Vol. 131 of *Dictionary of Literary Biography*. 3rd ser.

Canfield, J. Douglas, and Deborah C. Payne. *Cultural Readings of Restoration and Eighteenth-Century Theater*. Athens: U of Georgia P, 1995. Print.

Canfield, J. Douglas, and Maja-Lisa von Sneidern, eds. *The Broadview Anthology of Restoration and Eighteenth-Century Drama*. Peterborough: Broadview, 2001. Print.

Carracci, Annibale. *The Choice of Hercules*. 1596. Capodimonte Gallery, Naples. *Wikipedia*. Wikimedia, 12 Jan. 2006. Web. 28 Mar. 2012. <http://en.wikipedia.org/wiki/File:CarracciHercules.jpg>.

Catullus. Poem 101. *Carmina*. *Perseus Digital Library*. Tufts U, n.d. Web. 26 Dec. 2012.

Clark, Sandra. Introduction. Clark, *Shakespeare* xli–lxxviii.

———, ed. *Shakespeare Made Fit*. London: Dent, 1997. Print.

Congreve, William. *Incognita*. *The Complete Works of William Congreve*. Ed. Montague Summers. Vol 1. London: Nonesuch, 1923. 107–53. Print. 3 vols.

Conlon, Michael J. "The Rhetoric of *Kairos* in Dryden's *Absalom and Achitophel*." *Rhetorics of Order: Ordering Rhetorics in English Neoclassical Literature*. Ed. J. Douglas Canfield and J. Paul Hunter. Newark: U of Delaware P, 1989. 85–97. Print.

Corman, Brian. *Genre and Generic Change in English Comedy, 1660–1710*. Toronto: U of Toronto P, 1993. Print.

Corneille, Pierre. *Discourse of the Three Unities*. 1660. Trans. Walter Jackson Bate. *Criticism: The Major Texts*. Ed. Bate. San Diego: Harcourt, 1970. 118–19. Print.

Cotterill, Anne. "Dryden's Fables and the Judgment of Art." Zwicker, *Cambridge Companion* 259–79.

———. "The Obscure Progress of Satire in Dryden's Late Preface." *Digressive Voices in Early Modern English Literature*. Oxford: Oxford UP, 2004. 245–77. Print.

Crane, David. Introduction. *Marriage a-la-Mode*. By John Dryden. London: Black, 2002. iii–xv. Print.

Cressy, Serenus. *Fanaticism Fanatically Imputed*. N.p., 1672. Print.

Damrosch, David, et al., eds. *The Longman Anthology of British Literature*. 2nd ed. 2 vols. New York: Longman, 2003. Print.

Davenant, William. *A Proposition for the Advancement of Moralitie*. Ed. James R. Jacob and Timothy Raylor. *Seventeenth Century* 6 (1991): 242–50. Print.

Davis, Paul. "Dryden and the Invention of Augustan Culture." Zwicker, *Cambridge Companion* 75–91.

———. *Translation and the Poet's Life: The Ethics of Translating in English Culture, 1646–1726*. Oxford: Oxford UP, 2008. Print.

DeMaria, Robert, ed. *British Literature, 1640–1689*. Malden: Blackwell, 2001. Print.

Dennis, John. *Critical Works*. 2 vols. Ed. Edward N. Hooker. Baltimore: Johns Hopkins UP, 1939–43. Print.

———. "Reflections Critical and Satyrical." *Dryden: The Critical Heritage*. Ed. James Kinsley and Helen Kinsley. New York: Barnes, 1971. 252–60. Print.

Descartes, René. *The Passions of the Soul*. Trans. Stephen H. Voss. Indianapolis: Hackett, 1989. Print.

Dobrée, Bonamy. *Restoration Comedy, 1660–1720*. London: Oxford UP, 1924. Print.

Donaldson, E. Talbot. "Chaucer the Pilgrim." *PMLA* 69.4 (1954): 928–36. Print.

Donnelly, Jerome. "John Dryden and the Failure of Political Categories." *Studies in Voltaire and the Eighteenth Century* 305 (1992): 1392–94. Print.

Douglas, Mary. *Purity and Danger: An Analysis of Concepts of Pollution and Taboo*. New York: Routledge, 2002. Print.

Draghi, Giovanni Battista, and John Blow. *Odes to St. Cecilia's Day*. Dir. Peter Holman. Perf. Parley of Instruments, Playford Consort. Helios, 2007. CD.

Dryden, John. *King Arthur; or, The British Worthy*. Burden, *Henry Purcell's Operas* 255–335.

———. *The Major Works*. Ed. Keith Walker. Oxford: Oxford UP, 2003. Print. Oxford World's Classics.

———. *The Poems and Fables of John Dryden*. Ed. James Kinsley. London: Oxford UP, 1967. Print.

———. *The Poems of John Dryden*. 5 vols. Ed. Paul Hammond. London: Longman, 1994–2005. Print.

———. *Selected Poems*. Ed. Paul Hammond and David Hopkins. Harlow: Pearson, 2007. Print.

———. *Selected Poems*. Ed. David Hopkins. London: Everyman, 1998. Print.

———. *Selected Poems: John Dryden*. Ed. Steven N. Zwicker and David Bywaters. London: Penguin, 1997. Print.

———. *Virgil's* Aeneid. Ed. Frederick Keener. London: Penguin, 1997. Print.

———. *The Works of John Dryden*. Ed. Edward Niles Hooker and H. T. Swedenberg, Jr., et al. 20 vols. Berkeley: U of California P, 1956–2002. Print.

Dugaw, Dianne. "'The ~~Rationall~~ Spirituall Part': Dryden and Purcell's Baroque *King Arthur*." Lewis and Novak 271–89.

Durant, Jack D. "*Religio Laici*: The Poem as Product." *College Language Association Journal* 35 (1992): 448–66. Print.

Eliot, T. S. "John Dryden." 1921. *Selected Essays*. London: Faber, 1932. 305–16. Print.

Elyot, Thomas. "The Value of Poetry in Education." 1531. *Oxford University Press*. Oxford UP, n.d. Web. 7 Jan. 2013. <http://fds.oup.com/www.oup.com/pdf/13/9780198186793.pdf>.

Engetsu, Katsuhior. "Dryden and Modes of Restoration Sensibility." Zwicker, *Cambridge Companion* 181–96.

Essays of Love and Marriage: Being Letters Written by Two Gentlemen; One Dissuading from Love, the Other an Answer Thereunto. London, 1673. Print.

Etherege, George. *The Man of Mode.* Womersley 287–335.

Evelyn, John. *Diary and Correspondence of John Evelyn*. Ed. William Bray. London: Routledge, 1906. Print.

Everett, Barbara. "Dryden's *Hamlet*: The Unwritten Masterpiece." Rawson and Santesso 263–77.

Farnsworth, Rodney. "'Hither, This Way': A Rhetorical-Musical Analysis of a Scene from Purcell's *King Arthur*." *Musical Quarterly* 74 (1990): 83–97. Print.

Ferguson, Margaret, Mary Jo Salter, and Jon Stallworthy, eds. *The Norton Anthology of Poetry*. 5th ed. New York: Norton, 2004. Print.

Fielding, Henry. *Joseph Andrews*. Joseph Andrews *[and]* Shamela. Ed. Douglas Brooks-Davies and Martin C. Battestin. Oxford: Oxford UP, 1999. 1–303. Print. Oxford World's Classics.

Findlay, Alison. "Licensed to Thrill: Early Restoration Drama." *Women and Dramatic Production, 1550–1700*. Ed. Findlay and Stephanie Hodgson-Wright. Harlow: Pearson Educ., 2000. 123–50. Print.

Fisk, Deborah Payne, ed. *The Cambridge Companion to English Restoration Theatre*. Cambridge: Cambridge UP, 2000. Print.

Flores, Stephan P. "Negotiating Cultural Prerogatives in Dryden's *Secret Love* and *Sir Martin Mar-all*." *Papers on Language and Literature* 29.2 (1993): 170–96. Print.

Gagen, Jean. "Anomalies in Eden: Adam and Eve in Dryden's *The State of Innocence*." *Milton's Legacy in the Arts*. Ed. Albert Labriola and Edward Sichi, Jr. University Park: Penn State UP, 1988. 135–50. Print.

Gallantry a-la-mode, a Satyrical Poem, in Three Parts: Representing the Vanities of Several Humours of this Present Age. London, 1674. Print.

Gardiner, John Eliot, dir. *King Arthur*. By Henry Purcell. Perf. English Baroque Soloists. CD.

Garth, Samuel. Preface. *Ovid's* Metamorphoses *in Fifteen Books*. Trans. Garth et al. London, 1717. i–xx. Print.

Gentileschi, Artemisia. *Allegory of Painting*. 1630s. Royal Collection, Kensington Palace, London. *Autoritratti / Self-Portraits*. WordPress.com, 16 Sept. 2009. Web. 29 Mar. 2012.

Gentileschi, Artemisia, and Orazio Gentileschi. *Allegory of Peace and the Arts*. 1638–39. Marlborough House, London. *The Life and Art of Artemisia Gentileschi*. Christine Parker, n.d. Web. 29 Mar. 2012.

Godden, Thomas. *Catholicks No Idolaters*. London, 1672. Print. N. pag.

Grabu, Louis. *Albion and Albanius*. Ed. Bryan White. London: Stainer, 2007. Print. Purcell Society Ed. Companion Ser. 1.

———. "Concert of Venus." *Baroque Music for the Restoration Violin Band*. Dir. Peter Holman. Perf. Parley of Instruments. Hyperion, 1993. CD.

Gransden, K. W. "Milton, Dryden, and the Comedy of the Fall." *Essays in Criticism* 26.2 (1976): 116–33. *Oxford Journals Archive*. Oxford UP, n.d. Web. 10 July 2009.

Green, Susan, and Steven N. Zwicker, eds. *John Dryden: A Tercentenary Miscellany*. San Marino: Huntington Lib., 2001. Print.

Greenblatt, Stephen, et al. *The Norton Anthology of English Literature*. 9th ed. Vol. 1. New York: Norton, 2012. Print.

Greene, Donald. *The Age of Exuberance: Backgrounds to Eighteenth-Century English Literature*. New York: Random, 1970. Print.

Griffin, Dustin. "Dryden's 'Oldham' and the Perils of Writing: 'To the Memory of Mr. Oldham.'" *Modern Language Quarterly* 37.2 (1976): 133–50. Print.

Griffith, Richard. *Something New*. 1762. *Internet Archive*. Internet Archive, 7 July 2006. Web. 7 Jan. 2013.

Hagstrum, Jean. *Sex and Sensibility: Ideal and Erotic Love from Milton to Mozart*. Chicago: U of Chicago P, 1980. Print.

Hammond, Paul. *Dryden and the Traces of Classical Rome*. Oxford: Oxford UP, 1999. Print.

———. "The King's Two Bodies: Representations of Charles II." *Culture, Politics and Society in Britain, 1600–1800*. Ed. Jeremy Black and Jeremy Gregory. Manchester: Manchester UP, 1991. 13–46. Print.

Hammond, Paul, and David Hopkins, eds. *John Dryden: Tercentenary Essays*. Oxford: Clarendon, 2000. Print.

Harris, Tim. *London Crowds in the Reign of Charles II*. Cambridge: Cambridge UP, 1987. Print.

Harth, Phillip. *Contexts of Dryden's Thought*. Chicago: U of Chicago P, 1934. Print.

Hathaway, Baxter. *The Age of Criticism: The Late Renaissance in Italy*. Ithaca: Cornell UP, 1962. Print.

———. "John Dryden and the Function of Tragedy." *PMLA* 58.3 (1943): 665–73. Print.

Haynes, Bruce. *The End of Early Music: A Period Performer's History of Music for the Twenty-First Century*. Oxford: Oxford UP, 2007. Print.

Herman, Peter. *Destabilizing Milton:* Paradise Lost *and the Poetics of Incertitude*. New York: Palgrave, 2005. Print.

Hey for Horn Fair . . . a Merry Progress of Nine Several Sorts of Cuckolds. London, 1674. Print.

Hobbes, Thomas. *Leviathan*. Ed. Noel Malcolm. London: Oxford UP, 2012. Print.

Hodges, Thomas. *A Treatise of Marriage*. . . . London, 1673. Print.

Holland, Peter. *The Ornament of Action: Text and Performance in Restoration Comedy*. Cambridge: Cambridge UP, 1979. Print.

Hopkins, David. "Dryden and His Contemporaries." *Oxford History of Literary Translation in English, Volume 3: 1660–1790*. Ed. Stuart Gillespie and Hopkins. New York: Oxford UP, 2005. 55–66. Print.

———. *John Dryden*. Cambridge: Cambridge UP, 1986. Print.

Hopkins, Gerard Manley. *Letters of Gerard Manley Hopkins to Robert Bridges*. Ed. C. C. Abbott. Oxford: Oxford UP, 1935. Print.

Howe, Elizabeth. *The First English Actresses: Women and Drama, 1660–1700*. Cambridge: Cambridge UP, 1992. Print.

Hoxby, Blair. "Dryden's Baroque Dramaturgy: The Case of *Aureng-Zebe*." Lewis and Novak 244–72.

———. "Passion." *Twenty-First-Century Interpretations of Early Modern Theatricality*. Ed. Henry Turner. Oxford: Oxford UP, forthcoming.

Hughes, Derek. "*Aphrodite katadyomene*: Dryden's Cleopatra and the Cydnos." *Comparative Drama* 14 (1980): 35–45. Print.

———. "Art and Life in *All for Love*." *ELH* 42 (1975): 38–61. Print.

———. *English Drama, 1660–1700*. Oxford: Oxford UP, 1996. Print.

———. "Heroic Drama and Tragicomedy." Owen 195–210.

———. "The Significance of *All for Love*." *ELH* 37 (1970): 540–63. Print.

———. "The Unity of Dryden's *Marriage à-la-Mode*." *Philological Quarterly* 61.2 (1982): 125–42. Print.

Hume, Robert D. "Marital Discord in English Comedy from Dryden to Fielding." *Modern Philology* 74 (1977): 269–70. Print.

———. "The Myth of the Rake in Restoration Comedy." *Studies in the Literary Imagination* 10 (1977): 25–55. Print.

———. "The Politics of Opera in Late Seventeenth-Century London." *Cambridge Opera Journal* 10 (1998): 15–43. Print.

———. *The Rakish Stage: Studies in English Drama, 1660–1800*. Carbondale: Southern Illinois UP, 1983. Print.

Humphreys, A. R. *The Augustan World: Life and Letters in Eighteenth-Century England.* London: Methuen, 1954. Print.

Hunter, J. Paul. "Couplets and Conversation." *The Cambridge Companion to Eighteenth-Century Poetry*. Ed. John Sitter. Cambridge: Cambridge UP, 2001. 11–35. Print.

Hutton, Ronald. *The Restoration: A Political and Religious History of England and Wales, 1658–1667.* Oxford: Oxford UP, 1985. Print.

Hyde, Edward, earl of Clarendon. *A History of the Rebellion: A New Selection*. Ed. Paul Seaward. Oxford: Oxford UP, 2009. Print.

Jensen, H. James. *A Glossary of John Dryden's Critical Terms*. Minneapolis: U of Minnesota P, 1969. Print.

Johnson, Samuel. *Dictionary of the English Language*. London, 1755. Print.

———. "Dryden." *The Lives of the Most Eminent English Poets; with Critical Observations on Their Works*. Ed. Roger Lonsdale. Vol. 2. Oxford: Clarendon, 2006. 79–164. Print.

———. *The Major Works*. Ed. Donald Greene. Oxford: Oxford UP, 1984. Print. Oxford World's Classics.

———. *The Vanity of Human Wishes*. Johnson, *Major Works* 12–21.

Jones, Emrys. "Dryden's Persius." Rawson and Santesso 123–38.

Jonson, Ben. "To the Memory of My Beloved, the Author, Mr. William Shakespeare, and What He Hath Left Us." *Ben Jonson and the Cavalier Poets*. Ed. Hugh Maclean. New York: Norton, 1974. 85–88. Print.

Kaufman, R. J. "On the Poetics of Terminal Tragedy: Dryden's *All for Love*." *Dryden: A Collection of Critical Essays*. Ed. Bernard Schilling. Englewood Cliffs: Prentice, 1963. 86–94. Print.

Kavenik, Frances M. *British Drama, 1660–1779: A Critical History*. London: Twayne, 1995. Print.

Keats, John. *Poems of John Keats*. Ed. Miriam Allott. London: Longman, 1970. Print.

Keeble, N. H. *The Restoration: England in the 1660s*. Oxford: Oxford UP, 2002. Print.

Keener, Frederick. Preface. Dryden, *Virgil's* Aeneid vii–xliii.

Kelchner, Heidi. "Dryden's *Absalom and Achitophel*." *Explicator* 51.4 (1993): 216–19. Print.

Kewes, Paulina. "Dryden's Theatre and the Passions of Politics." Zwicker, *Cambridge Companion* 131–55.

Killigrew, Anne. *Poems*. 1686. Introd. Richard Morton. Gainesville: Scholars' Facsims. and Rpts., 1967. Print.

King, Bruce. "The Significance of Dryden's *State of Innocence*." *SEL: Studies in English Literature, 1500–1900* 4.3 (1964): 371–91. *JSTOR*. Web. 20 June 2008.

Kirsch, Arthur. *Dryden's Heroic Drama*. Princeton: Princeton UP, 1965. Print.

Kishlansky, Mark. *A Monarchy Transformed: Britain, 1603–1714*. London: Lane, 1996. Print.

Klinkenborg, Verlyn. "Keeping Bees among Us." *New York Times*. New York Times, 22 Feb. 2007. Web. 30 Apr. 2012.

Knights, L. C. "Restoration Comedy: The Reality and the Myth." 1946. McMillin 572–82.

Kroll, Richard. "Instituting Empiricism: Hobbes and Dryden's *Marriage a la Mode*." Kroll, *Restoration Drama* 207–27.

———. *Restoration Drama and "The Circle of Commerce."* Cambridge: Cambridge UP, 2007. Print.

Krook, Anne K. "Satire and the Constitution of Theocracy in *Absalom and Achitophel*." *Studies in Philology* 91.3 (1994): 339–58. Print.

Lamb, Charles. "On the Artificial Comedy of the Last Century." 1822. McMillin 567–72.

Langhans, Edward. "The Theatre." Fisk 1–18.

Leacroft, Richard. *The Development of the English Playhouse: An Illustrated Survey of Theatre Building in England from Medieval to Modern Times*. Ithaca: Cornell UP, 1973. Print.

Leader, Zachary. *The Life of Kingsley Amis*. New York: Pantheon, 2006. Print.

Leavis, F. R. "*Antony and Cleopatra* and *All for Love*: A Critical Exercise." *Scrutiny* 5 (1936): 158–69. Print.

Leckie, Barbara. *Culture and Adultery: The Novel, the Newspaper, and the Law, 1857–1914*. Philadelphia: U of Pennsylvania P, 1999. Print.

L'Estrange, Roger. *Seneca's Morals Abstracted: In Three Parts: I: Of Benefits; II: Of a Happy Lie, Anger, and Clemency; III: A Miscellany of Epistles*. London: T. N. for Henry Brome, 1679. Print.

Levine, Carole Freed. "*All for Love* and Book IV of the *Aeneid*: The Moral Predicament." *Comparative Literature* 33 (1981): 239–57. Print.

Levy, Sharon. "The Vanishing." *On Earth* Summer 2006: 14–21. Print.

Lewis, Jayne. "'The Type of a Kind'; or, The Lives of Dryden." *Eighteenth-Century Life* 25 (2001): 3–18. Print.

Lewis, Jayne, and Maximillian E. Novak, eds. *The Enchanted Ground: Reimagining John Dryden*. Toronto: U of Toronto P, 2004. Print.

Locke, John. *An Essay concerning Human Understanding*. Ed. Peter H. Nidditch. Oxford: Clarendon, 1975. Print.

Lockhart, J. G. *Memoirs of the Life of Sir Walter Scott*. 1806. 3 vols. Edinburgh: Cadell, 1839. Print.

Loewenstein, Joseph. *The Author's Due: Printing and the Prehistory of Copyright*. Chicago: Chicago UP, 2002. Print.

Loftis, John. "Commentary" [on *Secret Love*]. Dryden, *Works* 9: 331–51.

Love, Harold. "Dryden's London." Zwicker, *Cambridge Companion* 113–30.

———. "Dryden's Unideal Vacancy." *Eighteenth-Century Studies* 12.1 (1978): 74–89. Print.

———. "Fixity Versus Flexibility in 'A Song of Tom of Danby' and Dryden's *Absalom and Achitophel*." *Agent of Change: Print Culture Studies after Elizabeth L. Eisenstein*. Ed. Sabrina Alcorn Baron et al. Amherst: U of Massachusetts P, 2007. 140–56. Print.

Lowell, James Russell. "Dryden." *North Atlantic Review* 107 (1868): 190–229. Print.

Lubbock, Allan. *The Character of John Dryden*. London: Hogarth, 1923. Print.

Lynch, Jack, ed. *The State of Innocence and the Fall of Man*. *Electronic Texts*. Rutgers U, n.d. Web. 11 Aug. 2008.

Macaulay, T. B. "John Dryden." *Edinburgh Review* 47 (1828): 1–36. Print.

MacCallum, Hugh. "The State of Innocence: Epic to Opera." *Milton Studies* 31 (1994): 109–31. Print.

Mackie, Erin. *Market à la Mode: Fashion, Commodity, and Gender in the* Tatler *and the* Spectator. Baltimore: Johns Hopkins UP, 1997. Print.

MacLean, Gerald. *Culture and Society in the Stuart Restoration: Literature, Drama, History*. Cambridge: Cambridge UP, 1995. Print.

Maguire, Nancy Klein. *Regicide and Restoration: English Tragicomedy, 1660–1671*. New York: Cambridge UP, 1992. Print.

Maher, Lillian. "To the Memory of Mr. Dryden." Dec. 2008. TS.

The Maid's Complaint against the Batchelors . . . Passionately Setting Forth the Unkindness of Men, with Their Slighting the Good Old Way of Matrimony. London, 1675. Print.

Malone, Edmond. *Some Account of the Life and Writings of John Dryden*. London: Cadell, 1800. Print. Vol. 1, pt. 1, of *The Critical and Miscellaneous Prose Works of John Dryden*.

Manley, Delarivier. *New Atalantis*. Ed. Rosalind Ballaster. New York: New York UP, 1992. Print.

Marriage Asserted: In Answer to a Book Entituled Conjugium Conjurgium. . . . London, 1674. Print.

Martz, Louis. "Dryden's Poem of Paradise: *The State of Innocence, and Fall of Man*." Rawson and Santesso 181–93.

Marvell, Andrew. "On Paradise Lost." *Paradise Lost*. By John Milton. London, 1674. 209–10. Print.

Mason, H. F. "Dryden's Dream of Happiness." *Cambridge Quarterly* 9 (1980): 218–71. Print.

Maurer, A. E. Wallace. "The Form of Dryden's *Absalom and Achitophel*, Once More." *Papers on Language and Literature* 27 (1991): 320–37. Print.

McGirr, Elaine. *Heroic Mode and Political Crisis, 1660–1745*. Newark: U of Delaware P, 2009. Print.

McKeon, Michael. "Historicizing *Absalom and Achitophel*." *The New Eighteenth Century: Theory, Politics, English Literature*. Ed. Felicity Nussbaum and Laura Brown. New York: Methuen, 1987. 23–40. Print.

———. "Marxist Criticism and *Marriage à la Mode*." *Eighteenth Century: Theory and Interpretation* 24.2 (1983): 141–62. Print.

———. *Politics and Poetry in Restoration England*. Cambridge: Harvard UP, 1975. Print.

McMillin, Scott, ed. *Restoration and Eighteenth-Century Comedy*. 2nd ed. New York: Norton, 1997. Print.

Milhous, Judith, and Robert D. Hume. *Producible Interpretation: Eight English Plays, 1675–1707*. Carbondale: Southern Illinois UP, 1985. Print.

Miller, John. *The Restoration and the England of Charles II*. London: Longman, 1997. Print.

Miller, Shannon. *Engendering the Fall: John Milton and Seventeenth-Century Women Writers*. Philadelphia: U of Pennsylvania P, 2008. Print.

Milton, John. *John Milton: Complete Poems and Major Prose*. Ed. Merritt Y. Hughes. Indianapolis: Hackett, 1957. Print.

———. "Lycidas." Milton, *John Milton* 116–26.

———. *Paradise Lost*. Milton, *John Milton* 207–469.

Miner, Earl. *Dryden's Poetry*. Bloomington: Indiana UP, 1967. Print.

———. "On Reading Dryden." *John Dryden*. Ed. Miner. Oxford: U of Ohio P, 1972. 1–22. Print.

Montagu, Mary Wortley. "The Reasons That Induced Dr. Swift to Write a Poem Called the Lady's Dressing Room." *The Norton Anthology of English Literature*. Ed. Lawrence Lipking and James Noggle. 8th ed. New York: Norton, 2005. 2593–95. Print.

Mora, Maria Jose. "Type-casting in the Restoration Theatre: Dryden's *All for Love*, 1677–1704." *Atlantis* 27.2 (2005): 75–86. Print.

Mr. C. "Song: Against Marriage." *Bristol Drollery*. London, 1674. 6–7. Print.

Muir, Kenneth. "The Imagery of *All for Love*." *Proceedings of the Leeds Philosophical and Literary Society* 5 (1940): 140–47. Print.

Mullan, John. "Dryden's Anonymity." Zwicker, *Cambridge Companion* 156–80.

Nettleton, George, Arthur Case, and George Winchester Stone, Jr., eds. *British Dramatists from Dryden to Sheridan*. Carbondale: Southern Illinois UP, 1969. Print.

The New Way of Marriage; or, A Pleasant Contract between John and Kate. London, [1680?]. Print.

The Nine Muses; or, Poems Written by Nine Several Ladies upon the Death of the Late Famous John Dryden, Esq. London: Richard Basset, 1700. *Early English Books Online*. Web. 1 June 2009.

Novak, Maximillian E. "Commentary." Dryden, *Works* 13: 363–89.

———. "Criticism, Adaptation, Politics, and the Shakespearean Model of Dryden's *All for Love*." *Studies in Eighteenth-Century Culture*. Ed. Roseann Runte. Madison: U of Wisconsin P, 1978. 375–87. Print.

———. "John Dryden's Politics: The Rabble and Sovereignty." Rawson and Santesso 86–105.

———. "Libertinism and Sexuality." Owen 53–68.

———. "Margery Pinchwife's 'London Disease': Restoration Comedy and the Libertine Offensive of the 1670s." *Studies in the Literary Imagination* 10 (1977): 1–23. Print.

Oden, Richard L. Introduction. *Dryden and Shadwell, the Literary Controversy and* Mac Flecknoe, *1668–1679*. Ed. Oden. Delmar: Scholars' Facsims. and Rpts., 1977. v–xii. Print.

Ogden, James. "Dryden's Satirical Tendency." *Forum for Modern Language Studies* 31 (1995): 215–22. Print.

Orgel, Stephen. "Prospero's Wife." *Representations* 8 (1984): 1–13. Print.

Owen, Susan J., ed. *A Companion to Restoration Drama*. Oxford: Blackwell, 2001. Print.

Parry, Graham. *The Seventeenth Century: The Intellectual and Cultural Context of English Literature, 1603–1700.* New York: Longman, 1989. Print.

Patterson, Annabel. "'Crouching at Home, and Cruel When Abroad': Restoration Constructions of National and International Character." *The Stuart Court and Europe: Essays in Politics and Political Culture*. Ed. R. Malcolm Smuts. Cambridge: Cambridge UP, 1996. 210–27. Print.

Paulson, Ronald. "Dryden and the Energies of Satire." Zwicker, *Cambridge Companion* 37–58.

Pepys, Samuel. *The Diary of Samuel Pepys*. Ed. Robert Latham and William Matthews. 11 vols. Berkeley: U of California P, 1970–83. Print.

Philips, Katherine. "On the Fair Weather Just at the Coronation." *The Collected Works of Katherine Philips, the Matchless Orinda*. Ed. Patrick Thomas. Vol. 1. Cambridge: Stump Cross, 1990. 509–10. Print.

Picard, Liza. *Restoration London*. London: Weidenfeld, 1997. Print.

Pinnock, Trevor, dir. *King Arthur*. By Henry Purcell. Perf. Choir of the English Concert. Arkiv Produktion, 1991. CD.

Piper, William Bowman. "The Invulnerability of Poetic Experience." *South Central Review* 4.1 (1987): 11–23. Print.

Plutarch. From *Lives of the Noble Grecians and Romans*. Trans. Thomas North. *The Bedford Companion to Shakespeare*: *An Introduction with Documents*. Ed. Russ MacDonald. New York: Bedford, 2001. 186–87. Print.

———. "Of Isis and Osiris." *The Philosophie, Commonlie Called, the Morals*. Trans. Philemon Holland. London: Arnold Hatfield, 1603. 1286–319. Print.

Pohli, Carol Virginia. "Formal and Informal Space in Dryden's Ode 'To the Pious Memory of Anne Killigrew.'" *Restoration* 15 (1991): 27–40. Print.

Poor Anthony's Complaint and Lamentation against the Miseries of Marriage, Meeting with a Scolding Wife. [London], [between 1662 and 1688]. Print.

Pope, Alexander. *The Dunciad*. Ed. James Sutherland. New Haven: Yale UP, 1963. Print. Vol. 5 of *The Twickenham Edition of the Poems of Alexander Pope*. 3rd ed. 11 vols.

———. *An Essay on Criticism*. Pastoral Poetry *and* An Essay on Criticism. Ed. E. Audra Williams and Aubrey Williams. New Haven: Yale UP, 1961. 233–326. Print. Vol. 1 of *The Twickenham Edition of the Poems of Alexander Pope*. 11 vols.

———. *An Essay on Man*. Ed. Maynard Mack. New Haven: Yale UP, 1950. Print. Vol. 3.1 of *The Twickenham Edition of the Poems of Alexander Pope*. 3rd ed. 11 vols.

———. *Poems of Alexander Pope*. Ed. John Butt. New Haven: Yale UP, 1963. Print.

———. *The Rape of the Lock*. Pope, *Poems* 217–42.

———. "To Allen Lord Bathurst." Pope, *Poems* 570–85.

Pound, Ezra. *Poems and Translations*. New York: Lib. of Amer., 2003. Print.

Price, Curtis. *Henry Purcell and the London Stage*. Cambridge: Cambridge UP, 1984. Print.

Price, Martin, ed. *The Oxford Anthology of English Literature: The Restoration and the Eighteenth Century*. Oxford: Oxford UP, 1973. Print.

Pritchard, William H. "Dryden Rules." *On Poets and Poetry*. Athens: Swallow, 2009. 3–30. Print.

A Protestant Antidote against Popery: With a Brief Discourse of the Great Atheisticalness and Vain Amours Now in Fashion. London, 1674. Print.

Purcell, Henry. *King Arthur*. Cond. Trevor Pinnock. Perf. Choir of the English Concert. Arkiv Produktion, 1991. CD.

———. *King Arthur*. Cond. John Eliot Gardiner. Perf. Monteverdi Choir and English Baroque Soloists. Erato, 1992. CD.

———. *King Arthur*. Dir. William Christie. Perf. Les Arts Florissants. Erato, 1995. CD.

———. *King Arthur*. Dir. Jürgen Flimm. Cond. Nikolaus Harnoncourt. EuroArts Music Intl., 2005. DVD.

———. *Purcell Songs and Dialogues*. Perf. Emma Kirkby, David Thomas, and Anthony Rooley. Hyperion, 1993. CD.

———. *Theatre Music*. Cond. Christopher Hogwood. Perf. Acad. of Ancient Music. Decca; L'Oiseau-Lyre, 2004. 6 CDs.

———. *Works*. London: Novello, 1968–2007. Print.

———. *Works*. London: Stainer, 2008–. Print

"Quickness." *Oxford English Dictionary*. Oxford UP, n.d. Web. 14 May 2013.

Rapin, René. *Monsieur Rapin's Reflections on Aristotle's Treatise of Poesie: Containing the Necessary, Rational, and Universal Rules for Epic, Dramatick, and Other Sorts of Poetry*. Trans. Thomas Rymer. London: T. Warren for H. Herringman, 1694. Print.

Rawson, Claude, and Aaron Santesso, eds. *John Dryden, 1631–1700: His Politics, His Plays, and His Poets*. Newark: U of Delaware P, 2004. Print.

Reedy, Gerard. *The Bible and Reason*. Philadelphia: U of Pennsylvania P, 1985. Print.

Reinert, Thomas. "Theater and Civility in Dryden's Essay." *ELH* 65 (1998): 857–76. Print.

Remarques on the Humours and Conversations of the Town: Written in a Letter to Sr. T. L. London, 1673. Print.

Reverand, Cedric D., II. "Dryden's *Essay of Dramatick Poesie*: The Poet and the World of Affairs." *SEL* 22 (1982): 375–93. Print.

———. *Dryden's Final Poetic Mode: The Fables*. Philadelphia: U of Pennsylvania P, 1988. Print.

Ricks, Christopher. "Dryden's Triplets." Zwicker, *Cambridge Companion* 92–110.

Roach, Joseph R. *The Player's Passion: Studies in the Science of Acting*. Newark: U of Delaware P, 1985. Print.

Roberts, David. *The Ladies: Female Patronage of Restoration Drama, 1660–1700*. Oxford: Oxford UP, 1989. Print.

Robertson, Randy. "The Delicate Art of Anonymity: The Case of *Absalom and Achitophel*." *Restoration* 27 (2003): 41–60. Print.

Roper, Alan. *Dryden's Poetic Kingdoms*. Baltimore: Johns Hopkins UP, 1969. Print.

———. "Who's Who in *Absalom and Achitophel*?" *Huntington Library Quarterly* 53 (2000): 99–138. Print.

Rose, Craig. *England in the 1690s: Revolution, Religion, and War*. Malden: Blackwell, 1999. Print.

Rosenthal, Laura J. "'All Injury's Forgot': Restoration Sex Comedy and National Amnesia." *Comparative Drama* 42.1 (2008): 7–28. Print.

———. *Playwrights and Plagiarists in Early Modern England: Gender, Authorship, Literary Property*. Ithaca: Cornell UP, 1996. Print.

———. "Reading Masks: The Actress and the Spectatrix in Restoration Shakespeare." *Broken Boundaries: Women and Feminism in Restoration Drama*. Ed. Katherine M. Quinsey. Lexington: UP of Kentucky, 1996. 201–18. Print.

Rothstein, Eric, and Frances Kavenik. "Marriage a-la-Mode." *The Designs of Carolean Comedy*. Carbondale: Southern Illinois UP, 1988. 138–64. Print.

S[mith], W[illiam]. *Joyfull Tidings to the Begotten of God in All: With a Few Words of Counsel unto Friends concerning Marriage*. [London], 1672. Print.

Saintsbury, George. *Dryden*. London: Macmillan, 1881. Print.

Savage, Roger. "The Theatre Music." *The Purcell Companion*. Ed. Michael Burden. Portland: Amadeus, 1994. 313–83. Print.

Savile, George, marquis of Halifax. "A Character of King Charles II." *The Works of George Savile, Marquis of Halifax*. Vol. 2. Ed. Mark N. Brown. Oxford: Clarendon, 1989. 484–505. Print.

Scolnicov, Hanna, and Peter Holland. *Reading Plays: Interpretation and Reception*. Cambridge: Cambridge UP, 1991. Print.

Scott, Walter. *The Life of John Dryden*. London: Paterson, 1882. Print. Vol. 1 of *Works of John Dryden*.

———. *The Pirate*. 1821. 3 vols. Edinburgh: Constable, 1822. Print.

Seymar, William [William Ramsey]. *Conjugium Conjurgium; or, Some Serious Considerations on Marriage*. London, 1673. Print.

Shakespeare, William. *Antony and Cleopatra*. Ed. Michael Neill. Oxford: Oxford UP, 1994. Print.

———. *The Tempest*. Ed. Stephen Orgel. Oxford: Oxford UP, 1987. Print.

———. *The Works of Mr. William Shakespear in Six Volumes*. Ed. Nicholas Rowe. London: Jacob Tonson, 1709. Print.

Sherman, Stuart. "Dryden and the Theatrical Imagination." Zwicker, *Cambridge Companion* 15–36.

Simon, Richard. *Critical History of the Old Testament*. Trans. Henry Dickinson. London, 1682. Print.

Smith, John Harrington. *The Gay Couple in Restoration Comedy*. Cambridge: Harvard UP, 1948. Print.

Spurr, John. *England in the 1670s: "This Masquerading Age."* Oxford: Blackwell, 2000. Print.

———. "The Piety of John Dryden." Zwicker, *Cambridge Companion* 237–58.

———. *The Restoration Church of England, 1646–1689*. New Haven: Yale UP, 1991. Print.

Stage Beauty. Dir. Richard Eyre. Perf. Billy Crudup, Claire Danes, and Rupert Everett. Lionsgate, 2004. Film.

Stark, Jonathan, prod. *All Is Loveless* [scene from *All for Love*, by John Dryden]. 2008. *YouTube*. Web. 20 Mar. 2012.

———. "Re: All Is Loveless." Message to the author. 21 Aug. 2009. E-mail.

Staves, Susan. *A Literary History of Women's Writing in Britain, 1660–1789*. Cambridge: Cambridge UP, 2006. Print.

———. *Players' Scepters: Fictions of Authority in the Restoration*. Lincoln: U of Nebraska P, 1979. Print.

Stephen, Leslie. "John Dryden." *Dictionary of National Biography*. Ed. Stephen and Sidney Lee. Vol. 6. New York: Macmillan, 1908. 203–10. Print.

Sterne, Laurence. The Life and Opinions of Tristram Shandy, Gentleman*: The Florida Edition*. Ed. Joan New and Melvyn New. New York: Penguin Classics, 2003. Print.

Stewart, Susan. *Poetry and the Fate of the Senses*. Chicago: U of Chicago P, 2002. Print.

Stillingfleet, Edward. *Discourse concerning the Idolatry Practiced in the Church of Rome.* London, 1671. Print.

Stove, R. J. "Dryden in His Time and Ours." *New Criterion* 25 (2006): 24–28. Print.

Swift, Jonathan. "The Lady's Dressing Room." *The Poems of Jonathan Swift*. Ed. Harold Williams. Vol. 2. Oxford: Clarendon, 1937. 524–30. Print.

Templer, John. *The Saints Duty in Contending for the Faith*. London, 1659. Print.

Thompson, Ann. "'Miranda, Where's Your Sister?': Reading Shakespeare's *The Tempest*." The Tempest*: A Case Study in Critical Controversy*. Ed. Gerald Graff and James Phelan. Boston: Bedford, 2000. 337–47. Print.

Tillotson, Geoffrey, Paul Fussell, and Marshall Waingrow, eds. *Eighteenth-Century English Literature*. New York: Harcourt. 1969. Print.

Tillyard, E. M. W. "Dryden: 'Ode on Anne Killigrew,' 1686." *Five Poems: 1470–1870*. London: Chatto, 1948. 49–65. Print.

Tomlinson, Gary. *Music in Renaissance Magic: Toward a Historiography of Others*. Chicago: U of Chicago P, 1993. Print.

Turner, David M. *Fashioning Adultery: Gender, Sex, and Civility in England, 1660–1740*. Cambridge: Cambridge UP, 2002. Print.

Turner, James Grantham. *Libertines and Radicals in Early Modern London: Sexuality, Politics, and Literary Culture, 1630–1685.* Cambridge: Cambridge UP, 2002. Print.

Van Doren, Mark. *John Dryden: A Study of His Poetry*. New York: Holt, 1940. Print.

Vieth, David. "Irony in Dryden's *Ode to Anne Killigrew*." *Studies in Eighteenth-Century Culture* 14 (1985): 193–222. Print.

A Vindication of a Marriage Life: In Answer to the Broad-side against Marriage. [London], [1675]. Print.

Visconsi, Elliott. *Lines of Equity: Literature and the Origins of Law in Later Stuart England.* Ithaca: Cornell UP, 2008. Print.

Von Maltzahn, Nicholas. "Dryden's Milton and the Theater of Imagination." Hammond and Hopkins 32–56.

Waith, Eugene M. *Ideas of Greatness: Heroic Drama in England.* London: Routledge, 1971. Print.

Wallace, John M. "John Dryden's Plays and the Conception of Heroic Society." *Culture and Politics: From Puritanism to Enlightenment.* Ed. Perez Zagorin. Berkeley: U of California P, 1980. 113–34. Print.

Wasserman, Earl R. "The Pleasures of Tragedy." *ELH* 14 (1947): 283–307. Print.

Wasserman, George. *John Dryden.* New York: Twayne, 1964. Print.

Weber, Harold. *The Restoration Rake-Hero: Transformations in Sexual Understanding in Seventeenth-Century England.* Madison: U of Wisconsin P, 1988. Print.

Webster, Jeremy W. *Performing Libertinism in Charles II's Court: Politics, Drama, Sexuality.* New York: Palgrave, 2005. Print.

Weinbrot, Howard. *Britannia's Issue: The Rise of British Literature from Dryden to Ossian.* Cambridge: U of Cambridge P, 1993. Print.

Welch, Anthony. "Losing Paradise in Dryden's *State of Innocence.*" *Uncircumscribed Mind: Reading Milton Deeply.* Ed. Charles W. Durham and Kristin A Pruitt. Selinsgrove: Susquehanna UP, 2008. 222–42. Print.

W. H. "A Just, True, and Honourable Description of Marriage." *London Drollery: or, The Wits Academy.* London, 1673. 54. Print.

Wilde, Oscar. "The Critic as Artist." *Collins Complete Works of Oscar Wilde.* Glasgow: Harper, 1999. 1108–55. Print. Centenary ed.

Wilmot, John, earl of Rochester. *An Allusion to Horace. The Works of John Wilmot, Earl of Rochester.* Ed. Harold Love. Oxford: Oxford UP, 1999. 71–74. Print.

———. *The Complete Poems of John Wilmot, Earl of Rochester.* Ed. David M. Vieth. New Haven: Yale UP, 1968. Print.

Winn, James Anderson. "Dryden's Songs." Lewis and Novak 287–314.

———. *John Dryden and His World.* New Haven: Yale UP, 1987. Print.

———. *"When Beauty Fires the Blood": Love and the Arts in the Age of Dryden.* Ann Arbor: U of Michigan P, 1992. Print.

Wittreich, Joseph. *Feminist Milton.* Ithaca: Cornell UP, 1987. Print.

———. "Milton's Transgressive Maneuvers: Receptions (Then and Now) and the Sexual Politics of *Paradise Lost.*" *Milton and Heresy.* Ed. Stephen B. Dobranski and John Rumrich. Cambridge: Cambridge UP, 1998. 244–66. Print.

Womersley, David, ed. *Restoration Drama: An Anthology.* Oxford: Blackwell, 2000. Print.

Wordsworth, William. *Letters of William and Dorothy Wordsworth.* Ed. E. de Selincourt. Vol. 1. Oxford: Clarendon, 1967. Print.

Wykes, David. *A Preface to Dryden*. London: Longman, 1977. Print.

Xenophon. *Memorabilia*. Trans. Amy Bonnette. Ithaca: Cornell UP, 1994. Print.

Z. C. *Marriage-Musick or Nuptial-Duties, Directed in a Fatherly Admonition, to William Beard and Sarah Whiskard.* London, 1670. Print.

Zwicker, Steven N., ed. *The Cambridge Companion to John Dryden*. New York: Cambridge UP, 2004. Print.

———. "Composing a Literary Life." Zwicker, *Cambridge Companion* 3–14.

———. "Dryden and the Invention of Irony." *Swift's Travels: Eighteenth-Century British Travel and Its Legacy*. Ed. Nicolas Hudson and Aaron Santesso. Cambridge: Cambridge UP, 2008. 74–90. Print.

———. "Dryden and the Poetic Career." *The New Cambridge History of English Literature, 1660–1780*. Ed. John Richetti. Cambridge: Cambridge UP, 2004. 132–59. Print.

———. *Dryden's Political Poetry: The Typology of King and Nation.* Providence: Brown UP, 1972. Print.

———. *Politics and Language in Dryden's Poetry*. Princeton: Princeton UP, 1984. Print.

INDEX OF DRYDEN'S WORKS

INDEX OF NAMES

Modern Language Association of America

Approaches to Teaching World Literature

Achebe's Things Fall Apart. Ed. Bernth Lindfors. 1991.
Arthurian Tradition. Ed. Maureen Fries and Jeanie Watson. 1992.
Atwood's The Handmaid's Tale *and Other Works*. Ed. Sharon R. Wilson, Thomas B. Friedman, and Shannon Hengen. 1996.
Austen's Emma. Ed. Marcia McClintock Folsom. 2004.
Austen's Pride and Prejudice. Ed. Marcia McClintock Folsom. 1993.
Balzac's Old Goriot. Ed. Michal Peled Ginsburg. 2000.
Baudelaire's Flowers of Evil. Ed. Laurence M. Porter. 2000.
Beckett's Waiting for Godot. Ed. June Schlueter and Enoch Brater. 1991.
Beowulf. Ed. Jess B. Bessinger, Jr., and Robert F. Yeager. 1984.
Blake's Songs of Innocence and of Experience. Ed. Robert F. Gleckner and Mark L. Greenberg. 1989.
Boccaccio's Decameron. Ed. James H. McGregor. 2000.
British Women Poets of the Romantic Period. Ed. Stephen C. Behrendt and Harriet Kramer Linkin. 1997.
Charlotte Brontë's Jane Eyre. Ed. Diane Long Hoeveler and Beth Lau. 1993.
Emily Brontë's Wuthering Heights. Ed. Sue Lonoff and Terri A. Hasseler. 2006.
Byron's Poetry. Ed. Frederick W. Shilstone. 1991.
Works of Italo Calvino. Ed. Franco Ricci. 2013.
Camus's The Plague. Ed. Steven G. Kellman. 1985.
Writings of Bartolomé de Las Casas. Ed. Santa Arias and Eyda M. Merediz. 2008.
Cather's My Ántonia. Ed. Susan J. Rosowski. 1989.
Cervantes' Don Quixote. Ed. Richard Bjornson. 1984.
Chaucer's Canterbury Tales. Ed. Joseph Gibaldi. 1980.
Chaucer's Troilus and Criseyde *and the Shorter Poems*. Ed. Tison Pugh and Angela Jane Weisl. 2006.
Chopin's The Awakening. Ed. Bernard Koloski. 1988.
Coleridge's Poetry and Prose. Ed. Richard E. Matlak. 1991.
Collodi's Pinocchio *and Its Adaptations*. Ed. Michael Sherberg. 2006.
Conrad's "Heart of Darkness" and "The Secret Sharer." Ed. Hunt Hawkins and Brian W. Shaffer. 2002.
Dante's Divine Comedy. Ed. Carole Slade. 1982.
Defoe's Robinson Crusoe. Ed. Maximillian E. Novak and Carl Fisher. 2005.
DeLillo's White Noise. Ed. Tim Engles and John N. Duvall. 2006.
Dickens's Bleak House. Ed. John O. Jordan and Gordon Bigelow. 2009.
Dickens's David Copperfield. Ed. Richard J. Dunn. 1984.
Dickinson's Poetry. Ed. Robin Riley Fast and Christine Mack Gordon. 1989.
Narrative of the Life of Frederick Douglass. Ed. James C. Hall. 1999.
Works of John Dryden. Ed. Jayne Lewis and Lisa Zunshine. 2013.

Duras's Ourika. Ed. Mary Ellen Birkett and Christopher Rivers. 2009.
Early Modern Spanish Drama. Ed. Laura R. Bass and Margaret R. Greer. 2006.
Eliot's Middlemarch. Ed. Kathleen Blake. 1990.
Eliot's Poetry and Plays. Ed. Jewel Spears Brooker. 1988.
Shorter Elizabethan Poetry. Ed. Patrick Cheney and Anne Lake Prescott. 2000.
Ellison's Invisible Man. Ed. Susan Resneck Parr and Pancho Savery. 1989.
English Renaissance Drama. Ed. Karen Bamford and Alexander Leggatt. 2002.
Works of Louise Erdrich. Ed. Gregg Sarris, Connie A. Jacobs, and James R. Giles. 2004.
Dramas of Euripides. Ed. Robin Mitchell-Boyask. 2002.
Faulkner's As I Lay Dying. Ed. Patrick O'Donnell and Lynda Zwinger. 2011.
Faulkner's The Sound and the Fury. Ed. Stephen Hahn and Arthur F. Kinney. 1996.
Fitzgerald's The Great Gatsby. Ed. Jackson R. Bryer and Nancy P. VanArsdale. 2009.
Flaubert's Madame Bovary. Ed. Laurence M. Porter and Eugene F. Gray. 1995.
García Márquez's One Hundred Years of Solitude. Ed. María Elena de Valdés and Mario J. Valdés. 1990.
Gilman's "The Yellow Wall-Paper" and Herland. Ed. Denise D. Knight and Cynthia J. Davis. 2003.
Goethe's Faust. Ed. Douglas J. McMillan. 1987.
Gothic Fiction: The British and American Traditions. Ed. Diane Long Hoeveler and Tamar Heller. 2003.
Poetry of John Gower. Ed. R. F. Yeager and Brian W. Gastle. 2011.
Grass's The Tin Drum. Ed. Monika Shafi. 2008.
H.D.'s Poetry and Prose. Ed. Annette Debo and Lara Vetter. 2011.
Hebrew Bible as Literature in Translation. Ed. Barry N. Olshen and Yael S. Feldman. 1989.
Homer's Iliad *and* Odyssey. Ed. Kostas Myrsiades. 1987.
Hurston's Their Eyes Were Watching God *and Other Works*. Ed. John Lowe. 2009.
Ibsen's A Doll House. Ed. Yvonne Shafer. 1985.
Henry James's Daisy Miller *and* The Turn of the Screw. Ed. Kimberly C. Reed and Peter G. Beidler. 2005.
Works of Samuel Johnson. Ed. David R. Anderson and Gwin J. Kolb. 1993.
Joyce's Ulysses. Ed. Kathleen McCormick and Erwin R. Steinberg. 1993.
Works of Sor Juana Inés de la Cruz. Ed. Emilie L. Bergmann and Stacey Schlau. 2007.
Kafka's Short Fiction. Ed. Richard T. Gray. 1995.
Keats's Poetry. Ed. Walter H. Evert and Jack W. Rhodes. 1991.
Kingston's The Woman Warrior. Ed. Shirley Geok-lin Lim. 1991.
Lafayette's The Princess of Clèves. Ed. Faith E. Beasley and Katharine Ann Jensen. 1998.
Works of D. H. Lawrence. Ed. M. Elizabeth Sargent and Garry Watson. 2001.
Lazarillo de Tormes *and the Picaresque Tradition*. Ed. Anne J. Cruz. 2009.
Lessing's The Golden Notebook. Ed. Carey Kaplan and Ellen Cronan Rose. 1989.

Works of Naguib Mahfouz. Ed. Waïl S. Hassan and Susan Muaddi Darraj. 2011.
Mann's Death in Venice *and Other Short Fiction*. Ed. Jeffrey B. Berlin. 1992.
Marguerite de Navarre's Heptameron. Ed. Colette H. Winn. 2007.
Medieval English Drama. Ed. Richard K. Emmerson. 1990.
Melville's Moby-Dick. Ed. Martin Bickman. 1985.
Metaphysical Poets. Ed. Sidney Gottlieb. 1990.
Miller's Death of a Salesman. Ed. Matthew C. Roudané. 1995.
Milton's Paradise Lost. First edition. Ed. Galbraith M. Crump. 1986.
Milton's Paradise Lost. Second edition. Ed. Peter C. Herman. 2012.
Milton's Shorter Poetry and Prose. Ed. Peter C. Herman. 2007.
Molière's Tartuffe *and Other Plays*. Ed. James F. Gaines and Michael S. Koppisch. 1995.
Momaday's The Way to Rainy Mountain. Ed. Kenneth M. Roemer. 1988.
Montaigne's Essays. Ed. Patrick Henry. 1994.
Novels of Toni Morrison. Ed. Nellie Y. McKay and Kathryn Earle. 1997.
Murasaki Shikibu's The Tale of Genji. Ed. Edward Kamens. 1993.
Nabokov's Lolita. Ed. Zoran Kuzmanovich and Galya Diment. 2008.
Works of Ngũgĩ wa Thiong'o. Ed. Oliver Lovesey. 2012.
Works of Tim O'Brien. Ed. Alex Vernon and Catherine Calloway. 2010.
Works of Ovid and the Ovidian Tradition. Ed. Barbara Weiden Boyd and Cora Fox. 2010.
Poe's Prose and Poetry. Ed. Jeffrey Andrew Weinstock and Tony Magistrale. 2008.
Pope's Poetry. Ed. Wallace Jackson and R. Paul Yoder. 1993.
Proust's Fiction and Criticism. Ed. Elyane Dezon-Jones and Inge Crosman Wimmers. 2003.
Puig's Kiss of the Spider Woman. Ed. Daniel Balderston and Francine Masiello. 2007.
Pynchon's The Crying of Lot 49 *and Other Works*. Ed. Thomas H. Schaub. 2008.
Works of François Rabelais. Ed. Todd W. Reeser and Floyd Gray. 2011.
Novels of Samuel Richardson. Ed. Lisa Zunshine and Jocelyn Harris. 2006.
Rousseau's Confessions *and* Reveries of the Solitary Walker. Ed. John C. O'Neal and Ourida Mostefai. 2003.
Scott's Waverley Novels. Ed. Evan Gottlieb and Ian Duncan. 2009.
Shakespeare's Hamlet. Ed. Bernice W. Kliman. 2001.
Shakespeare's King Lear. Ed. Robert H. Ray. 1986.
Shakespeare's Othello. Ed. Peter Erickson and Maurice Hunt. 2005.
Shakespeare's Romeo and Juliet. Ed. Maurice Hunt. 2000.
Shakespeare's The Tempest *and Other Late Romances*. Ed. Maurice Hunt. 1992.
Shelley's Frankenstein. Ed. Stephen C. Behrendt. 1990.
Shelley's Poetry. Ed. Spencer Hall. 1990.
Sir Gawain and the Green Knight. Ed. Miriam Youngerman Miller and Jane Chance. 1986.
Song of Roland. Ed. William W. Kibler and Leslie Zarker Morgan. 2006.

Spenser's Faerie Queene. Ed. David Lee Miller and Alexander Dunlop. 1994.
Stendhal's The Red and the Black. Ed. Dean de la Motte and Stirling Haig. 1999.
Sterne's Tristram Shandy. Ed. Melvyn New. 1989.
Works of Robert Louis Stevenson. Ed. Caroline McCracken-Flesher. 2013.
The Story of the Stone (Dream of the Red Chamber). Ed. Andrew Schonebaum and Tina Lu. 2012.
Stowe's Uncle Tom's Cabin. Ed. Elizabeth Ammons and Susan Belasco. 2000.
Swift's Gulliver's Travels. Ed. Edward J. Rielly. 1988.
Teresa of Ávila and the Spanish Mystics. Ed. Alison Weber. 2009.
Thoreau's Walden *and Other Works*. Ed. Richard J. Schneider. 1996.
Tolstoy's Anna Karenina. Ed. Liza Knapp and Amy Mandelker. 2003.
Vergil's Aeneid. Ed. William S. Anderson and Lorina N. Quartarone. 2002.
Voltaire's Candide. Ed. Renée Waldinger. 1987.
Whitman's Leaves of Grass. Ed. Donald D. Kummings. 1990.
Wiesel's Night. Ed. Alan Rosen. 2007.
Works of Oscar Wilde. Ed. Philip E. Smith II. 2008.
Woolf's Mrs. Dalloway. Ed. Eileen Barrett and Ruth O. Saxton. 2009.
Woolf's To the Lighthouse. Ed. Beth Rigel Daugherty and Mary Beth Pringle. 2001.
Wordsworth's Poetry. Ed. Spencer Hall, with Jonathan Ramsey. 1986.
Wright's Native Son. Ed. James A. Miller. 1997.